Edward Milward-Oliver was born in London in 1948. He has spent twenty years in the leisure industry, including book publishing and TV and movie production. A director of a New York-based company developing regional satellite systems, he currently lives in West Germany, the 'high-density Mecca of espionage.'

He is the author of *Len Deighton: An Annotated Bibliography, 1954–1985*.

By the same author
Len Deighton: An Annotated Bibliography, 1954–1985

EDWARD
MILWARD-OLIVER

The Len
Deighton
Companion

GRAFTON BOOKS

A Division of the Collins Publishing Group

LONDON GLASGOW
TORONTO SYDNEY AUCKLAND

Grafton Books
A Division of the Collins Publishing Group
8 Grafton Street, London W1X 3LA

Published by Grafton Books 1988

First published in Great Britain by
Grafton Books 1987

The author gratefully acknowledges the permission
of Jonathan Cape Ltd and Century Hutchinson Ltd
to quote short extracts from the works of Len
Deighton.

ISBN 0-586-07000-1

Printed and bound in Great Britain by
Collins, Glasgow

Set in Times

For the watchers and station-keepers
of the Hong Kong network,
but most particularly Anita and Anson Wang

Contents

Preface and Acknowledgements   7

Key to Abbreviations and Acronyms   9

Interview with Len Deighton   11

Twenty-five-year Chronology of British
   and American First Editions   27

The Len Deighton Companion A–Z   31

Alphabetical List of Themes Explored   301

Register of Characters by Nationality   305

Bibliography: Fiction 1962–1987   311

Bibliography: Non-Fiction 1954–1987   321

Quiz Answers   327

Sources   331

PREFACE AND
ACKNOWLEDGEMENTS

This guide to the themes, characters, plots, settings, tradecraft and jargon found in Len Deighton's fiction and non-fiction spans twenty-five years from *The IPCRESS File* to *Winter*.

The entries are arranged alphabetically, from abandoned novels and abduction, to Zeppelins and the 'Ziggurat'. There's no index since the whole book is one vast index; however, a list of themes explored in the text, and a register of characters given individual mention, are included in an appendix for easy reference. I've kept cross-referencing to a minimum, for common sense should lead you to most associated entries. For example, if you look up 'Normannenstrasse'—the East German State Security block where Bernard Samson encounters his treacherous wife at the close of *Berlin Game*—you will find the text includes references to several other entries which together provide a picture of East Germany's secret intelligence apparat. (You'll also learn the East Berlin telephone number of 'Normannenstrasse', should you have need of it.)

This book could not have been undertaken without the kind assistance of many individuals. I am indebted to Jürgen Becker, Jonathan Clowes, Ray Hawkey and James Pepper for their advice and encouragement, to Michael and Susan Johnson for their inspiring friendship, to the staffs of the British Council Library in Cologne and the Militärgeschichtliches Forschungsamt in Freiburg, who responded to all my requests with sedulity, to my wife Ursula, who provided so many useful suggestions along the way, and to John Boothe and Nick Austin at Grafton Books, who have been constantly forthcoming and supportive. Finally, a special word of thanks to Len Deighton, whose unfailing patience and readiness to answer all my queries immeasurably lightened my task. This guide barely scratches the surface of his singular talent; I hope it is a worthy companion to the witty, thoughtful and entertaining books he has given us this past quarter century.

Edward Milward-Oliver

KEY TO ABBREVIATIONS
AND ACRONYMS

B&E	breaking and entering	Grepo	Grenzpolizei
BfV	Bundesamt für Verfassungsschutz	GRU	Glavnoye Razvedyvatelnoye Upravleniye
BND	Bundesnachrichtendienst		
BOAC	British Overseas Airways Corporation	GSFG	Group of Soviet Forces Germany
BUF	British Union of Fascists	HUMINT	Human Intelligence
CIA	Central Intelligence Agency	HVA	Hauptverwaltung Aufklärung
COCOM	Coordinating Committee for Multilateral Export Controls	IMT	International Military Tribunal, Nuremberg
		IPCRESS	*Induction of Psycho-neuroses by Conditional Reflex with Stress*
COS	Chief of Station		
CRO	Criminal Records Office		
C-SICH	Combined Services Information Clearing House (*fictional*)	IRAC	Intelligence Resources Advisory Committee
		JIC	Joint Intelligence Committee
DGSE	Direction Général de Sécurité Extérieur	KGB	Komitet Gosudarstvennoi Bezopastnosti
DIS	Defence Intelligence Staff		
DST	Direction de la Surveillance du Territoire	Kripo	Kriminalpolizei
		LSIB	London Signals Intelligence Board
ELINT	Electronic Intelligence		
Fluko	Flugwachkommando	MfS	Ministerium für Staatssicherheit
FO	Foreign Office		
FTP	Francs-Tireurs et Partisans	NATO	North Atlantic Treaty Organisation
GCHQ	Government Communications Headquarters	NSA	National Security Agency
		NSDAP	Nationalsozialistische Deutsche Arbeiterpartei (Nazi Party)
Gestapo	Geheimstaatspolizei		

OBZ	Obranne Zpravodajstvi	SIGINT	Signals Intelligence
OEIC	Overseas Economic Intelligence Committee	Sipo	Sicherheitspolizei
		SIS	Secret Intelligence Service, MI6
ONI	Office of Naval Intelligence	SS	Schutzstaffel
PHOTINT	Photographic Intelligence	Stasi	Staatssicherheitspolizei
PRC	People's Republic of China	STUCEN	Studies Centre (*fictional*)
		Teno	Technische-Nothilfe
PSIS	Permanent Secretaries Committee on the Intelligence Services	UFA	Universum Film Aktiengesellschaft
		USAAF	United States Army Air Force
RADINT	Radar Intelligence		
RADwJ	Reichsarbeitsdienst weiblichen Jugend	USAF	United States Air Force
		USIB	United States Intelligence Board
RAF	Royal Air Force		
RG	Renseignements Généraux	USMD	United States Medical Department
RSHA	Reichssicherheits-hauptamt	VNV	Vós não vedes (*fictional*)
		Vopo	Volkspolizei
SA	Sturmabteilung	WAAF	Women's Auxiliary Air Force
SAC	Strategic Air Command		
SB	Special Branch	WOOC(P)	The full name of Deighton's fictional intelligence department is never disclosed.
SD	Sicherheitsdienst		
SDECE	Service de Documentation Extérieure et de Contre-Espionage		

Film and television credits

a.d.	art director	*m.d.*	musical director
ch.	choreography	*p.*	producer
cost.	costumes	*p.c.*	production company
d.	director	*p.d.*	production designer
ed.	editor	*ph.*	director of photography
exec.p.	executive producer	*sc.*	screenplay
l.p.	listed players	*sfx.*	special effects
m.	music	*tls.*	titles

Interview with
Len Deighton

*My conversations with Len Deighton were conducted in London and within the shadow of the Berlin Wall in West Berlin.**

EMO: Before we talk about your novel *Winter*, I'd like to learn something of how you came to be an author. Had you attempted any other novels before *The IPCRESS File*?

DEIGHTON: No. I wrote a non-fiction piece when I came back from living in America. A description of what life was like in the States. But that was my only previous attempt at writing, and it wasn't really a book.

EMO: You were earning a good living as an illustrator. Why did you turn to writing?

DEIGHTON: I wasn't completely happy as an illustrator. Not that there's anything wrong with being one. In some ways there is more satisfaction to be gained from completing a picture than from writing a book. But some of the people you have to work for make life extremely depressing. When you're dealing with words, you never have to spend too much time taking advice and instructions from people who are totally illiterate; but when you're a commercial artist, almost all your instructions come from people who are unable to draw.

EMO: Did the transition from drawing to writing come naturally?

DEIGHTON: When I left the Royal College of Art in 1955, I wanted to see something of the world, so I worked for a while as an airline steward. And just as I have a sketchbook with me now, I did

* Portions of this interview first appeared in my book *Len Deighton: An Annotated Bibliography 1954–1985*.

drawings wherever I went. Looking back, I find that whereas at one time I had simply written 'brown', or 'rusty' or 'bright pink' to indicate what the colours were, on many of these drawings I wrote much longer, more detailed descriptions.

EMO: And as these descriptive pieces grew longer, was there something inevitable about a novel emerging somewhere down the line?

DEIGHTON: I don't think so. *The IPCRESS File* was started while I was living in France in 1960. I was earning a living as a freelance illustrator, and for fun I started writing in the evenings, without any clear idea of what I was doing or how it would turn out. Then I put it aside when I returned to live in England.

EMO: With no burning ambition to complete it, and see it published?

DEIGHTON: None. I didn't do anything with it until I went on holiday the following year. I remember deciding I'd take this 'thing' with me—I didn't really think of it as a book—with the idea of finishing it. After I came back it went into a drawer, and stayed there until I met Jonathan (Clowes) at a party. When he mentioned he was a literary agent I told him I had a manuscript at home, and he asked whether it had been submitted to any publishers. I said no, and he offered to read it.

EMO: Was it immediately accepted for publication?

DEIGHTON: Hutchinson and Cape turned it down, but both said they'd like to meet the author! Then Hodder & Stoughton accepted it. I think Jonathan persuaded them to increase the first print-run from about 2,500 to 4,000 copies,* with the pre-publication sale of the serial rights.

EMO: Harry Saltzman snapped up the film rights, and the book is still selling twenty-five years later. But I wonder, would you have continued writing if it hadn't enjoyed such a critical and early success?

---

* A fine copy of this first edition, in its dust-jacket, today commands a price of one hundred pounds or more. Deighton's early works are among collectors' gems encountered in *Hardcover* (New York, 1985), the debut thriller by former *Life* magazine correspondent Wayne Warga. The story is set against the background of the international rare book trade.

DEIGHTON: I was very lucky, and because it *was* a big success, all of a sudden my income was dramatically different. But the irony is that already as an illustrator I was making the sort of money that a fairly successful writer makes. So if *IPCRESS* had been only a moderate, even a warm success, I'm not sure what I would have decided.

EMO: And if it had been a failure?

DEIGHTON: Then I think I'd have changed direction again. I've always regretted that I've not been involved in the musical stage. It does attract me enormously. When I did *Oh! What a Lovely War*, that really brought together two passions of mine—the First World War and popular music. And I've always been interested in business and the world of economics. I find it very sad the way people have contempt for businessmen. I mean there are contemptible businessmen, but there's nothing contemptible about being a businessman. So I think I'd probably have been drawn to one of these two areas.

EMO: How close is the published novel to your original manuscript?

DEIGHTON: After accepting it, Hodder & Stoughton suggested I could improve certain passages, and I made considerable changes, not only the ones on which they'd insisted. Their acceptance put me in a positive mood of wanting to improve it.

EMO: Had you already written your second novel *Horse Under Water* before *The IPCRESS File* was published?

DEIGHTON: It was in first draft. I took it to Hodder & Stoughton and asked them to read it through, because they'd warned me that second books always get slaughtered by the critics. So I got a bit nervous about this, and took a long time writing it—even today I must be one of the world's slowest writers—until finally I had it ready. I took it to them, and they said they didn't want to read it. They told me they had a policy of not dealing with a second book until the first had come out.

EMO: Tom Maschler at Jonathan Cape published *Horse Under Water*.

DEIGHTON: That's right. And that enraged some people, who

claimed I was now going to be trained as the successor to Ian Fleming, who Cape also published.*

EMO: Back to the beginning for a moment. You were earning enough as an illustrator to write anything you chose. Why a spy novel?

DEIGHTON: There's a style of writing that's known as a 'Police Procedural', which I find very good and sound, and certainly works well against what we read in the newspapers. It has an authenticity, and you believe the author knows exactly how, for instance, the New York police operate, right down to the paperwork. It's probably true to say that I had an instinctive desire to write a 'Spy Procedural', and I think that's probably what I still write today.

EMO: Most people would agree that it's much more than procedural descriptions that make your books so satisfying. I'm thinking in particular of the dialogue.

DEIGHTON: I was always interested in dialogue, even before I started writing. And although the early books contain a lot of purple passages that read as though they were written by an art student—which of course is entirely correct—a great deal of information is transmitted through dialogue. This remains today one of the things I work hardest at, seeing how much I can delete from descriptive passages and convey by means of dialogue, because I think this is a healthy influence on a book and keeps it light and keeps it moving.

EMO: You also very successfully explore how people deliberately and at times inadvertently, mis-communicate.

DEIGHTON: Well, I feel it's one of the comedies, and tragedies, of our social life that very few people are able to communicate clearly, and very few people worry about it. Consequently there is a lot of misinformation being exchanged. I think in England we are probably masters of telling people not quite what we want them to know. This is why we like a language every word of which must

* Deighton met Ian Fleming only once, at a private luncheon arranged by journalist Peter Evans whose subsequent feature on the encounter appeared in the London *Daily Express*, 27 March 1963. Evans had astutely anticipated Deighton's literary success in his column in the *Daily Express*, 5 November 1962, one week prior to the publication of *The IPCRESS File*, in what was almost certainly the first article on the author to appear in the national press.

have at least a hundred meanings, and preferably none of the meanings the Englishman understands will be listed in the dictionary, thus preventing a foreigner ever communicating successfully in the English language. So when I began toying with the idea of writing, you can see that a spy story provided an ideal arena in which all this could be exaggerated and used.

EMO: Are you happy with the genre description 'spy story'? Do you find it too limiting?

DEIGHTON: Not at all. I think it's very beneficial for books to have a label if it's going to give them more chance of reaching the right public. It's one of the functions of the jacket, the blurb and advertising to prevent readers who *won't* like your book from buying it. That's even more important than attracting people who will like it. But it can sometimes work against you. According to my mail, a lot of women read and enjoyed *Goodbye Mickey Mouse*. They were surprised, because its 'war novel' label suggested it would be full of swearing marines storming the beaches and so on.

EMO: Do you get many letters from readers?

DEIGHTON: More than I can answer, and this makes me feel rather guilty. Perhaps I can use this interview to say thank you to people who write such pleasant and interesting letters. I read every letter with great care and take notice of all criticism and suggestions even if I don't actually write a reply.

EMO: You mentioned book jackets. Ray Hawkey's black-and-white jackets for your first three novels were very distinctive, and widely praised. How did Ray's involvement arise?

DEIGHTON: We were students together at the Royal College. When Hodder & Stoughton accepted *The IPCRESS File*, I asked how much they paid for book jackets and they said fifteen guineas. Ray had been doing jackets for fifty guineas, so I said I'd pay the difference, because I wanted him to do it. I felt it was unhealthy to design my own. Of course Hodder were delighted with the result; the jacket was a classic.

EMO: And Ray's involvement with your books continues to this day.

DEIGHTON: That's right. All Ray's work is one hundred per cent his own, in as much as I know that when I was illustrating, the more that people left me alone the better job I did. Publishers have been very co-operative, and over the years it's given Ray a freedom which is difficult to achieve in a commercial environment.

EMO: How did the celebrated promotional material come about?

DEIGHTON: It was immediately apparent to me that when launching books, publishers were too often just content to flatter the authors—they'd throw a small party, lay on a couple of bottles of sweet sherry and invite a few people along. I felt that a publishing house should use its skills as a publisher to promote books. In those days, very small amounts of money could produce very intriguing promotional items.

EMO: Were they all your ideas?

DEIGHTON: It's difficult to remember now. I think the small notebook for *Billion-Dollar Brain* was my idea. The 'Top Secret' wallet which accompanied *An Expensive Place to Die* was entirely Ray Hawkey's. I'd always said I didn't like blurbs that made it unnecessary to read the first three chapters. It can remove some of the excitement of a book, and often makes for a not very interesting blurb. So I think what Ray did in the case of that book, was to take the story and write for himself a scenario of events which might have preceded the action. He then made that into a set of documents. It was one of the most successful pieces he did.

EMO: In those first eight years, 1962 through to 1970, you had eleven books published, you worked on two screenplays, produced two feature films, served as Travel Editor on *Playboy* and wrote your cookstrips for the *Observer*. It suggests a tremendous head of creative energy was released with the publication of *The IPCRESS File*.

DEIGHTON: Well, eight years is a long time, and I've never been very keen on holidays of any sort. I think when you're in your early thirties—as I was—and you have a book published and you've never until that time wanted to, suddenly you *do* explode with energy and ideas. I remember saying that I could write two books a year in those early years, but I was dissuaded by my publishers. They were right; it's better to give time for rewriting and planning.

EMO: How did you come to books? Were you encouraged to read as a child?

DEIGHTON: I was a very poor scholar. I'd come home from the grammar school with these bad reports and my father, who didn't believe in corporal punishment, told me that he wouldn't punish me if he saw that I was regularly reading books. So whenever my father was around, I made sure I was reading, which wasn't very difficult because I quite enjoyed books.

EMO: What did you read?

DEIGHTON: Many of the same books I see my own children reading today: Conan Doyle, Jules Verne, *Treasure Island*, biographies, history and so on.

EMO: Ever play truant from school?

DEIGHTON: Yes, and I still have nightmares about it. I haven't been to school for like a month, and I'm thinking . . . they're going to find out, they're going to catch me!

Yes, sometimes I'd skip classes, and to stay off the streets I'd go to the British Museum or the Marylebone Public Library. I particularly liked the reference section—I think the seating was more comfortable—and I'd read all the magazines, and of course the encyclopaedias. I think in a funny sort of way that was very beneficial to me as a writer, and still today I read reference books for pleasure.

EMO: You're largely self-taught, and I know you have an enduring concern for the limitations of formal education. As a writer, do you feel particular responsibilities in addition to entertaining your readers?

DEIGHTON: Writers become very good at communicating information, and because of this skill, many people think that the information is of itself good. Writers have a very protected sort of life. We are well looked after, we work in a warm, sheltered environment and tap out our messages. We have to beware of sitting in judgement on the people who actually get things done. It's tempting to do so, when writing fiction, and even more when writing history. I think a writer should destroy clichés and make people rethink assumptions, but few writers, if any, are clever enough to tell people what to think.

EMO: You've been quoted as wanting 'goodness and brains to triumph over badness and muscle' in your books. To what extent do you deliberately set out to underwrite certain values?

DEIGHTON: If we accept that all art is the imposing of order upon the chaos of nature, it's extremely tempting to inflict on this chaos a totalitarian pattern. All artists are inclined to be fascistic because they are, by the very nature of what they do, imposing by force of will an artificial arrangement of elements. Now one of the kinds of arrangement that I don't like is the meeting of force with brutal counterforce, because it doesn't lead to anything except the acceptance of force as benign. I think what we do have to promote as writers is the benefit of people using their brains.

EMO: Let's talk some more about the actual process of writing. The evolution of each book is clearly unique, but speaking generally, can you describe the stages your novels go through?

DEIGHTON: I usually have plans for, say, the next six books. Right now, I'm collecting material for a book I'll not write for maybe four years.

EMO: What's the starting-point, the catalyst that sets you off?

DEIGHTON: For me it's much more a technical decision than one of story and environment, which are the excuses for achieving what I want to do. I knew, for example, that when I finished *Goodbye Mickey Mouse* (a story set in 1944), I'd want to write a book in contemporary speech. Checking every word to make sure no modern expressions slip in is fascinating, but it's tremendously restricting. A very early decision is whether the story is going to be told in the first person, or the third person. And then I get to the central characters, who are always thought of in terms of their job and environment.

EMO: Is it easier to write a first-person narrative?

DEIGHTON: Not at all. It's often assumed the writer just has to draw on his own personality and experience. None of the central characters in my first-person books are myself. For instance, in the *Game, Set & Match* trilogy, Bernard Samson is a male chauvinist with a chip on his shoulder. The intention is that the reader sees through his vanity and bitterness, and learns to live with his ego, and still likes him. I find I have to work longer and harder to create these first-person narratives than I do when writing a novel in the third person.

EMO: Is all this evolving on notes in a box-file, or in your head?

DEIGHTON: Entirely in my head. All that goes into the box-file is research material. Just recently, I was reading an article about the German Intelligence Service, and I tore it out because I know it's good background information for one of two books I'm planning—though I'm not sure which one. But everything about the actual story I allow to evolve in my head, because I find once it's written down I get hypnotised by it. I start writing as late as I can, for whilst the idea—however complex—is in the brain, it can still be radically changed.

EMO: Has the idea for a novel ever come from someone else?

DEIGHTON: I think SS–GB was the only time a whole book has been suggested to me. I was sitting with Tony Colwell and Ray Hawkey in Cape's offices, and we were going over promotional material for *Fighter*. Tony asked what I thought might have happened had Hitler actually invaded Britain. I said I'd seen quite a lot of the German planning, and outlined what probably would have happened. Ray immediately suggested the subject would make a marvellous novel—what he called an 'Alternative World' book. I'd never heard the expression before. Anyway, I went home without too much enthusiasm for it, but the idea kept coming back to me, and the more I thought about it the more attractive it became. But then I thought, the readers aren't going to buy a central character who's a highly placed collaborator, and I didn't want someone who was sweeping the floor at the German High Command and listening at the keyhole. The hero had to be English, I wanted him at the centre of affairs, but I just couldn't crack the problem of finding a sympathetic role for him. Then one night in bed I suddenly had an idea. He could be a policeman, doing something like crowd control, nothing controversial . . . then I thought murder! He's going to be investigating a murder—no one is going to mind him co-operating with the enemy if he's doing such a socially okay job. It was the key to making Ray's idea work, and without it SS–GB would probably never have been written.

EMO: What percentage of ideas for books do you cast away, or deliberately suppress?

DEIGHTON: Ninety per cent! Ideas for books are plentiful. It's making them work that's difficult. One is stuck with the writing for years, so I try and make sure that I only start on projects I can live with.

EMO: Are there stories you've taken through several of the stages and then abandoned?

DEIGHTON: Yes. I've put aside two or three books when they were almost complete. Others I've started over again. *SS–GB* was originally written in the first person, then rewritten in the third person from page one. *Goodbye Mickey Mouse* was restructured because technical problems came up. I'd planned for each chapter to explore a different point of view of life at the American airfield, and I wanted to use the different points of view to tell the story. It wasn't until I was a quarter of the way through writing that I realised the ending wouldn't work using this technique. So I scrapped what I'd written, and started again.

EMO: Is the abandoned material wasted?

DEIGHTON: Nothing is ever really abandoned, it's just set aside temporarily. I was going to write a non-fiction book about confidence tricksters, and I talked to dozens of tricksters and victims. That book was never written, but I used the research to write the novel *Only When I Larf*.

EMO: Once you're satisfied with the structure, and the research is complete, do you sit down and write a lengthy synopsis with chapter outlines?

DEIGHTON: I usually plan the novel on scraps of paper, with a lot of diagrams and arrows. Then finally I take one A4 sheet of paper for each chapter and block out rather lengthy descriptions. By this time a lot of problems have solved themselves.

EMO: Do you follow a regular 'eve-of-fight' routine before commencing a new novel?

DEIGHTON: I find there's something inevitable about starting a book. I've started some books working on the back of an envelope in a bus. When the time comes, you just have to start.

EMO: To what extent do you allow the story to develop its own direction?

DEIGHTON: The structure is established right at the beginning, but there has to be room for the characters to change and develop. The conflict between the plan, and the direction the story wants to go, provides the tension a writer suffers, and *needs*, to produce a book.

EMO: And do you work through sequentially from the first chapter to the last?

DEIGHTON: Not necessarily. Sometimes research opportunities make me get down to writing a rough draft of a later chapter. But I prefer to work through from the beginning.

EMO: Has a story ever developed an ending you hadn't planned?

DEIGHTON: No. I think if this ever happened I would dump the book. But there are always minor twists and turns in an ending that weren't originally anticipated.

EMO: How about the actual writing, do you enjoy it?

DEIGHTON: Once I start writing I'm obsessed. I work almost without stopping because I have to. I can't truly say I like writing, but once I start on a book it's difficult to stop even for a day.

EMO: Do you need to hide yourself away?

DEIGHTON: No. I do the mail and that's by far the worst distraction for a writer. The door to my workroom is always open, so I can hear the sounds of the house, and the children don't hesitate to wander in and start talking. If I had to isolate myself from my family to write, I would find some other job.

EMO: You said you scrapped *Goodbye Mickey Mouse* a quarter way through because of structural problems and started over again. How much rewriting do you do?

DEIGHTON: It's a matter of constant revision hour by hour as I write. Then I reread yesterday's work, and I go on revising the whole book over and over again.

EMO: Few writers I know are ever satisfied with their work. By the time the book is published they know better than any critic where the faults lie.

DEIGHTON: Yes, and for that reason I've never reread any of my novels. I remember that when it was decided to publish *Berlin Game*, *Mexico Set* and *London Match* in one volume, I was very tempted to modify some passages. But then I decided it wouldn't be a good idea to have two versions of the same texts.

EMO: *Game, Set & Match* was an ambitious undertaking. What was the genesis of the trilogy?

DEIGHTON: After *SS–GB*, *XPD* and *Goodbye Mickey Mouse* I wanted to write a novel in the first person again. Normally everything I write is pared right down, so it's as cryptic and tight as I can make it. But this time I deliberately wanted to allow the central character to talk more. I thought, I'm going to let him anticipate some of what's coming along and let him comment on everything. In most of my other first-person novels, it was all given to the reader who could make of it whatever he or she wished.

EMO: What drew you to use Berlin as a principal background again, some twenty years after writing *Funeral in Berlin*?

DEIGHTON: Over the years I'd talked to a lot of Germans and made many visits to Germany, particularly while researching the three non-fiction books *Fighter*, *Airshipwreck* and *Blitzkrieg*. But I hadn't been in Berlin for a long time and I felt I wanted to go back, with no idea of using it as a background. When you like a city very much, you have to be careful not to misunderstand its suitability in a story. At the time I was thinking about the trilogy. I had the central character in his spy headquarters in London, that was fixed, and I was trying to work out his sphere of operations, which could have been anywhere. Then returning to the city, I found I very much wanted to write about it again. So the first book became *Berlin Game* and I used the city as a major setting in *London Match*.

EMO: Which points up the value of holding the idea in your head for as long as possible.

DEIGHTON: That's right. I don't have a rule about not putting down notes or anything, but I think the free association of ideas, which can only take place in the head, is a great advantage.

EMO: Did you find writing the trilogy a formal challenge? It has a very solid, carefully structured plot.

DEIGHTON: Let me tell you, I was very, very nervous about it. I was worried a lot of people might say it was a long, overblown treatment for a story which would have been better done short. But once I started writing it, I felt it was absolutely the way it should be done. Of course, there were limitations. I had to plan all three books together. I couldn't introduce major new characters in each book, and I couldn't kill important characters off. It meant I didn't get quite the slam-bang finishes I would if I were writing only one book.

EMO: Several of the characters from *Game, Set & Match*, and their parents, appear in your novel *Winter*. Did the novel arise from a continuing interest in the characters, or was *Winter* planned before you embarked on the trilogy?

DEIGHTON: *Winter* was planned many years ago. I suppose it's a book I have wanted to write ever since finishing *Blitzkrieg*. A lot of the research I did for that book produced personal stories and anecdotes that couldn't be used in a history book. I started to think about a novel set in the 1930s and when I began to plan the *Game, Set & Match* trilogy, *Winter*—which covers the first half of the century—fitted into the plan.

EMO: You must have enjoyed working out how these characters in the trilogy came to be where they are and what they are. It's delightful to see Lisl Hennig as a young girl in Berlin, to encounter Werner Volkmann's parents and meet Bernard Samson's father.

DEIGHTON: The trilogy is quite long—some might say too long—and by the time I'd finished it I knew the characters in considerable detail. I only had to relate them to each other. I hope the reader has the same sort of fun following the twists and turns of all that planning and work.

EMO: *Winter* is the story of a Berlin family from the turn of the century through to the end of World War II. In terms of subject and style it marks a radical departure from your previous novels.

DEIGHTON: In many ways *Winter* was more interesting to write than anything I have done before. The idea of writing a 'family saga' was in itself quite daunting. I read several books of this type before deciding that I couldn't follow the technique of continuing time. That is to say, I felt I couldn't keep writing '. . . and then three months later . . . it wasn't more than a year after that . . .' and so on. I decided to write detailed episodes—some of them covering only a few minutes of time—and then move forward to another such detailed episode. I wrote the whole first draft of the book without being totally confident that this device would work. I showed the typescript to a couple of people who I knew would give me their real opinion, however disturbing, and they found the format satisfactory. It was only after that first draft that I was able to relax and work into the book. Of course one of the casualties of a book so filled with history is dialogue. The style of the dialogue is quite different from *Game, Set & Match* but since I'd always intended *Winter* to be written in the third person this didn't make it incompatible with the other books. However it required constant monitoring and took ages to write. I'm sure this book was written more slowly than any previous one because there were so many different aspects to worry about.

EMO: The emotional centre of *Winter* is Paul Winter; a bright, charming, nice fellow in many ways, who rises to become a senior administrator in the Gestapo. Realising this character can't have been without difficulty.

DEIGHTON: It provided countless ways to go wrong. I didn't want the book to become an apologia for the Nazis, and yet I wanted to say that it could happen here. I have never been able to see Hitler as an extraordinary man. Hitler was an ordinary man given extraordinary power by people who were prepared to do anything they were told without questioning it. Perhaps Germans are particularly vulnerable to such a tyranny but it would be dangerous to think they are unique in this respect. Paul Winter is a loyal and efficient bureaucrat who looks at life in the dispassionate and ruthless way that such people look at all of us, which is to say as paperwork. That idea guided me throughout the writing of the book.

EMO: Do you judge him victim or begetter of his time?

DEIGHTON: Paul is an apolitical, rather liberal individual who has always respected his parents and admired everything about his elder brother. Peter Winter is an authoritarian figure as first children sometimes are, and he's nostalgic for the old *Kaiserzeit*. And yet it's Paul who smooths the way for the tyranny: Peter who fights it. I didn't want the brothers to be stereotypes. I didn't want to say this is the sort of person who becomes a fascist: while this nice chap is anti-fascist. There have been far too many stories like that already. I wanted two people who were complex enough to make the story interesting, although in a family saga covering such a period of time there's a limit to how complex even the major characters can be. I don't write books to give messages to anyone,

I'd consider that arrogant. I'm an entertainer not a politician. But privately, that is to say when I'm not writing, my feeling is that all questions demand individual answers. Obeying any political party sounds rather like leaving others to do your thinking for you.

EMO: One asks, how could a nation have so blindly followed Hitler? How could the camps have happened? There's no single explanation, yet I wondered to what extent the novel is a working out of your own need to answer some of these questions?

DEIGHTON: While working on the book, and talking to countless Germans including many who'd been very close to horrendous episodes, I sometimes felt I could answer them. But now I confess myself just as puzzled as I ever was. However, the more I learn about the Third Reich the more it confirms my belief that the power of government, and the way that civil servants are permitted to interpret the law, and modify it to their own convenience and views, has, with the coming of the computer data base, become a serious threat to a free society.

EMO: Can you explain this continuing fascination that Germany holds for you?

DEIGHTON: First of all there is the enigma about the nature of the German. No less importantly there is the geography. Germany's Elbe has long been a place where East meets West. If I may quote from *Mexico Set* '. . . Lombard from Slav, Frank from Avar, Christian from barbarian, Catholic from Protestant and Communist from Capitalist' to say nothing of being the place where the two greatest military powers, and vastly different political systems, face each other. As if that wasn't difficult enough to comprehend, we have Germany split into two: one committed to the East, the other to the West. There is even a town, a rather wonderful old town, split into two like a living virus dabbed onto a slide under a microscope. I find it quite irresistible.

EMO: You're planning a further trilogy featuring some of these same characters. How do you recharge your creative batteries for the next book?

DEIGHTON: I try and forget that I write.

Edward Milward-Oliver

TWENTY-FIVE-YEAR CHRONOLOGY OF BRITISH AND AMERICAN FIRST EDITIONS, 1962–1987

1962
November
   The IPCRESS File *London*

1963
October
   Horse Under Water *London*
October
   The IPCRESS File *New York*

1964
September
   Funeral in Berlin *London*
November
   Drinks-man-ship (ed.) *London*

1965
January
   Funeral in Berlin *New York*
March
   Action Cook Book *London*
October
   Où est le garlic *London*

1966
January
   The Billion Dollar Brain *New York*
March
   Billion-Dollar Brain *London*
September
   Cookstrip Cook Book *New York*

1967
March
   The Assassination of President Kennedy (co-author) *London*
April
   An Expensive Place to Die *New York*
April
   Len Deighton's London Dossier *London*
May
   An Expensive Place to Die *London*
October
   El Alamein and the Desert War (contr.) *London*

1968
January
   Horse Under Water *New York*
April
   Only When I Larf *London*
July
   El Alamein and the Desert War (contr.) *New York*
November
   Len Deighton's Continental Dossier *London*

1970
September
   Bomber *London*
September
   Bomber *New York*

1971
October
  Declarations of War   *London*

1972
June
  Close-Up   *London*
June
  Close-Up   *New York*

1974
January
  The Valley of Fear (intr.)   *London*
May
  Spy Story   *London*
September
  Spy Story   *New York*

1975
March
  Eleven Declarations of War   *New York*
May
  Yesterday's Spy   *London*
October
  Yesterday's Spy   *New York*
October
  Guilt-Edged (foreword)   *London*

1976
June
  Twinkle, Twinkle, Little Spy   *London*
September
  Catch a Falling Spy   *New York*

1977
March
  Où est le garlic   *New York*
May
  The Valley of Fear (intr.)   *New York*
September
  Fighter   *London*

October
  How to be a Pregnant Father (recipes)   *Secaucus*

1978
May
  Fighter   *New York*
August
  SS–GB   *London*
October
  Airshipwreck (co-author)   *London*

1979
February
  SS–GB   *New York*
March
  Airshipwreck (co-author)   *New York*
March
  Basic French Cooking   *London*
September
  Blitzkrieg   *London*
October
  Tactical Genius in Battle (ed/intr.)   *London*
October
  Tactical Genius in Battle (ed/intr.)   *New York*

1980
March
  How to be a Pregnant Father (recipes)   *London*
May
  Blitzkrieg   *New York*
September
  The Battle of Britain   *London*
October
  The Orient Flight L.Z.127-Graf Zeppelin (co-author)   *Maryland*

1981
March
  XPD   *London*
April
  XPD   *New York*

September
   The Egypt Flight L.Z.127-Graf
   Zeppelin (co-author)   *Maryland*

1982
August
   Whodunit? (contr.)   *London*
August
   Whodunit? (contr.)   *New York*
September
   Goodbye Mickey Mouse   *London*
October
   Goodbye, Mickey Mouse   *New
   York*

1983
October
   Berlin Game   *London*

1984
January
   Berlin Game   *New York*
September
   The French Foreign Legion
   (intr.)   *London*
September
   The French Foreign Legion
   (intr.)   *New York*
October
   Mexico Set   *London*

1985
February
   Mexico Set   *New York*
August
   The Adventure of the Priory School
   (intr.)   *Santa Barbara*
October
   London Match   *London*

1986
January
   London Match   *New York*
October
   Game, Set & Match   *London*

1987
March
   Only When I Laugh   *New York*
October
   Winter   *London*
October
   Literary Agents (intr.)   *Oxford*

1988
January
   Winter   *New York*

THE LEN DEIGHTON
COMPANION

A–Z

abandoned novels. *See Mamista!*

abduction, conducted on a massive scale, is investigated by the unnamed narrator of *The IPCRESS File*. Deighton's first novel opens with the disappearance of a top British biochemist, the latest victim of Jay's plot to brainwash the entire framework of the nation. Subsequently, the narrator himself is abducted from an American nuclear test site on Tokwe Atoll by members of Jay's network. When it serves to advance the cause, it is ruthlessly practised by both sides in the intelligence war: in *XPD*, the CIA identify Willi Kleiber as a KGB agent, lift him out of Europe and covertly fly him to the United States for interrogation; in *Berlin Game*, Bernard Samson fears for the safety of his children, and ensures they have armed police protection before exposing his wife as the KBG mole within London Central; in *Mexico Set*, Erich Stinnes reveals a KGB contingency plan to abduct Samson to Moscow, while in *London Match*, they brazenly kidnap him on the streets of West Berlin.

ABROAD IN LONDON. Deighton's first published writing, a portrait of London's Soho district, appeared in Issue 10 of *Ark* (1954), the journal of London's Royal College of Art. It's a short illustrated piece of some 400 words, yet is early evidence of his keen eye and his ability to bring to life a person or a place in a phrase.

The Abwehr. The German military intelligence service was engaged in vicious rivalry with the SS's own intelligence organisation, the Sicherheitsdienst, for the greater part of World War II. This conflict lies at the heart of *SS–GB*, in which British resistance leader George Mayhew plays off one against the other to deny both the fruits of Britain's atomic research. In June 1944, control of the Abwehr was finally seized by the SS, which merged it into the Reichssicherheitshauptamt, leading to a unified German intelligence service under the Nazi Party's control.

Abwehr officers encountered in the novels include Captain Hans Hesse, General Georg von Ruff and Dr Hans Starkhof. Willi Kleiber is said to have made quite a name for himself in the service, and Claude Winkler admits to having been one of its agents while active with the Guernica Network in Nazi-occupied France.

Acacia Drive. An unremarkable street in one of those districts where the suburbs creep stealthily in towards London, where Jay's sidekick Housemartin is arrested impersonating a police Chief Inspector in *The IPCRESS File*. This leads the narrator to raid No. 42 in the hope of recovering the missing biochemist Raven, but he finds the house's cell-like rooms empty. The only clues to the mysterious former occupants are a few hundred feet of unedited 16mm silent cine-film, and a spool of recording tape sounding like 'the "Messiah" heard through a wall and played at half speed'—an enigma solved when the narrator escapes from the Hungarian prison in the novel's finale.

access controls. The three Anglo-American secret classifications, Top Secret (or 'Cosmic' for NATO documents), Secret and Confidential, are only the tip of the iceberg, for classifiers have a tendency to invent new secrecy labels at every opportunity. In *XPD*, all MI6 documents are said to have an '*ultra*-secret' classification.

You'll sometimes hear officials talking of 'clearances' rather than 'classifications', but the two terms are generally complementary. For example, a person having a 'TS clearance' is permitted to read classified documents up to and including the level of Top Secret. Laminated on to these are Special Intelligence clearances—GH7 'non-stopped', in the case of Jean Tonnesen in *The IPCRESS File*.

acoustic couplers are small devices which enable computers to talk to each other over the telephone. Colonel Schlegel impresses Charles Bonnard in *Yesterday's Spy* with his latest toy—an acoustic coupler looking like a portable typewriter, which enciphers, transmits, receives and deciphers secret communications over open lines.

ACTION. Short story in the collection *Declarations of War*. Thirty years after World War II, former RAF Medical Officer Stanley Childs and Air Marshal John Dover observe the making of a war film, and see their past adventures unfold before their eyes—but not as they remember them.

action codes employed by WOOC(P) are deciphered in a footnote in *Horse Under Water*. All jobs requested have RI (Relative Importance) codes and are then given D of C (Difficulty of Completion) codes. A low RI (i.e. not very important job) will be attended to if it gets a low D of C (i.e. if it's easy to do). Similarly, a high D of C job requires a high RI to get it approved for action.

ACTION COOK BOOK: Len Deighton's Guide to Eating (Jonathan Cape, London, 18 March 1965/**Cookstrip Cook Book**, Bernard Geis, New York, 9 September 1966; non-fiction). Eighty cookstrips from Deighton's popular *Observer* series, which complement *Où est le garlic* and *Basic French Cooking*, being mostly English-style cooking and basic information. 'It's his freshness, in all his text as well as in the brilliant idea of the strips themselves, which puts him among the most attractive and usable cookery writers we have,' wrote *The Journal of the Wine & Food Society*.
See also: the Cookstrip.

actors, and showbusiness in general, are intimately portrayed in *Close-Up*. This study of a celebrated English film actor in decline had its origins in Deighton's experience of producing *Only When I Larf* and *Oh! What a Lovely War*—'It was a safety valve; something I did instead of murdering certain movie people.'[1] And while it is said there's something of an actor in every spy, the narrator of *Billion-Dollar Brain* is surprised to learn his old pal Harvey Newbegin once trod the boards. 'Well I wasn't really an actor. I just barn-stormed around after I left college. I was serious about acting in those days, but the hungrier I got the more my resolution sagged, until a guy I'd known at college talked me into a job with the Defense Department.'

ADAGIO. Short story in the collection *Declarations of War*, in which one minute in the life of an RAF pilot during the Battle of Britain is reconstructed in action-filled slow motion.

Adem, ——. Minor character in *The IPCRESS File*, a stringer for British Intelligence in the Middle East. In his mid-sixties, he's a fine judge of horses, wines and illegal substances, and has an encyclopaedic knowledge of an area stretching from Northern Turkey to Jerusalem.

adultery. A guileless Harvey Newbegin is spellbound by Midwinter's teenage assassin Signe Laine ('Look at her: the texture of her hair, soft hands, her skin. She has youth') in *Billion-Dollar Brain*. Frank Harrington's surprise mistress hidden away in Berlin-Lübars turns out to be Werner's young wife, Zena Volkmann, in *Berlin Game*. Tessa Kosinski's wayward eye settles on Giles Trent ('He's a handsome brute . . . and George was away watching the Japanese making motorcars') in *Berlin Game*, then Dicky Cruyer in *Mexico Set* ('It wasn't an affair, darling. No one could have an affair with Dicky; he's having an imperishable affair with himself')—a liaison recklessly renewed in *London Match*. And the family saga *Winter* is peppered with adulterous liaisons: Harald Winter and Martha Somló, Inge Winter and Deputy Reichsminister Fritz Esser, and most surprising of all, Veronica Winter and Alan 'Boy' Piper.

Unexpected consequences follow Red Bancroft's lesbian seduction of Elena Bekuv in *Twinkle, Twinkle, Little Spy* and Marshall Stone's fling with Ingrid Rainbow in *Close-Up*, while Vera Hardcastle's ruthless disregard for her soldier husband in Burma leads to a bloody *crime passionnel* at the conclusion of *Goodbye Mickey Mouse*.

THE ADVENTURE OF THE PRIORY SCHOOL by Arthur Conan Doyle. *Introduced by Len Deighton* (Santa Teresa Press, Santa Barbara, August 1985). Deighton was brought up with the Sherlock Holmes stories and his continuing enthusiasm is evident in his original essay which accompanies this facsimile of the autograph manuscript in The Marvin P. Epstein Sherlock Holmes Collection.

See also: Watson roles.

advertising. Having graduated from the Royal College of Art and worked as an airline steward for BOAC, Deighton spent several years illustrating advertising and publicity material in New York and London, where he served briefly as art director of an advertising agency. In *Horse Under Water*, the narrator sardonically observes a group of advertising executives in London's Ritz bar, '. . . with not enough chin and too much cuff. They were buying drinks with a generosity that an expense account brings. They prodded and discussed their product in low respectful tones. Sliced, sterilized and Cellophane wrapped; a loaf.'

aerial warfare decisively changed the nature of armed conflict in this century, and is the subject of some of Deighton's finest writing; notably *Bomber*, one of the classic novels about World War II, *Goodbye Mickey Mouse* and the short stories *Winter's Morning* and *Lord Nick Flies Again*, both set in World War I, and *Action*, *Adagio* and *Brent's Deus Ex Machina*, set in World War II. It also figures in *Winter*, in which Harald Winter grows rich supplying airframes to the German military during World War I and both Glenn Rensselaer and Alan Piper enter service with Britain's Royal Flying Corps.

A perceptive and lucid analysis of the Battle of Britain ('a pivotal point of the history of this century') is to be found in the two non-fiction studies *Fighter* and *Battle of Britain*, while the role of aircraft in the radical German strategy of the 'lightning war' is examined in *Blitzkrieg*.

agents. Qualifications, access to targets, forms of payment—these all vary, but it's axiomatic that one man's agent is another man's traitor. 'Agents come in many shapes and sizes,' observes Bernard Samson in *Mexico Set*. 'Some are waiting for the socialist millennium, some hate their parents, some get angry after being ripped off by a loan company. Some simply want more money. But usually it begins with opportunity. A man finds himself handling something secret and valuable . . .' Dedicated communist agents encountered in the novels include Gerry Hart, Willi Kleiber, Douglas Reid-Kennedy and Fiona Samson; numbered among London's men are Adem, Aziz, Walter von Munte, Johnnie Vulkan/Paul Louis Broum and Werner Volkmann.

agents of influence. Disguised voices in foreign governmental, political and journalistic circles, whose overriding mission is to manipulate opinion and policy—e.g. Gerry Hart in *Twinkle, Twinkle, Little Spy*.

airports serve as incidental locations in several novels. Joe MacIntosh is killed by a car-bomb at London-Heathrow in *Horse Under Water*; a package of supposedly lethal eggs is stolen by Harvey Newbegin at London's BEA Terminal in *Billion-Dollar Brain*; Douglas Archer first encounters SS-Standartenführer Oskar Huth at London's Croydon Airport in *SS–GB*; Gerry Hart is revealed as Moscow's man when he takes Senator Greenwood hostage at Washington-Dulles in *Twinkle, Twinkle, Little Spy*; Charles Stein is kidnapped by Rocky Paz at Los Angeles International in *XPD*; Paul Biedermann is murdered at Paris-Charles de Gaulle and Bernard Samson is unexpectedly contacted by his treacherous wife at London-Heathrow in *Mexico Set*; and Paul Winter receives a dramatic summons to Munich's

Oberwiesenfeld airport in the early hours of 30 June 1934, as Hitler sets in motion the bloody purge of the SA in *Winter*. Wartime airfields are portrayed in *Bomber* (Warley Fen and Kroonsdijk) and *Goodbye Mickey Mouse* (Steeple Thaxted), and military airfields feature in *The IPCRESS File* (Lay Field on Tokwe Atoll) in *Berlin Game* (RAF Berlin-Gatow) and in the short story set in war-torn Vietnam, *First Base*.

airships were historically short-lived, but for Deighton they have a magic that the aeroplane cannot replace. His enthusiasm is evident in *Airshipwreck*, *Flying the Atlantic*, and the two aerophilately books *The Orient Flight L.Z.127-Graf Zeppelin* and *The Egypt Flight L.Z.127-Graf Zeppelin*. Typically, he has also made this private pursuit work for him in his fiction. In the massive novel *Winter*, he convincingly recreates a Zeppelin raid over England in World War I, and captures the excitement of passengers crossing the Atlantic aboard the *Graf Zeppelin* in 1929—ten years before the first commercial aircraft travelled this route. Picture postcards of airships are used as contact codes by Melodie Page in *Yesterday's Spy*, and Egypt's plan to convince Israel that it is in possession of stolen atomic shells is foiled when Charles Bonnard destroys Champion's modern airship at the climax of the novel.

AIRSHIPWRECK (Jonathan Cape, London, 5 October 1978/Holt Rinehart Winston, New York, 15 March 1979; non-fiction.) *Co-authored by Len Deighton and Arnold Schwartzman*. The age of the commercial airship was brief, and the incidence of disastrous failure was high, yet Deighton maintains that the airship was one of the greatest triumphs of structural engineering the world has known. Drawing on a rare collection of photographs, he records how the dream went wrong and pays tribute to the master builders and their aluminium marvels.

Albufeira. The small fishing town in Portugal which provides the setting for much of *Horse Under Water*. 'To wake up in the sun of Albufeira is to be reborn' suggests the narrator, though visitors there today will find it rather different from the place Deighton wrote about all those years ago.

'Alforreca'. Cryptonym for the WOOC(P) operation to raise material from the sunken wartime U-boat off Albufeira in *Horse Under Water*.

Algeria, and that part of the Sahara desert within its borders, serve as unfamiliar settings for the opening and closing chapters of *Twinkle, Twinkle, Little Spy*. More at home in an urban environment, Deighton was prompted to write about the region after participating (as a member of one of the control parties) in the Sahara stages of a motor rally organised by Wylton Dickson, co-publisher of *Len Deighton's Continental Dossier*. 'It was awe inspiring to drive through the desert at night: it produces a curious optical illusion of being in a big tunnel. To find people alone in the middle of this wasteland is a surprise, and to find them selling ancient Roman arrowheads, dug from its sand, was enough to send me back to my history books.'[2]

Algiers. North African capital briefly visited by Major Mann and the narrator of *Twinkle, Twinkle, Little Spy* to intercept Soviet fugitives, Professor and Mrs Bekuv. 'It is a city of narrow alleys and steep staircases, hovels and office blocks, secret gardens and boulevards. At its feet there is a busy port. Behind it, the roads hairpin up into the lush green hills and pine forests, climbing ever higher into the Atlas Mountains.'

Allenby, Professor. Smug young Cambridge professor of modern history encountered at the Foxwell's elegant soirée in *Spy Story*, who champions the German reunification talks being held in Copenhagen. 'Marx designed his theories round the belief that Germany—not Russia—would be the first socialist land. A unified Germany would provide a chance to see Marxism given a real chance . . .': a scenario that sends tremors through the Foreign Office and British Intelligence.

Altgarten. The fictional German country town near the Netherlands border, whose fate it is to lie in the path of the 700 RAF bombers as they fly from the coast towards Krefeld in *Bomber*. For when Alan Hill's Mosquito is shot down by a Luftwaffe night-fighter, the target indicators are jettisoned over the south-east edge of Altgarten, and ten million pounds of high explosives and phosphorous incendiaries intended for Krefeld are unleashed on the town's 5,000 terrified inhabitants.

Amalgamated Minerals Inc. The multi-national company dreamed up by Silas Lowther as a front to swindle a quarter of a million dollars from New York marks Karl Poster and Johnny Jones, in *Only When I Larf*.

'Ambrose'. The CIA cryptonym for its 'A' code employee Red Bancroft, a member of the Psychological Advisory Directorate in *Twinkle, Twinkle, Little Spy*.

America. Deighton first visited North America whilst on vacation from the Royal College of Art, and wrote of his experience in *Impressions of New York*. Later, he moved to New York to earn a living as a freelance illustrator, but after three months he found he couldn't abide the hot weather in the city and took the Greyhound trail, seeing something of the West and exploring Mexico, before returning to London. He has been back many times since, and American locations appear in several novels: *Billion-Dollar Brain* (New York and Texas), *Only When I Larf* (New York), *Close-Up* (Hollywood), *Twinkle, Twinkle, Little Spy* (Miami, New York, Washington and Virginia), *XPD* (Los Angeles, New York and South Carolina) and *Winter* (New York, Washington and the San Fernando Valley).

American Civil War (1861–5). The struggle between the Confederate 'slavers' and the Union 'abolitionists', which resulted in the devastation of the South, is the meticulously realised historical setting for the short story *Discipline*. Over half a century later it is apparent that the bitter conflict continues to haunt

Americans when Glenn Rensselaer suggests to his sister in *Winter* that Europe in 1910 stands on the brink of a similar cataclysm.

American Intelligence. A maze of interlocking and overlapping agencies, principal among which are: the Central Intelligence Agency, the National Security Agency, the Defense Intelligence Agency, the Offices of Army Intelligence, Naval Intelligence and Air Force Intelligence (including the National Reconnaissance Office), the State Department's Bureau of Intelligence and Research, the FBI's Internal Security Division, the Atomic Energy Commission's Division of Intelligence and the Treasury Department. The Director of the CIA is statutory head of the entire community, and his two principal management tools are the Intelligence Resources Advisory Committee (IRAC) and the United States Intelligence Board (USIB).

American Intelligence officers with a significant role in the novels include Red Bancroft, Barney Barnes, Joe Brody, Hank Dean, 'Skip' Henderson, Melvin Kalkhoven, Major Mickey Mann, Harvey Newbegin, Glenn Rensselaer, Colonel Charles Schlegel, Sam Seymour and Todd Wynn.

Americans are cast in many notable roles. Deighton is one of the few English writers able to create convincing characters who speak credible American. Especially noteworthy are the novels *Goodbye Mickey Mouse*, the story of a group of US Air Force fighter pilots based in wartime England, and *Winter*, the saga of a German-American family through the first half of this century.

'Americans are not noted for assuming failure to be possible before starting something,' suggests the narrator of *The IPCRESS File* on his arrival at Tokwe Atoll, which inside ninety days has been equipped with an airfield, accommodation, extensive R&R facilities for the rock happy servicemen, a mess capable of serving 9,000 meals a day, and a 24-hour radio station! A reactionary Texan billionaire, General Midwinter, leads the fanatical anti-communist crusade in *Billion-Dollar Brain*, aided by former US Foreign Service officer Harvey Newbegin, first encountered in *Funeral in Berlin*. Three novels team a British Intelligence officer with an American boss, *Spy Story*, *Yesterday's Spy* and *Twinkle, Twinkle, Little Spy*, and the *Game, Set & Match* trilogy features an utterly believable American who has wormed his way up into the British spy hierarchy.

See also: field agents.

————, **Anna-Luisa.** Beautiful, twenty-two-year-old German RADwJ social worker, daughter of a high-ranking official in the Propaganda Ministry in *Bomber*. Having looked after the young son of August Bach since his wife died in an air raid on Krefeld, she and Bach discover that they are in love—only hours before she and ten-year-old Hans are killed in the RAF bombing error that destroys Altgarten.

anonymous narrators. The nameless first person narrators of *The IPCRESS File*, *Horse Under Water*, *Funeral in Berlin* and *Billion-Dollar Brain* are generally regarded to be the same laconic British Intelligence officer, despite the fact that he was at school in Burnley in 1940 in *The IPCRESS File*, yet working for British Intelligence in Lisbon that same year in *Horse Under Water*. 'There were advantages to having an anonymous hero,' says Deighton. 'He might or he might not be the same man. This gave me a chance to make minor modifications as and when I wanted them.'[3] The protagonist of *An Expensive Place to Die* is similarly unnamed, and *Spy Story* features a close relative of the earlier narrator operating with the assumed name 'Patrick Armstrong'. In the subsequent novel *Yesterday's Spy*, the narrator shares the same American boss but is referred to throughout by his wartime cover name 'Charles Bonnard', and the otherwise anonymous narrator of *Twinkle, Twinkle, Little Spy* adopts the unlikely alias of one 'Frederick L. Antony'.

Anson, Mary. Energetic, brunette lawyer, happily married to Peter Anson in *Close-Up*. Former wife of superstar actor Marshall Stone, she proves to have relearnt the values of the world outside Hollywood when drawn into Stone's life a second time.

Anson, Peter. British narrator of *Close-Up*. A former Hollywood contract writer turned entertainments editor of an up-market Sunday newspaper, who embarks on a biography of the international superstar and charismatic member of Hollywood's elite, Marshall Stone. The fact of having written the script for Stone's first, acclaimed film, and of being married to his one-time wife, seem to give him all the cards. And he is candid about his motives; he believes Stone to be a rare talent, wants to revisit the big-daddy world of Hollywood, and 'to some extent I wanted to know more about the life that my wife had exchanged for mine'.

anti-heroes. Following the publication of *Horse Under Water*, one critic wrote that 'the most obviously new thing about Mr Len Deighton's spy stories is the anti-heroic quality of his central character'.[4] This is true of the narrators of all his mainstream spy novels; they are neutral meritocrats, whose allegiance is to their own abilities and the job they're paid to do. They feel little or no moral superiority over their opponents, but engage our support with their professionalism, compassion and laconic humour.

Antony, Frederick L. The otherwise anonymous British Intelligence narrator of *Twinkle, Twinkle, Little Spy*. Superficially cast in the same mould as the heroes of *The IPCRESS File*, *Horse Under Water*, etc., he's lost that chip on his shoulder and certainly proves more sensitive to his emotions. Teamed with feisty CIA officer Major Mickey Mann, he takes custody of a defecting Soviet scientist in the Sahara desert and assists Mann in exposing a major KGB source of secret American scientific data on Capitol Hill, before returning halfway back across Africa to find a covert Soviet listening post tapping American comsats.

'Apocalypse'. Cryptonym for the Nazi Sicherheitsdienst's operation to secure Britain's wartime atomic secrets in *SS–GB*.

appendices. The battery of footnotes and appendices in *The IPCRESS File*, *Horse Under Water*, *Funeral in Berlin*, *Billion-Dollar Brain* and *An Expensive Place to Die*, evinced a new style of spy thriller not successfully imitated by anyone since. Deighton delights in entertaining us with instruction on subjects ranging from handling unfamiliar pistols and wire-tapping, to Soviet Security Systems and the neutron bomb.

Appleyard, Bob. Lively, rootless, twenty-six-year-old junior partner in the trio of confidence tricksters in *Only When I Larf*. Having graduated from gas meter banditry to six-figure scams, he covets the respect enjoyed by Silas Lowther as leader and seizes an opportunity to mastermind the team's final venture—an audacious plan to swindle a quarter of a million dollars from the Honourable Gerald Spencer.

Arabs. The Egyptians are Steve Champion's paymaster in *Yesterday's Spy*, with a plan to convince the world they are in possession of atomic artillery shells; a Lebanese 'stringer' for WOOC(P) assists in the recovery of an abducted British biochemist in *The IPCRESS File*; Algerians are briefly encountered in *Twinkle, Twinkle, Little Spy*; and Silas Lowther impersonates an Arab businessman in the swindle pulled on the Honourable Gerald Spencer in *Only When I Larf*.

Archer, Douggie. Detective Superintendent Archer's young motherless son, whose future is secured when Harry Woods agrees to act as SS-Gruppenführer Kellerman's informant in *SS–GB*.

Archer, Detective Superintendent Douglas. Renowned thirty-three-year-old detective in Scotland Yard's Murder Squad, with the leading role in *SS–GB*. A good professional policeman, forced to lead a strangely ambiguous life working in collaboration with the German occupation forces, he becomes embroiled in the feuding between two rival SS officers and is led into an espionage battle whose outcome will determine the future of Europe.

The Arctic is the setting for a chilling sequence at the climax of *Spy Story*, when the American nuclear submarine USS *Paul Revere* manoeuvres beneath the ice and then surfaces to rendezvous with an alleged Soviet defector, Rear-Admiral Remoziva.

Mr Aristo. According to Dalby in *The IPCRESS File*, the alias used by Christian Stakowski when he helped arrange the hurried defection of the Foreign Office spies, Burgess and Maclean, in 1951.

Ark. The journal of London's Royal College of Art, in which appeared Deighton's first published writing: *Abroad in London* (1954) and *Impressions of New York* (1955). Deighton won a scholarship to the Royal College in 1952, having studied at St Martin's School of Art on an ex-service grant, and graduated in 1955.

Arkwright, Sergeant. Special Branch alias adopted by Chico—since WOOC(P), like MI5, has no powers of arrest—when he and Lt.-Col. Harriman snatch Dr Felix Pike in *Billion-Dollar Brain*.

Armstrong, Patrick. Work name of the narrator of *Spy Story*, who if not our overweight friend from *The IPCRESS File*, is certainly a close relative. Formerly with British Intelligence, he is now employed at the war-gaming centre STUCEN, where NATO defence strategies are matched against theoretical Soviet strike threats. Happy in his job, the past gone forever, he declines George Dawlish's offer to return to fieldwork but is soon propelled into a cunning operation to sabotage German reunification talks that are opposed by the Foreign Office.

————, Arthur. Well-informed London villain, doing a nice trade in stolen wine and cigarettes in *SS–GB*, whose asides to Detective Superintendent Douglas Archer persuade the young detective to invite himself to Sydney Garin's glittering Portman Square party—where he finds George Mayhew and Sir Robert Benson contemplating an attempt to release King George VI from the Tower.

Ashton, Private Joshua. Infantryman in the Union Army in *Discipline*. One of a Michigan family of thirteen, he earned a living from timber before being conscripted, and never once considers that he might be killed in the Civil War.

Ashton, Nora. Young, vivacious WAAF officer working in the Royal Air Force Bomber Command headquarters at High Wycombe in *Bomber*, whose love for Simon Cohen irrevocably links her to the outcome of the night's bombing raid over Germany.

THE ASSASSINATION OF PRESIDENT KENNEDY (Jonathan Cape, London, 23 March 1967; non-fiction). *Compiled and edited by Michael Rand, Howard Loxton and Len Deighton.* An original and graphic presentation of the key evidence of the Warren Commission and its critics, in a portfolio containing twelve reproductions of contemporary documents, a cut-out model and five explanatory broadsheets.

Deighton's interest in the subject arose when Bertrand Russell lent him an advance copy of Mark Lane's book *Rush to Judgement*. Without subscribing to any one of the conspiracy theories, he was impressed by the weight of evidence that conflicted with the Warren Commission's conclusions.

Deighton wrote the broadsheets, the portfolio was art-directed by Michael Rand of *The Sunday Times*, and Howard Loxton contributed original research arising from his work with Mark Lane.

assumed identities (not to be confused with *cover names*) are exposed with varying degrees of significance. Johnnie Vulkan is revealed to be Paul Louis Broum, and Major Bailis to be a civilian named Wilson, in *Funeral in Berlin*. Manuel da Cunha and Fernie Tomas are respectively unmasked in *Horse Under Water* as Fregattenkapitän Knobel—a former scientific officer of the wartime German Navy—and Bernard Thomas Peterson, a former British naval officer convicted of collaborating with the Nazis during World War II. Renegade American Harvey Newbegin travels with papers identifying him as a Swedish national, named Eriksson, to circumvent Finnish passport control as he flees to Leningrad in *Billion-Dollar Brain*. The murder victim, identified as antiques dealer Peter Thomas in *SS–GB*, is later discovered to be the nuclear physicist, Dr William Spode. The mysterious Nazi Reichsbank Director, Dr Frank, and the West German businessman Peter Friedman, both turn out to have been Willi Kleiber in *XPD*. And the trio of confidence tricksters in *Only When I Larf* assume a wide range of identities during their crooked adventures.

The Atelier. The (fictional) French artillery testing range—a barren region of scrub and rock north of the Côte d'Azur—from which Steve Champion allegedly intends to steal atomic artillery shells in *Yesterday's Spy*.
See also: Valmy Complex.

atomic weapons. *See* nuclear devices.

Austria. Many forget that until the collapse of the Habsburg monarchy in 1918, the country was a dominant power in central Europe. The Imperial capital of Vienna at the turn of the century is the setting for the opening of *Winter*, while the planning and execution of the Nazi *Anschluss* of March 1938 is one of many historical events portrayed in this saga of a Berlin family through the first half of the century.

autobiographical content. Although there is a recurring link between British authors of spy fiction and the real life profession (Allbeury, Buchan, Chesterton, Fleming, Greene, Le Carré, Maugham), Deighton was never engaged in intelligence work. It is also worth mentioning in the light of his war fiction that he was only ten years old at the outbreak of World War II, though in a sense *SS–GB is* autobiographical in that he drew on memories of wartime—gas lights, tin baths, dimly-lit streets, food rationing—and of places he'd known in his childhood, when writing the novel. Personal traits shared with some of his fictional creations include a fascination for electronic hardware, an interest in cooking, military history and music, and a distrust of formal education.

avalizing provides Werner Volkmann with a precarious living in the *Game, Set & Match* trilogy. He raises loans in the West to finance exports to East Germany, and then collects the money from the East German Government, taking a tiny percentage on each deal. It isn't a banker's business; it's a free-for-all, in which many get their fingers burned. But it enables Werner to move in and out of the Eastern Sector with the minimum of fuss, making him a useful asset for British Intelligence.

Avenue Foch Clinic. Monsieur Datt's scandalous Paris establishment, a *maison de passe* rumoured to be owned by the Ministry of the Interior or the SDECE (neither of which proves true) in *An Expensive Place to Die*. Staffed by a cadre of intellectually and sexually high-powered hostesses, its hidden purpose is to compile 'research dossiers' of tape and film on influential political clients from East and West.

Awards. In 1973 the Commission d'Histoire, Arts et Lettres, de l'Aéro-Club de France awarded Len Deighton *un diplôme* in recognition of the novel *Bomber*. Founded in 1894, the Club is the world's foremost and oldest aviation authority. It pioneered the rules for competitive flying, which are still observed today, granted the world's first pilot's licences, and currently promotes and encourages research on the history of aviation. Eight years after this award, Deighton and his co-author Fred Blau were the recipients of the Federation of Air Mail Societies special FISA Medal for Literature, following the publication of their book *The Orient Flight L.Z.127-Graf Zeppelin*.

Awawa, Ibo. Ambitious African politician in his late forties, the War Minister of the newly emergent nation of Magazaria, whose brazen quest for weapons to mount a coup d'état and seize his country's throne makes him easy prey for the trio of confidence tricksters in *Only When I Larf*.

Aziz, ————. Minor character in *Yesterday's Spy*, who works for the World Meteorological Organisation in Geneva. His masters would be astonished, perhaps, to discover that he is a senior analyst for the Egyptian Intelligence agency, Mukhabarat el-Aam. Certainly his masters in Cairo would be devastated to learn that he's been on *London's* payroll for nearly ten years.

B

Bach, Oberleutnant August. Compassionate forty-six-year-old widower, holder of the coveted 'Blue Max' and Commanding Officer of the Luftwaffe coastal radar station 'Ermine' in *Bomber*. After evacuating his ten-year-old son, and his fiancée, from Krefeld to the safety of Altgarten, he plots the heavy raid by the 700 RAF bombers—unaware that little Hans and Anna-Luisa are among its victims.

bacteriological warfare. Despite the public condemnation of bacteriological and chemical weaponry, governments continue to fund research programmes. In *Billion-Dollar Brain*, deadly viruses are stolen from Britain's Porton Microbiological Research Establishment by members of Midwinter's network, and later, Harvey Newbegin attempts to defect to the Soviet Union with a second batch of pathogens. The subject also arises in *The IPCRESS File*, when Jay kidnaps a Porton chemical warfare biochemist, and in *Funeral in Berlin*, when the narrator is sent to Berlin to receive a Soviet enzyme scientist whom Colonel Stok is willing to sell to the West.

'Bad Monday'. A fateful day in the history of the 220th Fighter Group in *Goodbye Mickey Mouse*. They lose station commander Dan Badger and several other pilots over Berlin, Jamie Farebrother is fatally injured as his Mustang blows a tyre on take-off and Vince Madigan is the victim of a bloody *crime passionnel*.

Badger, Colonel Dan. Prickly, restless, USAF station

commander of the 220th Fighter Group based at Steeple Thaxted in *Goodbye Mickey Mouse*. Entered the Air Force after flying mail routes, and at thirty-six is thought too old to command a Fighter Group—though if he has any failings, they're social rather than operational. Killed in combat on 'Bad Monday', when a Luftwaffe fighter collides with his Mustang during a head-on attack.

Bailis, Major. Assumed identity of a civilian layabout named Wilson, playmate of Johnnie Vulkan in *Funeral in Berlin*.

Baix, Chief Inspector. Amiable senior officer of the Moroccan Sûreté Nationale, side-tracked in Marrakech by the narrator in *Horse Under Water*. 'A soft red fez rode side-saddle on a thin brown pointed face. His moustache was sad and well cared for, and a large nose drove a wedge between his small eyes. He tapped the nose with a silver-topped cane. He looked like something dreamed up by central casting . . .'

Baltic States. Collective name for Lithuania, Latvia and Estonia. Formerly part of the Tsarist Empire, they became independent states after World War I, but were reannexed by the Soviet Union in 1940.

The family homeland of Texan billionaire, General Midwinter, whose dreams of liberating the territory lead to the subversive incursions mounted by the Facts for Freedom organisation in *Billion-Dollar Brain*.

Bancroft, Red. Bisexual CIA officer, attached to the Psychological Advisory Directorate, whose seduction of Elena Bekuv in *Twinkle, Twinkle, Little Spy* is calculated to break Gerry Hart's network of KGB spies. 'It was the smile that I was to remember long after everything else about her had faded in my memory,' admits the narrator. 'It was a strange, uncertain smile that sometimes mocked and sometimes chided but was none the less beguiling for that, as I was to find to my cost.'

banks and bankers have critical roles in several novels. The discovery of a £250,000 Swiss bank deposit provides the key to Johnnie Vulkan's motives in *Funeral in Berlin*; an eminent West German banker unwittingly finances the KGB operation to secure the Hitler Minutes in *XPD* and Peter Friedman masterminds a one hundred million dollar fraud on the Swiss bank owned by Charles Stein and the 'Kaiseroda Raiders' in an attempt to force Stein to surrender the coveted document; the exfiltration of Dr Walter von Munte, a senior official of East Germany's Deutsche Notenbank, exposes the KGB mole within London Central in *Berlin Game*; a plot of land on the Obersalzburg pledged as collateral to Harald Winter's bank is fraught with destiny for his son Paul in *Winter*; and Lebanese banks prove the key to relieving the Honourable Gerald Spencer of a quarter of a million dollars in *Only When I Larf*.

Barbarossa Club. The Soho striptease and gambling club where Dalby and Jay attempt to set up the narrator of *The IPCRESS File* as the traitor responsible for the abduction of the missing Porton biochemist, Raven.

Barga, Barbara. Attractive American journalist on assignment in Nazi-occupied Britain in *SS–GB*, whose minor role in the conspiracy organising the King's escape to America, and ardent affair with Douglas Archer, lead to her accidental death at the hands of the Gestapo.

Barga, Danny. Barbara Barga's former husband, with a minor role in *SS–GB*. A US State Department officer, he's parachuted into Nazi-occupied Britain to inform the Resistance that the King won't be welcome in North America, and is later killed during the fire-fight at Bringle Sands.

Barnes, Barney. Jive-talking black CIA officer, who cryptically advises the narrator to leave Tokwe Atoll in *The IPCRESS File*. His subsequent death at the wheel of a generator truck suggests foul play by Jay's IPCRESS Network, but is later confirmed to have been a bona fide accident.

Baroni, Caterina. Former wife of Steve Champion, in *Yesterday's Spy*. Interviewed by Bonnard at the outset of his enquiry, she bitterly accuses him of hero-worshipping her ex-husband, and makes no attempt to hide the pain of rejection.

Baroni, Marius. Deceased brother of Caterina and Pina Baroni, betrayed by Steve Champion and murdered by the Gestapo during World War II.

Baroni, Pina. Sister of Caterina Baroni in *Yesterday's Spy*. Convinced Steve Champion betrayed their brother to the Gestapo during World War II, she conspires with Serge Frankel to murder him on an autoroute outside Nice, unaware that he is accompanied by son Billy and Charles Bonnard.

Barrett, Pete. Resentful Whitehall Special Branch detective encountered by Bernard Samson in *London Match*.

BASIC FRENCH COOKING (Jonathan Cape, London, 1 March 1979; non-fiction). Presents the fundamental facts of French home cooking, together with 50 of Deighton's celebrated cookstrips. Revised and enlarged from *Où est le garlic*.

Battersby, Sergeant Ted. Studious, eighteen-year-old RAF flight engineer, newly assigned to 'Creaking Door' in *Bomber*. Expected to know every nut and bolt of his aeroplane, as well as to help operate the controls on take-offs and landings, he doughtily assists Sam Lambert in bringing their crippled Lancaster safely back to Warley Fen following the raid on Altgarten.

Battersby, ———. The US Intelligence Department's logistic king—one of several well-laundered American specialists encountered on Tokwe Atoll by the narrator of *The IPCRESS File*.

The Battle of Britain. Few episodes in modern history have so captured the imagination as the battle for the skies over Britain in the summer of 1940. Deighton writes in his Foreword to *Battle of Britain*: '. . . the more I study the Battle of Britain the more convinced I become that it was a pivotal point of the history of this century. To anyone who says that it was not one of the most important battles of the Second World War I ask, without it what other battles would there have been?'

Fictionally portrayed in *Adagio*, it is rerun as a 'war-game' in *Spy Story*, and is analysed at length in *Fighter* and the previously mentioned *Battle of Britain*.

BATTLE OF BRITAIN (Jonathan Cape, London, 11 September 1980/Coward McCann & Geoghegan, New York, 12 September 1980; non-fiction). Having assembled new and contemporary drawings, diagrams, charts and maps, as well as unfamiliar archive photographs, Deighton embodies his text in this visual material to tell the story of one of the most important battles of World War II.

'Battle Opera House'. The massive Divisional Fighter Control bunker at Deelen visited by August Bach in *Bomber*. As high as an apartment building and as long as a city block, phone and teleprinter cables link it to airfields, watch-towers, radar stations, radio monitors and civil defence headquarters across Northern Europe.

Beamish, Stanley. Cover name used by the narrator of *The IPCRESS File* when first making contact with Jay in Leds coffee-house. (Jay blandly presents a business card identifying himself as 'Henry Carpenter—Import Export'.)

Beat the Devil (GB 1954). In his essay *Why Does My Art Go Boom?*, Deighton acknowledges that his first novel, *The IPCRESS File*, was inspired by this Humphrey Bogart-Peter Lorre film, with its offbeat satire of greed, fakery, and the English class system. Directed by John Huston, with a screenplay by Truman Capote and Huston from the novel by James Helvick (Claude Cockburn), the film was dismissed by most critics at the time, but it quickly became a cult favourite, which it remains today.

Beer, Leutnant. Reluctant Luftwaffe night-fighter pilot, stationed at Kroonsdijk in *Bomber*. A pre-war racing driver, he 'hosepipes his fire all over the sky' and has yet to be credited with a kill.

Beirut is today very different from the city Deighton used as an incidental location in *The IPCRESS File* and the setting for the final triple-cross in *Only When I Larf*. Back in the 1960s it was the financial and resort centre of the Middle East, a cosmopolitan playground with luxury hotels (the Phoenicia was one of the world's best) and the world's largest casino (whose gaming tables were used to launder the proceeds from local heroin operations).

Bekuv, Professor Andrei. Leading Soviet expert on masers and inter-stellar communications, lured to the West in *Twinkle, Twinkle, Little Spy*. Later betrayed by his wife, he's forced to return to his Sahara ground station—a covert Soviet listening post tapping secret American comsats stationed over the Atlantic, where he's killed by a Soviet smart-bomb that destroys all evidence of the audacious project.

Bekuv, Elena. Wife of Professor Bekuv in *Twinkle, Twinkle, Little Spy*, whom she joins in America on KGB instructions. Seduced by Red Bancroft, she accompanies her husband back to his Sahara ground station and dies in the Soviet air-strike.

Belgium. Time has healed the wounds, but death pervades the topsoil of this small country which has been invaded twice this century. The grim chaos of life in the German trenches on the Western Front in 1917 is graphically depicted in *Winter*, and the fearful battles of the Ypres salient ('There's scarcely an Englishman that didn't have a relative die here. Perhaps a piece of Britain died here too') recalled by the narrator of *An Expensive Place to Die*. A generation later, the frontier village of Brûly de Pesche is the setting for the alleged meeting between Winston Churchill and Adolf Hitler in *XPD*. The tactics and planning of the

German invasion in May 1940 are considered at length in *Blitzkrieg*, and briefly in *Fighter* and *Battle of Britain*.

The Bendlerblock. The huge building in Berlin from where the German High Command sent the Army to conquer Europe is the dramatic centre of preparations for the Austrian *Anschluss*, and later the anti-Hitler conspiracy, in *Winter*. The building still stands, converted to offices for a cosmetic manufacturer, but Bendlerstrasse has been renamed and a memorial to Count von Stauffenberg stands in the courtyard where in July 1944 he was summarily executed after placing the bomb intended to kill Hitler.

Benson, Sir Robert. Senior civil service mandarin who remains a powerful man in the corridors of Whitehall after the Nazi occupation of Britain in *SS–GB*. Later revealed as an ineffectual party to the King's release from the Tower of London.

Berger, SS-Obersturmführer. Senior full-time SS official of Altgarten in *Bomber*.

Berlin. No modern city evokes more contradictory images than the former capital of Bismark's Empire and Hitler's Third Reich. The atmosphere and ambience of those times are painstakingly recreated in Deighton's massive family saga *Winter*, while echoes of the city in the golden twenties and early thirties—the exuberant metropolis of Amusierkabaretts, the Wintergarten and the glamorous UFA film studios—animate the ageing Lisl Hennig in *Game, Set & Match*. At the same time Bernard Samson and Werner Volkmann reflect on the appalling history of wartime Berlin, events relived by Hans Wever in *XPD* when he recounts his role in the final Götterdämmerung of Spring 1945.

Postwar Berlin, the only city still officially under the martial command of foreign armies, is portrayed in Deighton's third novel *Funeral in Berlin*, again in *Game, Set & Match* (the endpapers of the English omnibus edition reproduce a map of the city identifying key locations which feature in the trilogy), and is unhappily recalled by Marjorie Reid-Kennedy in *Twinkle, Twinkle, Little Spy*.

A brief account of the Allied bombing in August 1940, one of the chain of events that led to the Battle of Britain, is provided in *Fighter*.

Berlin, East. In accordance with the London Protocol of September 1944, postwar Berlin was divided into four occupation zones: Soviet, American, British and French (the so-called 'Vodka', 'Coca-Cola', 'Whiskey' and 'Champagne' sectors). Nearly half of the city was allotted to the Soviets and it became the *de facto* capital of East Germany, notwithstanding the Western Allies' consistent refusal to recognise the sector boundary as an international frontier.

Until 1961, East Berliners were able to visit West Berlin's shops, theatres and cinemas, and see relatives, without real difficulty. But too many decided to remain in the West, and on 13 August 1961 the East German security forces suddenly sealed off sixty-eight of the eighty crossing points, and began building a wall of barbed wire and concrete along the sector boundary. The Allies strongly protested and publicly resolved to maintain a military presence in the city, though privately many Western leaders were relieved that the Soviets had stopped short of occupying West Berlin.

Although the Wall continues to divide the city, the Four Power status of Berlin guarantees that military personnel from the Allied garrisons can freely enter and leave East Berlin provided they are in uniform (Soviet access to West Berlin is similarly guaranteed). But the demilitarised status of Berlin forbids the presence of *German* soldiers on either side of the Wall (no West German soldier may appear in uniform in West Berlin and none of its male residents can be drafted), though this is regularly violated by the East Germans, who claim that East Berlin is a component of their nation. The Soviet Army's GSFG Strike Force maintains extensive facilities in the Karlshorst district, as does the KGB, which works closely with East Germany's Ministerium für Staatssicherheit in Normannenstrasse. (The regime's secret twelve-square-mile complex of underground bunkers built to withstand the twin threats of external attack or internal revolution, lies just outside East Berlin, in Strausberg.)

The whole sector is intensively targeted by Western Intelligence agencies, who themselves maintain a considerable presence in West Berlin. In *Funeral in Berlin*, the narrator slips into this world 'where communist isn't a dirty word' to negotiate the transfer of an important Soviet scientist with Colonel Stok. Bernard Samson is infiltrated into East Berlin through the underground railway tunnels to bring Brahms Four to safety in *Berlin Game*, while Werner Volkmann moves openly through the checkpoints in *Berlin Game* and *Mexico Set*, before being detained and held hostage on the wrong side of the Wall in *London Match*.

Berlin Field Unit. Runs active field agents into the East. One of several departments that together comprise MI6's Berlin Station, headed by Frank Harrington in the *Game, Set & Match* trilogy.

BERLIN GAME (Hutchinson, London, 3 October 1983/Alfred A. Knopf, New York, 5 January 1984; fiction). The first novel of the *Game, Set & Match* spy trilogy concerns treachery at the heart of London Central, and introduces fortyish Bernard Samson, a British intelligence officer who was born into the trade. His father, Brian Samson, was head of Berlin Station immediately after World War II, and saw to it that his son was raised and educated in the former German capital. The story is set in London, and of course Berlin, a city peopled with characters Samson has known since he was a streetwise *berliner Schuljunge*.

Berlin Network. *See* Brahms Network.

Berlin Resident. Head of MI6's Berlin Station; a position held by Frank Harrington in the *Game, Set & Match* trilogy, and formerly by Brian Samson.

Berlin Station. MI6 stations are customarily based in British embassies and sometimes consulates abroad; Berlin merits its own station, acting independently of that in Bonn. Local operations are run by the station's case officers, supervised by the Resident, who keeps London's desk officers informed of the progress and problems of these operations. (MI6 has a considerably smaller budget than its American counterpart, and according to ex-CIA officer Miles Copeland, in most parts of the world a primary duty of the British Resident is 'to use his superior prestige and cunning to persuade his CIA colleague to join with him in joint Anglo-American operations, for which he supplies the brains and the CIA colleague supplies the funds'.)[5]

See also: German Desk.

Berlin System. Network of MI6 agents established by John Koby in early postwar Berlin, subsequently dismantled by Bret Rensselaer. Nearly forty years later, this is cited by Koby in *London Match* as evidence of Rensselaer's long-time allegiance to Moscow.

Berlin Wall. At two o'clock on the morning of 13 August 1961, East German construction workers supported by armed industrial militia groups began erecting barbed-wire barriers around West Berlin. Five days later the wire was replaced by a concrete wall. Strengthened and made more elaborate in the years since, it is 165.7 km. long, of which 46 km. actually divides Berlin. At certain points the Wall doesn't stand exactly on the sector boundary, rather a bit behind it, and it's been known for the East German Grepos to unexpectedly emerge through a metal door in the Wall and seize 'border violators' trespassing on this no-mans-land. Border escapes are prevented by slalom courses, gates and sliding concrete barriers erected at the crossing points at Friedrichstrasse (better known as Checkpoint Charlie), Bornholmer Strasse, Chausseestrasse, Invalidenstrasse, Heinrich-Heine Strasse, Sonnenallee, Staaken, Stolpe and Drewitz. However, over the past twenty-five years about 5,000 people have managed to safely cross to West Berlin. At the time of writing, fifty-eight escapees have been shot dead by the Grepos.

A dramatic and irrefutable symbol of the ideological divide

between East and West, the Berlin Wall figures in *Funeral in Berlin*, *Berlin Game* and *London Match*.

See also: Checkpoint Charlie *and* Grepos.

Berlin, West. The term 'front line city' came into use when Berlin was the touchstone of cold-war politics; but West Berliners don't like to hear it used today. However its geographical location, and the grim Wall that has claimed so many lives, makes West Berlin quite unlike any other city.

Western access to this 'island in a red sea' is by air, by rail from West Germany and via the four motorway transit routes through East Germany. These links have been subject to periodic interference, most notably in 1948–9 when the Soviets halted all rail and road traffic, to which the Americans and British responded by organising an airlift of food and fuel as well as men and mail.

The Quadripartite Agreement of 1971 removed Berlin as a perennial source of conflict between East and West. However, West Berlin remains divided into three sectors—American, British and French—with their respective military garrisons, and sizeable offices are maintained by the CIA in Berlin-Dahlem, by the British Intelligence services at the Olympia Stadium and of course by the West German BND and BfV.

The early postwar years are recalled by Bernard Samson in the *Game, Set & Match* trilogy, much of which is set in contemporary West Berlin, while *Funeral in Berlin* provides a portrait of the city at the height of the Cold War following the construction of the Wall.

Berliners. Known for their distinctive sort of roguish wit—*Schalkheit*, but less renowned for modesty or simplicity, their fictional counterparts include Paul Biedermann, Poppy Biedermann, Max Binder, Max and Marie-Louise Breslow, Serge Frankel, Erich and Lisl Hennig, Gerda Koby, Lothar Koch, Leutnant Kokke, Axel Mauser, Rolf Mauser, Dr Isaac Volkmann, Werner Volkmann, Franz Wever, Harald Winter, Paul and Inge Winter, Peter Winter and Frau Wisliceny. (One is tempted to add the *berlinerisch* Bernard Samson to this list.) Johnnie Vulkan,

Lottie Winter and Veronica Winter are all residents of the city, as were SS-Standartenführer Huth and Erich Stinnes, but Douglas Archer knows it only from stories told by his mother, a former English governess in Berlin.

A *Berliner* is also a type of German doughnut. The day after President Kennedy made his famous proclamation, 'Ich bin ein Berliner', the cartoonists had a field day with talking doughnuts.

————, **Bernhard.** Youthful Cambridge-educated recruit to WOOC(P)—'apt to use one long word where eight short ones would do'—charged by the narrator of *Horse Under Water* with investigating the complex financial holdings of crypto-Fascist Cabinet Minister, Henry Smith.

'Bernhard'. The Nazi Sicherheitsdienst's operation to counterfeit Allied banknotes worth millions during World War II, a large sum of which is said to be aboard the sunken German U-boat lying off Albufeira in *Horse Under Water*. The plan's origins, and postwar attempts to locate a consignment supposedly abandoned near Lake Traunsee in Austria, are the subject of an appendix to the novel.

Berwick House. Otherwise known as the London Debriefing Centre (notwithstanding the weathered sign identifying it as a Ministry of Pensions training school) in the *Game, Set & Match* trilogy. A secluded eighteenth-century manor, originally taken over by the War Office in 1940, 'and like so many other good things siezed temporarily by the government, never returned to its original owners'. With its grounds ringed by infrared beams and sonic warning shields, it provides secure accommodation for Giles Trent in *Berlin Game* and Erich Stinnes in *London Match*.

betrayal of a cause or a country is revealed at the climax of many of the novels. Money and power prove irresistible to Dalby in *The IPCRESS File*. Communism motivates Gerry Hart and Douglas Reid-Kennedy in *Twinkle, Twinkle, Little Spy*, Willi Kleiber and Edward Parker in *XPD*, and notably Fiona Samson in

Berlin Game, but Harvey Newbegin claims to be 'returning home' when he defects to the Soviets in *Billion-Dollar Brain*. Henry Smith and Bernard Peterson are confronted with awkward reminders of wartime betrayal in *Horse Under Water*, as is Steve Champion in *Yesterday's Spy*, and the Nazi occupation of Britain gives rise to various permutations of treachery in *SS–GB*.

An exotic sexual betrayal humiliates Professor Bekuv in *Twinkle, Twinkle, Little Spy*, while greed lies behind Silas Lowther's betrayal of his partners in *Only When I Larf* and explains Johnnie Vulkan's multiple deceptions in *Funeral in Berlin*.

Biedermann, Paul. Wealthy West Berlin businessman who seeks Bernard Samson's protection in *Mexico Set* after unwisely laundering cash for the KGB. Later murdered at Charles de Gaulle airport in a KGB ploy to frame Samson and cast doubts on his loyalty.

Biedermann, Poppy. Jet-set daughter of Paul Biedermann, a guest at one of Frank Harrington's dinner parties attended by Bernard Samson in *Berlin Game*. Zena Volkmann is later 'mistaken' for Poppy by Erich Stinnes in *Mexico Set*, thereby alerting London Central to his presence in Mexico City.

'Big Friends'. Nickname given the American bombers by the escorting fighter pilots in *Goodbye Mickey Mouse*.

THE BILLION DOLLAR BRAIN (G. P. Putnam's Sons, New York, 11 January 1966/**Billion-Dollar Brain**, Jonathan Cape, London, 31 March 1966; fiction). The fourth of Deighton's novels to be narrated by the unnamed employee of WOOC(P) is the story of an anti-communist espionage network owned by a Texan billionaire, General Midwinter, run from a vast computer complex known as the Brain. After having been recruited by Harvey Newbegin, the narrator travels from the bone-freezing winter of Helsinki, Riga and Leningrad, to the stifling heat of Texas, and soon finds himself tangling with enemies on both sides of the Iron Curtain.

Billion-Dollar Brain (GB 1967). *p.c.*: Lowndes Productions. *exec.p.*: André de Toth. *p.*: Harry Saltzman. *d.*: Ken Russell. *sc.*: John McGrath. Based on the novel by Len Deighton. *ph.*: Billy Williams. *ed.*: Alan Osbiston. *p.d.*: Syd Cain. *a.d.*: Bert Davey. *m.*: Richard Rodney Bennett. *l.p.*: Michael Caine (*Harry Palmer*), Karl Malden (*Leo Newbegin*), Ed Begley (*General Midwinter*), Oscar Homolka (*Colonel Stok*), Françoise Dorleac (*Anya*), Guy Doleman (*Colonel Ross*), Vladek Scheybal (*Dr Eiwort*), Milo Sperber (*Basil*), Janos Kurutz, Alexei Jawdokimov, Paul Tamarin, Iza Teller (*Latvian Bandits*), Mark Elwes (*Birkinshaw*), Stanley Caine (*Postman*), Gregg Palmer, John Herrinton, Hans de Vries (*Dutch Businessmen*), Fred Griffiths (*Taxi Driver*), John Brandon (*Jim*), Tony Harwood (*Macey*), Donald Sutherland (*Computer Operator*), Michael Stayner (*Scientist*), George Roubicek (*Edgar*), Brandon Brady (*Midwinter's Security Chief*), Alex Marchevsky, Peter Forest (*Russian Radar Technicians*), Reed de Rouen (*Observer*), James Woolf (*Telephone Operator*), Miki Iveria (*Russian Woman*), Susan George, Jill Mai Meredith (*Russian Girls*), Dolly Brennan (*Old Latvian Woman*), Frederick Schrecker (*Old Russian Man*), Bill Mitchell (*Sentry*), Steve Emerson, Mark Ross (*Russian Secret Policemen*), Max Kirby (*Shoe Salesman*). 9,990 feet; 111 minutes.

Binder, Max. A boyhood friend of Bernard Samson, and member of the Brahms Network, with a minor off-stage role in *Berlin Game*. Resident in East Berlin, he narrowly escapes to the West after having been betrayed by the KGB mole within London Central.

Bingham, Albert. The sixty-year-old ex-Scots Guardsman employed as Bret Rensselaer's chauffeur in *Berlin Game*, whose compulsive garrulity when off duty leads Bernard Samson to suspect his wife of having an affair with the personable American.

Bishop, Helen. Short dark girl employed by British Intelligence under the cover name of Melodie Page in *Yesterday's*

Spy. Instructed by Schlegel to shadow Steve Champion, she's murdered after learning of Cairo's plan to convince Israel it possesses atomic artillery shells stolen from France.

'The Bishop'. Ageing tramp who befriends Charles Bonnard in *Yesterday's Spy* after his release from Wormwood Scrubs. Later revealed to be on Steve Champion's payroll.

'Black Peter'. Fierce-looking crippled Berliner encountered by Bernard Samson and Werner Volkmann during their childhood, and recalled in *London Match*. 'Even as a child I'd seen the irony of him sitting in the bombed rubble of central Berlin and making so lovingly the model B-17 bombers that the American airmen bought as souvenirs.'

blackmail ('biographic leverage') plays a significant role in *Horse Under Water* when British Cabinet Minister Henry Smith's pro-Nazi wartime activities are exploited by Fernie Tomas and Manuel da Cunha; again in *SS–GB*, when Harry Woods agrees to act as SS-Gruppenführer Kellerman's informant to save Douggie Archer from being sent to a Hitler Youth unit in Bohemia; and in *Close-Up*, when Leo Koolman reveals mob pressure on the studio and clinches a new film deal with a reluctant Marshall Stone. The most flagrant blackmailing operation is that run by Monsieur Datt in *An Expensive Place to Die*, whose 800 dossiers of film and tape on the influential political clients of his Avenue Foch 'pleasuredrome' seemingly make him immune from prosecution.

black marketeering. Fiddling in the army is said to have started Silas Lowther on a lifetime of swindles and confidence tricks ('When he got demobbed he couldn't get used to being without the luxuries') in *Only When I Larf*. Gefreiter Orth, the telephone operator at the Luftwaffe radar station 'Ermine' in *Bomber*, is said to be a notorious black marketeer, and the murder of 'Peter Thomas' at the beginning of *SS–GB* is initially considered to be an underworld killing following the discovery of petrol coupons, drinks and stolen cigarettes at the Shepherd Market apartment. The widespread black marketeering in Berlin after the war is evoked in *London Match*, when Bret Rensselaer attributes John Koby's downfall to his illegal profiteering with his brother-in-law, and Bernard Samson recalls how his father had smartly transferred Ted Riley out of the Intelligence Corps on finding that he'd become involved with some dealers on Potsdamer Platz.

Blantyre, ———. Languid Special Branch detective who accompanies Bonnard in *Yesterday's Spy* as he turns over Steve Champion's London hideaway in his search for the missing agent, Melodie Page.

Blessing, Feldwebel. Impulsive young Bavarian with a minor role in *Bomber*. Overseer of the local foreign labour force at the Luftwaffe night-fighter station at Kroonsdijk, he identifies himself as an undercover Sipo officer and sets in motion the arrest of the popular young pilot Christian Himmel.

BLITZKRIEG: From the Rise of Hitler to the Fall of Dunkirk (Jonathan Cape, London, 3 September 1979/Alfred A. Knopf, New York, 22 May 1980; non-fiction). The second volume in Deighton's planned twelve-volume series examining important World War II battles and their technology. It opens with an account of Hitler's rise to power, then traces the idea, the planning and the realisation of the German High Command's strategy of the 'lightning war'. With a foreword by General W. K. Nehring, a.D., former Chief of Staff to General Heinz Guderian.

Bloom, Alice. Memorable minor character in *The IPCRESS File*, *Horse Under Water*, *Funeral in Berlin* and *Billion-Dollar Brain*. A cross between a librarian and a concierge, she fiercely guards the portals to WOOC(P)'s offices in Charlotte Street, and it is said no one can do anything in that building without first having her approval.

The Blue Admiral. The player commanding NATO forces during war games at the Studies Centre (STUCEN) in *Spy Story*.

The Blue Suite. Quarters for the Blue Admiral and his Blue Ops staff at the Studies Centre in *Spy Story*. Blue Suite, like the opposing Red Suite in the basement, receives only the results of reports and analysis, for neither side is allowed access to the big War Table displaying the true state of the game. Since the teams may be locked in battle for several days, the Suites have bedrooms, bathrooms, a well-stocked bar and a sentry to make sure nobody tries to sneak a look at that Table.

'Blue-jacket'. Resistance cryptonym for King George VI in *SS–GB*. ('It was a fine code-word for King George the Sixth, the sailor king, nautical and classless. It would be right for the history books.')

Bock, Paul. Young computer operator in the London branch of Dr Böttger's German bank, viciously murdered after uncovering details of the Trust and Operation Siegfried in *XPD*.

Bohnen, Colonel Alexander. Imperious USAAF officer serving in London in the winter of 1943–4, with a major role in *Goodbye Mickey Mouse*. One of many eminent American businessmen drafted into khaki to further the Allied war effort, he has mixed feelings when joined by his estranged son Jamie Farebrother—newly posted to the 220th Fighter Group at Steeple Thaxted. Yet as he seeks to overcome the barriers between them, so Bohnen succeeds in building new ones by failing to accept the transformation of his son into a man, until he's forced to relinquish the role of father by the tragic events of 'Bad Monday'.

Böll, Gerd. August Bach's cousin, one of Altgarten's most prosperous tradesmen, in *Bomber*. After expressing reservations about Bach's intention to marry Anna-Luisa, he's killed by a 600-lb delayed action bomb dropped by the RAF, as he tries to release her and young Hans from beneath a collapsed building.

BOMBER (Jonathan Cape, London, 10 September 1970/Harper & Row, New York, 30 September 1970; fiction). Deighton's seventh novel is a devastating indictment of war. It follows the air and ground progress of a routine RAF raid on the industrial Ruhr that goes terribly wrong when ten million pounds of high explosives and phosphorous incendiaries, intended for Krefeld, are mistakenly unleashed on the small town of Altgarten. Chosen by Anthony Burgess as one of the best ninety-nine novels published in English since 1939.[6]

See also: Awards.

Bonn. The birthplace of Beethoven was a controversial choice in 1949 as the capital of West Germany. The Parliamentary Council's rejection of Frankfurt, by the narrow majority of four votes, owed much to the persuasive powers of the Federal Republic's future Chancellor, Konrad Adenauer, who was unwilling to move from the nearby village of Rhöndorf. And Berlin's members of parliament needed no convincing that Frankfurt would constitute a serious rival to their city if Germany were reunited. Today, with the country still divided, Bonn is no longer the 'provisional' seat of federal agencies, and a quarter of the town's population comprises diplomats, bureaucrats and journalists. It has a singular history of espionage scandals, and West Germans have got used to the notion of their civil servants working for the other side.

London Match opens with Bernard Samson and a BfV team detaining the thirty-two-year-old secretary of a senior Bonn politician, formerly employed in the Defence Ministry—one of three KGB agents blown by Erich Stinnes in a calculated bid to establish his bona fides with London. And a series of embarrassing disclosures in Bonn, just as the government is warming up for an election, precipitates the investigation of Steve Champion in *Yesterday's Spy*, and explains the presence in Nice of BND officer Claude Winkler. The Dreesen Hotel in the present suburb of Bad Godesberg was very often used by Hitler before the war. It was from here that he flew to Munich in June 1934 to set in motion the 'Night of the Long Knives', the bloody purge of the SA dramatised in *Winter*. Four years later, it was the scene of his first meeting with Neville Chamberlain at the height of the Czechoslovakia crisis.

Bonnard, Charles. Wartime cover name of the otherwise anonymous narrator of *Yesterday's Spy*, who has worked for British Intelligence since having been sent as a green recruit into Nazi-occupied France in 1940. But the magic of those early days, when a premium was placed on the cunning loner who played his hunches, has been replaced by the soulless efficiency of great corporate departments run by confident bullies like his boss, Charles Schlegel. Yet it's these very skills that are required of him when ordered to shake down his wartime mentor and former colleague Steve Champion.

BONUS FOR A SALESMAN. Short story in the collection *Declarations of War*. A former British arms salesman recalls in a letter to an old colleague how a 1920s revolution in Latin America provided the opportunity for his self-advancement—to President of the unnamed country.

Bookbinder, Kagan. Barrel-chested emigré producer of Marshall Stone's first acclaimed film. As a party to the dark secrets behind Stone's rise to stardom, he becomes a valued background source for biographer Peter Anson in *Close-Up*.

Booth, Flight Sergeant. The RAF officer in Warley Fen's Photographic Section endowed with the poignant, final lines of *Bomber*—'The attack hasn't hit Krefeld, sir, I've just been studying the negs. Street patterns are nothing like it. I don't know, sir. It doesn't look like anywhere. It doesn't look like anywhere.'

Bordeaux. Briefly visited by the narrator of *Funeral in Berlin* to confer with his friend and counterpart in the DST, Grenade. 'Bordeaux occupies a special semantic importance in the minds of all Frenchmen (as Munich does to Britons). In 1871, in 1914 and in 1940 Bordeaux was the city to which the French Government fled, yelling "Stand firm!" over their shoulders. Each large hotel knew the influx of folding chairs and filing cabinets, typewriters and armed sentries. As I drove past them I remembered June 1940; Bordeaux was the halfway house between Verdun and Vichy.'

border crossings. *See* exfiltrations *and* infiltrations.

Borg, Erich. Former Wehrmacht Colonel-General, now living in East Berlin, whose large collection of German wartime military records provides conclusive evidence of Johnnie Vulkan's real identity in *Funeral in Berlin*.

Böttger, Dr Paul. Eminent West German banker who's persuaded to support Willi Kleiber's efforts to acquire the Hitler Minutes in *XPD*, unaware that the Trust is being used as a front for an operation masterminded by Moscow Centre.

'Box Four'. WOOC(P)'s latest cryptonym for Christian Stakowski, formerly known as 'Jay'—divulged in the prologue to *The IPCRESS File*. 'I'm in a very confusing business,' admits the narrator to his perplexed Minister.

Boyer, Staff Sergeant Harry. By common consent, the most experienced airman at Steeple Thaxted in *Goodbye Mickey Mouse*, though he enjoys greater renown as an organiser of crap games.

'Brahms Four'. Cryptonym for Dr Walter von Munte, a senior official of East Germany's Deutsche Notenbank and long-time MI6 spy in the *Game, Set & Match* trilogy.

Brahms Network. Cut-outs used by London Central to channel material from Brahms Four. Members of the network include Werner Volkmann, Rolf Mauser and Max Binder.

The Brain. The large computer complex housed in three buildings sunk deep into a Texas hillside, which masterminds the anti-communist espionage network owned by General Midwinter in *Billion-Dollar Brain*. So called, because each part of the computer is named after a section of the human brain: the Medulla, Pons and Midbrain.

brainwashing, a translation of the Chinese 'hsi nao' (wash-brain), has been practised under other names for centuries, but not until the Korean War did it achieve worldwide notoriety. There are two major methods of altering or controlling human behaviour: psychological, and pharmacological. In *The IPCRESS File* (the title derives from 'Induction of Psycho-neuroses by Conditioned Reflex with Stress'), Jay uses both for mutual reinforcement to create a network of highly-placed informers, as does Monsieur Datt in his clinic on Paris's Avenue Foch in *An Expensive Place to Die*, while Midwinter's organisation employs psychological techniques to indoctrinate agents sent behind the Iron Curtain in *Billion-Dollar Brain*.

Brand, Heinrich. Cruel tyrannical Bavarian in *Winter*, whose consuming envy dogs Paul Winter and Alex Horner for the best part of a quarter century, from the trenches of the Western Front to the final battles of World War II.

Brand, Sergeant John. Seasoned bemedalled officer in the Royal Fusiliers, commanding the firing squad despatched to Pooglui Camp in *Twelve Good Men and True*. But such is the tension, that no one knows that it is not his voice that gives the order to fire.

breaking and entering (B&E). Rarely will Western counter-espionage agencies admit to it, since these same agencies are charged with upholding the law and preserving democracy. However, the Watergate affair resulted in a flood of disclosures about the FBI's recent B&E activities, and in Britain, MI5 is reputed to have two teams of surreptitious entry specialists: the locksmiths and carpenters of the section known as A1(D), and the burglars of A1(A). (One of MI5's biggest ever coups was in 1955, when it burgled a Mayfair apartment where all 50,000 membership files of the British Communist Party were being kept. It removed them, copied them all in one night, and returned them before daybreak.)

As it occurs in the novels, the ends generally justify the means.

The WOOC(P) black-bag specialist, Ossie Butterworth, is employed in *Horse Under Water* to steal a vital radio recall unit from da Cunha's Moroccan home and in *Funeral in Berlin* to learn more about the mysterious Samantha Steel; in *Yesterday's Spy*, the narrator and Dawlish turn over Champion's London hideaway in their search for the missing MI6 agent Melodie Page, and in *XPD*, Melvin Kalkhoven leads a CIA team which breaks into a KGB safe house in New York to install sneakies ahead of a crucial meeting between Edward Parker and Willi Kleiber.

But Ted Riley finds the KGB's Cambridge Network treacherously forewarned as he breaks into their safe house in *London Match*, and Jean-Paul Pascal has cause to regret stealing classified papers from the narrator's Paris apartment in *An Expensive Place to Die*, for they've been treated with ninhydrine and the violet stains on his hands take days to wear off.

Brent, Flying Officer Michael. Young working-class RAF bomber pilot, based at Brimington airfield in *Brent's Deus Ex Machina*, whose request to be permanently grounded is denied by the station's snobbish Medical Officer, John Garrard. His fear of flying is subsequently eclipsed by his bitter hatred for Garrard, driving him on to become one of the squadron's most valiant pilots.

BRENT'S DEUS EX MACHINA. Short story in the collection *Declarations of War*. A World War II RAF bomber pilot has his request for permanent grounding denied by the squadron's disdainful Medical Officer, and the resulting feud drives him on to reckless heroism.

Breslow, Marie-Louise. Berlin-born wife of Max Breslow in *XPD*, whose fervid adaptation to life in California still surprises her husband.

Breslow, Mary. Comely daughter of Max and Marie-Louise Breslow, earnestly pursued by Billy Stein in *XPD*.

Breslow, Max. Minor-league Hollywood film producer, at pains to obscure his Nazi past in *XPD*. However, forty years after escorting Adolf Hitler's personal papers to a hiding place in the Kaiseroda Mine, he finds himself embroiled in Willi Kleiber's ruthless attempt to acquire the most sensitive of the documents, the Hitler Minutes.

Bringle Sands. Wartime atomic research establishment on the Devon coast, taken over by the German army following the Nazi occupation of Britain in *SS–GB*. Coveted by the SS, its destruction by American Marines in a daring commando raid deals a fatal blow to Nazi ambitions to develop the first atomic bomb.

British Intelligence. An organisation chart would reveal a pyramidal structure, with four principal intelligence agencies at its base: the Secret Intelligence Service or MI6, which conducts overseas espionage; the Security Service or MI5, responsible for counter-intelligence; the Government Communications Headquarters (GCHQ), which provides communications and cryptanalysed intelligence; and the Defence Intelligence Staff (DIS), representing the military intelligence departments of the armed forces.

The activities of these agencies are co-ordinated by the Joint Intelligence Committee (JIC), while a second major body, the Overseas Economic Intelligence Committee (OEIC), directs them in the gathering of commercial and economic information (some of which is fed to British companies whose commercial interests are considered identical to the national interest). Two further committees are concerned with specific agencies; the London Signal Intelligence Board (LSIB) which directly supervises GCHQ, and the Official Committee on Security, which is the supervising body for MI5. Long-term plans and priorities are examined by the Co-ordinator of Intelligence and Security.

These five are in turn supervised by the Permanent Secretaries Committee on Intelligence Services (PSIS) chaired by the Cabinet Secretary, and at the very top of the pyramid, of course, is the Prime Minister.

The contemporary reality of British Intelligence is the context for the fictional worlds portrayed in twelve of the novels: *The IPCRESS File*, *Horse Under Water*, *Funeral in Berlin*, *Billion-Dollar Brain*, *An Expensive Place to Die*, *Spy Story*, *Yesterday's Spy*, *Twinkle, Twinkle, Little Spy*, *XPD*, *Berlin Game*, *Mexico Set* and *London Match*.

See also: London Central *and* WOOC(P).

British Military Intelligence. The War Office department headed by Colonel Ross in *The IPCRESS File*, from which the narrator is discharged to work with the civilians in WOOC(P). ('Ross obviously thought my posting a very fine tentative solution until I could be got out of his life altogether.') The department is later accused by Olaf Kaarna in *Billion-Dollar Brain* of running a vast subversive operation in northern Europe, centred in Finland—speculative nonsense encouraged by the Facts for Freedom organisation to cover its own activities.

British Union of Fascists (BUF). Founded by Oswald Mosley in 1932, the Union immediately adopted the salute and blackshirt uniform of the Italian Fascists. It remained ineffectual, but given its increasing anti-Semitism and admiration of Hitler, its leaders were arrested on the outbreak of World War II.

It comes as no surprise to learn in *Horse Under Water* that Bernard Peterson joined the BUF in the mid-1930s, foreshadowing his treacherous work for the Germans during the war.

Brody, Joe. Quietly spoken American Intelligence officer in *Berlin Game*, who prefers to be described as an 'employee of Siemens'. Had his investigation of a Berlin Station leak to the Soviets back in 1978 correctly identified the source, the KGB mole within London Central would have been unmasked very much earlier.

Brooks, Angela. Long-suffering personal secretary to Marshall Stone in *Close-Up*.

Broum, Paul Louis. Principal antagonist in *Funeral in Berlin*. A former communist party assassin and scion of a wealthy Jewish family, he escaped from Treblinka at the end of the war after assuming the identity of a murdered camp guard named Johnnie Vulkan. But having impersonated Vulkan through the early postwar years—freelancing for British Intelligence in both sectors of Berlin—he spins a deadly web of deceit to acquire the documentation needed to prove his *real* identity, in order to collect £250,000 left by his family in a Swiss bank.

Brûly de Pesche. Small Belgian frontier village where, it is alleged in *XPD*, Winston Churchill had a clandestine meeting with Adolf Hitler in June 1940.

Brummage, Eddie. Real name of actor Marshall Stone in *Close-Up*. At one point he arrives unannounced at Heathrow airport and rediscovers what it is like to be a member of the general public—for his ticket and passport are in the name of a 'nobody', named Brummage.

Brummage, Sylvia. Mother of actor Marshall Stone in *Close-Up*, whom biographer Peter Anson finds to be 'unsympathetic to everything that is Eddie's life'.

bugging. There's a distinction, often misunderstood, between bugging, which means the secret surveillance of conversations by use of a hidden transmitter or microphone, and wire-tapping, the clandestine interception of telephone calls. Samantha Steel's phone is *tapped* in *Funeral in Berlin*, as is that in Patrick Armstrong's former apartment in *Spy Story*; whereas the KGB's New York safe house is *bugged* by Melvin Kalkhoven and his CIA team in *XPD*. Interestingly, the relentless search for the Hitler Minutes in this latter novel arises from Heinrich Himmler's decision to 'bug' the meeting between Winston Churchill and Adolf Hitler in 1940, and produce a written record of the proceedings.

Bundesamt für Verfassungsschutz (BfV). West Germany's counter-intelligence agency is headquartered in Cologne and has locally administered regional offices in each of the ten Federal States and Berlin. Currently run by Gerhard Boeden, the BfV was established by MI6 after World War II and first headed by Dr Otto John, a conspirator in the Hitler bomb plot. In a celebrated and bizarre turn of events, Otto John subsequently 'defected' to East Berlin, then claimed to have been kidnapped and brain-washed, and returned to the West in December 1955 to serve a prison sentence for treason. (In 1985, Hans Joachim Tiedge, head of the BfV's national department responsible for countering East German espionage, made a similar journey eastwards, but has yet to return.)

West Germany is the high-density Mecca of espionage—latest estimates suggest 10,000 foreign spies and agents of influence—and the BfV uncovers dozens of cases annually. Like Britain's MI5 it has no powers of arrest, which is the responsibility of the 14th Kommissariat of the Kripo, whose officers are stationed in every major West German city.

London Match opens with Bernard Samson and officers from the BfV's political office in Bonn detaining the thirty-two-year-old secretary of a senior West German politician, whom they remove from a high-society Christmas party for interrogation at the BfV's office in Berlin-Spandau. 'He made a fuss of course. He wanted his lawyer and wanted to talk to his boss and some friend of his in the government . . . He was still protesting when he departed with the arrest team. They were not impressed; they'd seen it all before.'

See also: Hauptverwaltung Aufklärung.

Bundesnachrichtendienst (BND). West Germany's foreign intelligence and espionage agency, headed by Dr Hans-Georg Wieck, is based at Pullach, near Munich. Established and originally funded by the Americans immediately after World War II, it was formerly known as the Gehlen Bureau, after its first chief—the legendary ex-Abwehr officer, General Reinhard Gehlen.

In *Funeral in Berlin*, it is the Gehlen Bureau that is called upon to arrange the covert transfer of Semitsa from East to West Berlin, subsequently losing some of its agents to KGB Colonel Stok; in *Yesterday's Spy*, Claude Winkler's coincidental appearance in Nice is certainly due to the BND's interest in Steve Champion; while in *XPD*, a luncheon between MI6 boss Sir Sydney Ryden and a senior officer of the BND leads to the vicious murder of bank employee Paul Bock.

See also: Reinhard Gehlen.

Bureau for the Rehabilitation of German Prisoners of War from the East. Cover name of the Gehlen Bureau cell in West Berlin visited by the narrator of *Funeral in Berlin*.

Burgess and Maclean. The notorious British Foreign Office diplomats, recruited by Soviet Intelligence in the 1930s, whose hurried flight to Moscow in May 1951—only hours before Maclean was due to be interrogated by MI5—precipitated Britain's biggest postwar spy scandal. The question of who tipped them off was inadequately resolved by the defection of the 'third man' Kim Philby in 1963, and the public unmasking of Anthony Blunt in 1979.

In *The IPCRESS File*, Dalby credits Jay with having played a role in their journey eastwards, for which he was paid £25,000 drawn on the Swiss Bank Corporation.

Busby, Lieutenant. Pushy US Counter-Intelligence Corps officer in *Winter*, who leads the hunt for Paul Winter along the Austrian frontier following his escape from Nuremberg.

business proprietaries are widely used by the intelligence community to provide ostensibly private and commercial cover for a multitude of clandestine activities.

In *The IPCRESS File*, 'Acme Films', 'The Dalby Inquiry Bureau', 'The Ex-Officers Employment Bureau' and 'B. Isaacs. Tailor', all conceal the affairs of WOOC(P) in Charlotte Street. A German merchant bank near Berlin's Ku'damm is used by British Intelligence as a clearing house for information in *Funeral in*

Berlin, while a travel agency is the cover for MI6's offices in Nice in *Yesterday's Spy* and a betting shop for London Central's Kilburn safe house in *London Match*.

Butcher, Ivor. Minor character in *Horse Under Water*. A former Home Office phone-tapper, he earns a living on the fringes of the intelligence community by trading chaff acquired from foolish people with access to secret, or semi-secret, information.

Butterworth, Ossie. Former common criminal, one of London's best B&E men, whose expertise is called upon by the narrator in *Horse Under Water* (the novel includes an appendix summarising his wicked career) and *Funeral in Berlin*. His wife Bessie, a switchboard operator at WOOC(P)'s offices in Charlotte Street, makes a brief appearance in *Billion-Dollar Brain*.

Byrd, Martin Langley. English painter resident in Paris, later revealed to be the narrator's MI6 case officer in *An Expensive Place to Die*. 'Byrd had killed, perhaps many times. It leaves a blemish in the eyeballs and Byrd had it.'

C

Café Leuschner. A big barn of a place near the remains of Berlin's Anhalter Bahnhof, chosen by Bernard Samson for clandestine meetings in *Berlin Game* and *London Match*. It stirs memories of his childhood in early postwar Berlin, when the Saturday visit for one of Herr Leuschner's genuine American ice creams was the high-point of his week. 'As a kid I'd always liked to sit at the counter rather than at the tables. In those days the chairs were old bentwood ones, painted olive green, the only colour of paint that one could get in the city. The furniture at Leuschner's café—like so many other painted things of that time—exactly matched the trucks of the US Army.'

Caine, Michael (1933–). The Oscar-winning British actor played for years in second features (*How to Marry a Rich Uncle*, *A Hill in Korea*, *Blind Spot*, *Solo for Sparrow*) before he found fame with his portrayal of Deighton's insolent nameless agent—christened 'Harry Palmer' in the films—in *The Ipcress File*, *Funeral in Berlin* and *Billion-Dollar Brain*. 'I knew Michael before they made *The Ipcress File*, and always thought he was a natural for the part,' recalls Deighton. 'They originally cast someone else (Christopher Plummer), but Michael gave the character an extra dimension, there's no doubt about it.'[7]

Callaghan, Colonel Bill. White-haired Bostonian lawyer at the Nuremberg IMT war crimes trial in *Winter*, but for whose surveillance order, Paul Winter might have made it to the Austrian border and found sanctuary in Switzerland.

Cambridge Network. KGB network of spies at the Ministry of Defence research laboratory in Cambridge, blown by Soviet defector Erich Stinnes in a calculated bid to establish his bona fides in *London Match*. However, the attempt to seize the network's coded files, and then entrap its members at a Hampstead stakeout, fatally miscarries, suggesting further treachery within London Central.

cars lend a deliberate symmetry to the *Game, Set & Match* trilogy: all three novels open and close with Bernard Samson seated in a hardtop. Elsewhere, they are associated with the deaths of several characters, proving fatal for Dalby in *The IPCRESS File*, Joe MacIntosh in *Horse Under Water*, Ingrid Rainbow in *Close-Up* and 'Elliot Castlebridge' in *XPD*—in which Bernie Lustig's mutilated body is found in the trunk of one, Colonel Pitman's fatal heart attack on a Swiss autoroute leads to the recovery of the Hitler Minutes and Boyd Stuart's life is saved by switching vehicles with a hapless young Washington embassy attaché.

On occasion they lead to some unexpected discoveries. The car shadowing the narrator in *Horse Under Water* is traced to a British Cabinet Minister; Spanish registration plates identify Johnnie Vulkan's white-haired contact in Hendaye-plage as former SS medical officer Dr Ernst Mohr in *Funeral in Berlin*; a breakdown leads Patrick Armstrong to find a 'double' occupying his former apartment in *Spy Story*; car registration records reveal Hank Dean's mystery visitor to have been Henry Hope Dean in *Twinkle, Twinkle, Little Spy*; Douglas Archer is led to an unexpected meeting between the Abwehr and the resistance after following Captain Hesse's car in *SS–GB*; and a parking ticket draws the CIA's attention to the KGB's 'illegal resident', Edward Parker, in *XPD*.

The narrator of *The IPCRESS File* is lured into a trap chasing Dalby's car across Tokwe Atoll, and high-speed chases across the Sahara figure prominently in the opening and closing chapters of *Twinkle, Twinkle, Little Spy*. Pina Baroni attempts to gun down Steve Champion on a French autoroute in *Yesterday's Spy*,

Bernard Samson is overpowered in his car and forced to drive to a meeting with his treacherous wife in *Mexico Set* and Carol Miller is observed using one as a 'dead drop' at the opening of *London Match*.

Deighton has a lot of fun recording the early days of the motor car in *Winter*. Harald Winter's expensive 'horseless carriage'—a Benz Viktoria—draws amazed crowds in Vienna at the turn of the century, yet barely ten years later we find Glenn Rensselaer describing to his homesick sister how he stood in New York's Herald Square 'and saw it jammed so tight with automobiles that none of them could get going'.

Carswell, Captain J. F. Substantive British army captain nudging sixty, with little or no prospect of a move past substantive major, seconded to WOOC(P) in *The IPCRESS File*. His statistical research to identify potential defectors and S1 targets is initially dismissed by the narrator, 'but it was a long time later that I understood how important was the work he was doing'.

Carter, Sergeant Tommy. Handsome former police constable from Newcastle, skipper of the RAF Lancaster 'Joe for King' in *Bomber*. Survives the raid over Germany and returns to Warley Fen to celebrate his twenty-first birthday, unaware that the mission has gone terribly wrong.

Cartwright, Private. British Army identity adopted by Bob Appleyard when the trio of confidence tricksters attempt to sell scrap metal as armaments in *Only When I Larf*.

case officer. Field intelligence officer, usually based in an overseas embassy station, responsible for specific local espionage operations and frequently the handling of an individual agent. A good case officer is said to combine 'the qualities of a master spy, a psychiatrist and a father confessor'.[8] The narrator of *Funeral in Berlin* is temporarily assigned to be Johnnie Vulkan's case officer during the covert transfer of Semitsa from East to West Berlin, Martin Langley Byrd reluctantly identifies himself as the narrator's case officer in *An Expensive Place to Die*, while Boyd Stuart hurriedly summons his case officer, Dr Curtiss, after narrowly escaping death in *XPD*.

The change-over of case officers presents one of the biggest problems in handling agents, and Silas Gaunt recalls in *Berlin Game* how, when Bret Rensselaer took over as Brahms Four's Berlin-based case officer, the transition was eased by having him continue to use Gaunt's code-name.

Cassel, Kevin. Moon-faced controller of C-SICH, the Combined Services Information Clearing House, consulted by the narrator of *Horse Under Water* to learn more about the meddlesome British Cabinet Minister, Henry Smith.

Castlebridge, Elliot. Young British colonel entrusted by Winston Churchill to deliver his rejection of Adolf Hitler's peace terms following their purported conference of June 1940, in *XPD*. Reportedly killed in a car crash in 1959, 'Elliot Castlebridge' is revealed to have been the wartime cover name used by current MI6 Director General Sir Sydney Ryden, and goes some way to explain his acute concern for the fate of the Hitler Minutes.

CATCH A FALLING SPY (Harcourt Brace Jovanovich, New York, 27 September 1976; fiction). American edition of *Twinkle, Twinkle, Little Spy*, first published in Britain in June 1976.

Cavendish, Charlie. Undercover agent for C-SICH and constant friend to the narrator of *The IPCRESS File*, whose cryptic cable forewarning of betrayal fails to prevent the narrator's abduction from Tokwe Atoll. Later mistaken for the narrator, he's needlessly slaughtered by a hoodlum working for Jay's IPCRESS Network.

Central Intelligence Agency (CIA). Established in 1947 to co-ordinate and analyse foreign intelligence reports for the

American President and his policy-makers, the CIA's activities have in recent years come to be dominated by covert operations. However, with the Agency facing some of its sharpest scrutiny in a decade as the Iran-Contra arms affair unfolded in 1987, the White House had to find someone untainted by clandestine affairs to replace ailing director William Casey, and in March 1987 nominated the head of the FBI, William Webster, as his successor.

The CIA has its headquarters eight miles from downtown Washington in Langley, Virginia. It is broadly organised into four directorates: Intelligence, Science and Technology, Management and Services, and—by far the largest—Operations, or Clandestine Services, which absorbs about two-thirds of the Agency's budget. Overseas stations are generally run from America's embassies, but for example in West Germany—largest site for CIA operations— while the Chief of Station sits in the Embassy in Bonn, the nub of the Agency's activities is the IG-Farbenhaus in Frankfurt. Defectors and escapees from the Soviet Union and Eastern Europe are processed at a reception centre maintained at Camp King, outside Frankfurt.

The CIA has special intelligence-sharing agreements with several English-speaking governments, particularly the British, and it is normal for the London COS to sit in on meetings of the Joint Intelligence Committee, withdrawing when 'domestic business' is up for discussion.

It comes as no surprise to learn that the Agency is siphoning money to General Midwinter's anti-communist crusade in *Billion-Dollar Brain*. A covert CIA plan to leak classified fall-out data to the Chinese government to silence the hawks who believe the PRC can survive a nuclear attack, lies behind the intrigues in *An Expensive Place to Die*. The later novel *Twinkle, Twinkle, Little Spy* features a joint CIA/British Intelligence operation centred on Soviet defector Professor Andrei Bekuv, and the CIA again plays a significant role in *XPD*, when it lifts Willi Kleiber out of Europe and flies him to the States for interrogation. Serving CIA officers encountered in the novels include Red Bancroft, Barney Barnes, Joe Brody, 'Skip' Henderson, Melvin Kalkhoven, Major Mickey Mann, Sam Seymour and Todd Wynn.

Central Registry. MI5's security index, mentioned in passing in *Horse Under Water* and *Funeral in Berlin*, grew out of the pre-World War I register of aliens compiled by local police forces throughout Britain. By 1917 it contained over 25,000 personal files, and today is reckoned to hold over two million computer dossiers on individuals and organisations considered a threat to national security.

Champion, Steve. Principal antagonist in *Yesterday's Spy*. A wealthy Englishman of about sixty, who by all accounts enjoyed a distinguished military and intelligence career before building a successful business empire in the South of France. However, behind this façade lurks a perfidious opportunist: the 'hero' who betrayed the wartime Guernica Network, and is now embarked on an Egyptian-sponsored plan to dramatically alter the military balance of the Middle East.

Chandler, Raymond (1888–1959). American crime novelist, whose hard-boiled detective fiction quickly attained literary acclaim and tremendous popularity, which it retains to this day. Deighton acknowledges a debt to this influential writer, '. . . for one of the things that Raymond Chandler did with his Philip Marlowe stories was to remove that last chapter where everything was explained. He began unravelling the mystery in Chapter Two, so that what you had was a mystery being unravelled and ravelled at the same time.'[9]

changing papers is a long and dreary process encountered by every entrant to the intelligence services, according to the narrator of *The IPCRESS File*. 'Your whole life is turned over like topsoil; new passport of course, but also new birth certificate, radio and TV licences, marriage certificates; and all the old ones are thoroughly destroyed. It takes four days.'

Charlotte Street. Established in the early novels as the London thoroughfare 'in the district that would be Soho, if Soho had the strength to cross Oxford Street' where the secret intelligence unit, WOOC(P), has its offices in 'a small piece of grimy real estate on the unwashed side of the street'.

'Charly'. *See* Charlotte Lucas-Mountford.

Chauvet, Maria. Chic thirty-two-year-old Parisienne, with an ambiguous role in *An Expensive Place to Die*. The illegitimate daughter of Monsieur Datt, and former wife of Chief Inspector Claude Loiseau, her loyalties are finally resolved when she fatally shoots Datt as he embarks for China with his coveted 'dossiers'.

Checkpoint Charlie. Scene of the confrontation between American and Soviet tanks shortly after the Berlin Wall was erected, the renowned international crossing point is located at the corner of Friedrichstrasse and Koch Strasse in the American sector. The name 'Charlie' derives from the NATO phonetic code: Checkpoint Alpha is the frontier crossing point between West and East Germany at Helmstedt-Marienborn, and Checkpoint Bravo is the crossing point between West Berlin and East Germany at Dreilinden-Drewitz. Checkpoint Charlie is the only crossing point on the Wall open twenty-four hours a day, but is restricted to diplomats and non-German nationals entering East Berlin by car or on foot (i.e. *not* West Berliners, who may only enter East Berlin via the crossing points at Bornholmer Strasse, Chausseestrasse, Invalidenstrasse, Oberbaumbrücke and Sonnenallee; *nor* West Germans, who must cross at Bornholmer Strasse, Prinzenstrasse/Heinrich-Heine-Strasse, or at the Kontrollpunkt located in Friedrichstrasse station).

Checkpoint Charlie is vividly depicted at the height of the Cold War in *Funeral in Berlin* ('Photo-flashes sliced instants from eternity. The pavement shone with water and detergent under the press-men's feet. Way down towards Hallesches Tor a US military ambulance flasher sped towards the emergency ward and was all set to change direction to the morgue . . . One by one the reporters gunned their V.W.s and began composing tomorrow's headlines in their minds. "Young Berliner killed in wall crossing" or "Vopos Gun Down Wall-Hopper" or "Bloody Sidewalk

Slaying at the Wall''. Or maybe he wouldn't die'). And it is the scene of frantic activity in *Berlin Game* and *London Match*.

See also: Berlin Wall *and* Grepos.

chess is frequently employed as a metaphor to illustrate the pattern of the 'intelligence game'. Fittingly, Colonel Stok is depicted as being an excellent player in *Funeral in Berlin*, though he concedes that Johnnie Vulkan is one of the few men in Berlin who can consistently beat him. Epigraphs from a chess book are used as chapter headings throughout the novel, and nearly twenty years later, Deighton chose the name of a chess opening as the title for the first of his *Game, Set & Match* trilogy, *Berlin Game*.

'Chico'. *See below*.

Chilcott-Oakes, Philip ('Chico'). Ex-Horse Guards upper-class supernumerary in WOOC(P), 'with the advantage of both a good brain and a family rich enough to save him using it', briefly encountered in *The IPCRESS File*, *Funeral in Berlin* and *Billion-Dollar Brain*.

children. The corrupting demands of a nation at war, with children exhorted to turn society upside down in return for pieces of coloured ribbon or a new promotion, worry a fearful August Bach in *Bomber*. 'Every fit, aggressive youngster who tries hard can get himself a bomber or a U-boat or an artillery battery and wreak havoc upon the world that it's taken us old men so long to put together. Nineteen-year-old children creep up on a 20,000-ton merchant ship, press a button, and watch it die, writhing like a wingless fly . . . Where have we failed, Max? What manner of children will they breed, and what manner of world will they shape?'

Children are pawns in the hands of often venal adults in several novels. Steve Champion wins a mean battle with ex-wife Caty for custody of their son Billy in *Yesterday's Spy*; Henry Hope Dean grows up unaware that his real father is communist agent Douglas Reid-Kennedy in *Twinkle, Twinkle, Little Spy*; SS-Gruppenführer

Kellerman bullies Harry Woods into acting as his informant by threatening to send young Douggie Archer to a Hitler Youth unit in Germany in *SS–GB*; and Bernard Samson is forced to order armed police protection for his children, Billy and Sally, before exposing his wife as Moscow's penetration agent in London Central in *Berlin Game*.

The sometimes irreconcilable relationship between parents and their children is a resonating theme in *Goodbye Mickey Mouse* and a bizarre subplot in *Close-Up*, in which Marshall Stone's desirable companion Suzy Delft is revealed to be his illegitimate daughter by Ingrid Rainbow. And seventeen-year-old Paul Winter is prompted to wonder if everyone feels guilty about neglecting their parents as he writes to his family from the Western Front in *Winter*, promising a longer letter but knowing he'll never get it on paper.

Shared childhood experiences in early postwar Berlin are recalled by Bernard Samson and Werner Volkmann in the *Game, Set & Match* trilogy, but in *Only When I Larf* the delinquent games of Silas and Bob drive an exasperated Liz Mason to declare: 'And my mother says wouldn't I like to have children. What I'd like is one adult man.'

Childs, Stanley. Former RAF Medical Officer in *Action*, who accompanies Air Marshal John Dover to see their wartime adventures unfold on a film set—but not as they remember them.

China. The People's Republic of China has infrequently figured in modern espionage fiction. However, in *An Expensive Place to Die*, Deighton develops the story around the American State Department's concern that the concept of nuclear deterrence is being jeopardised by the fact that China is not being deterred. Published reports of US nuclear tests have been deliberately sanitised to minimise fall-out, and these figures are being used by Chinese hawks to 'prove' that the PRC can survive a nuclear attack. Washington therefore decides to apprise the Chinese government of the true dangers of fall-out, and the CIA's Special Projects Division come up with a plan to leak genuine classified data to the Chinese Embassy expert in Paris—using a British cut-out to avoid compromising local CIA operatives.

Chlestakov, ———. KGB fieldman with a central role in the Soviet ploy to safeguard Fiona Samson in *Berlin Game*, laying a cynosural trail identifying Giles Trent as the traitor within London Central.

Christmas finds an irate Bernard Samson ordered to Berlin in *London Match*, and there's not much joy for Elena Bekuv after an apparent attempt on her life following midnight mass in *Twinkle, Twinkle, Little Spy*. Jamie Farebrother spends it in the arms of Victoria Cooper in *Goodbye Mickey Mouse*, but Marshall Stone's extra-marital activity during Christmas in Los Angeles draws the ire of studio executive Leo Koolman in *Close-Up*. And it's scarcely an occasion of festive goodwill in *Winter* either. Christmas 1918 is a time of madness in Berlin, leading Fritz Esser to abandon the Spartakists and throw in his lot with the Freikorps; Paul Winter's family celebration in 1930 breaks up after differences over his famous new neighbour on the Obersalzburg; and Christmas 1941 finds General Alex Horner and von Kleindorf trapped in the snow-covered approaches to Moscow.

Churchill, Winston (1874–1965). Distinguished British statesman and wartime Prime Minister, whose bulldog stubbornness and belief in ultimate victory did much to sustain the British people through World War II.
In *SS–GB*, a novel portraying the Nazi occupation of Britain in 1941, Churchill is reported as having been executed by a Luftwaffe firing squad in Berlin, apparently refusing a blindfold and holding up his fingers in that familiar V-for-victory sign. While in *XPD*, forty years after an alleged secret meeting between Churchill and Adolf Hitler in 1940 to discuss Britain's surrender, a ruthless espionage battle is fought by British Intelligence to suppress Hitler's minutes of the affair.
A factual assessment of Churchill's role and achievements in the

early years of World War II is contained in *Fighter*, *Blitzkrieg* and *Battle of Britain*.

See also: history as hypothesis.

ciphers. A cipher system breaks up the plaintext (the original message) into units of regular length, substituting individual letters or letter-pairs. Thus a cipher might split the *Vu* from *lkan* in *Vulkan*, whereas a code will substitute a single codenumber or codeword (e.g. KING for *Vulkan*). To transform a message using a cipher system is to encipher it, the unintelligible message is known as the ciphertext, and to reverse the transformation is to decipher it. Third parties not in possession of the cipher key engage in cryptanalysis.

cities. Spies tend to be metropolitan people, and whilst Deighton's heartland may be London and Berlin, all his cities (and towns) are observed with 'the sharpest of urban eyes'.[10] Portrayed in the novels are Albufeira, Algiers, Beirut, Berlin, Bordeaux, Geneva, The Hague, Hamburg, Helsinki, Hendaye-plage, Leningrad, London, Los Angeles, Madrid, Marrakech, Mexico City, Miami, Moscow, Munich, New York, Nice, Ostend, Paris, Prague, Riga, San Antonio, Vienna and Washington DC.

A non-fiction guide to London, compiled and edited by Deighton, *Len Deighton's London Dossier*, was published in 1967. If you can find a copy now, it offers a fascinating portrait of the 'swinging' city of the 1960s.

city drop. A hiding place in a busy urban location, accessible in the course of an agent's normal movements (e.g. railway station, theatre or car park), where messages and material can be deposited or collected. An anonymous London phone booth is used by the Facts for Freedom network to deposit messages for the narrator of *Billion-Dollar Brain*, whereas Brahms Four is said in *Berlin Game* to prefer working through the mail—always local addresses to avoid the East German censors—and to use a drop only in emergencies.

class. Deighton's protagonists tend to be resolutely working-class in background and point-of-view, and the class battles they must wage ('What chance did I stand between the Communists on the one side and the Establishment on the other—they were both out-thinking me at every move'—*The IPCRESS File*) add considerable wit, tension and complexity to the novels.

Claude *l'avocat.* *See* Claude Winkler.

'clean but not kosher'. Expression current in Nazi-occupied London in *SS–GB*, describing offences to which a London policeman will turn a blind eye.

Clevemore, Sir Henry. MI6's senescent Director-General in the *Game, Set & Match* trilogy, whose approaching retirement kindles an internecine battle of power, further debilitating an organisation already humiliated by treachery within its senior staff.

CLOSE-UP (Jonathan Cape, London, 1 June 1972/Atheneum, New York, 19 June 1972; fiction). Deighton's eighth novel is set in the big-daddy world of the film business, and linchpin of the story is a charismatic member of Hollywood's elite—English actor Marshall Stone. When Stone's ex-wife's husband, Peter Anson, starts researching his biography, painful memories and suppressed scandals are uncovered along with yesterday's triumphs, and Anson is forced to conclude that the true story can only be written as a novel—which he'll call *Close-Up*.

closing lines. Ten passages chosen for the quality of the writing, or the virtue of reminding us of the energy, style and prevalent concerns of the novels from which they are taken. Sources are given at the end of the entry. How many can you identify before checking the list?

Anytime I want Jay I know I can find him at the 'Mirabelle', and last Saturday morning I bumped into him at Leds. He wants Jean and me to go to dinner with him. He said he would cook it himself. I'd like to go but I don't think I will. It's not wise to make too many close friends in this business. **(a)**

Across the silent, wet street, a newspaper tumbles gently like an urban tumbleweed. It floats just buoyant on the wind, kisses a traffic sign, lightly dabs a slide trombone and plasters itself across army boots. The newspaper is rainsoaked to a dull yellow colour but the large headline is blunt and legible. 'Berlin—a new crisis?' **(b)**

. . . Very high, one bird flew purposefully and alone on a course as straight as a light beam. Farther along the shore, in and out of the dunes, a hedgehog wandered, aimlessly sniffing and scratching at the colourless grass and watching the gulls at their game. The hedgehog would fly higher and stronger than any of the birds, if only he knew how. **(c)**

'Flight Sergeant Booth here, sir, Photo Section. The attack hasn't hit Krefeld, sir, I've just been studying the negs. Street patterns are nothing like it. I don't know, sir. It doesn't look like anywhere. It doesn't look like anywhere.' **(d)**

The heavy blue notepaper crackled as the man signed his name. The signature was an actor's: a dashing autograph, bigger by far than any of the text. It began well, rushing forward boldly before halting suddenly enough to split the supply of ink. Then it retreated to strangle itself in loops. The surname began gently but then that too became a complex of arcades so that the whole name was all but deleted by well-considered decorative scrolls. The signature was a diagram of a man. **(e)**

. . . Ferdy had gone and Marjorie too: the comfortable little world I'd built up since leaving the department had disappeared as if it had never been.

'Are they treating you well in here?' said Dawlish.

'Pickled fish for breakfast,' I said.

'The reason I ask,' said Dawlish, 'is that we have a bit of a problem . . . It's a security job . . .'

I suppose I might have guessed that a man like that doesn't fly to Norway to bring anyone grapes. **(f)**

Now Steve was dead. The hotel was dead, and the café was gone. The chairs and tables were replaced by a corrugated iron hoarding. Upon it there was layer upon layer of posters, advertising everything from Communist Party candidates to Go-Go-clubs and careers in the Foreign Legion. Across them, someone had daubed '*Merde aux Arabes*' in red paint.

'Are you listening?' said Schlegel.

'Yes,' I said, but I wasn't. **(g)**

'I phoned England an hour ago,' said Werner. 'I knew it would be the first thing you'd ask. There's an armed police guard around your mother's house. Anything the Russians try won't work. The children are safe.'

'Thanks Werner,' I said. Thinking about the children made it easier not to think about Fiona. Better still would be not having to think at all. **(h)**

'. . . Moskvin's a desk man, is he?'

'Yes,' said Stinnes. 'And I hate desk men.'

'So do I,' I said feelingly. 'They're bloody dangerous.' **(i)**

'. . . Okay, there are wounds, and there will be scars, but it's not game, set and match to Fiona. It's not game, set and match to anyone. It never is.'

Werner opened the door and, as the light inside the car came on, I saw his weary smile. He wasn't convinced. **(j)**

(a) *The IPCRESS File*, (b) *Funeral in Berlin*, (c) *An Expensive Place to Die*, (d) *Bomber*, (e) *Close-Up*, (f) *Spy Story*, (g) *Yesterday's Spy*, (h) *Berlin Game*, (i) *Mexico Set*, and (j) *London Match*.

clubs. London's gentleman's clubs, centred around Pall Mall, have provided generations of privileged men with a discreet setting in which to order the nation's affairs. White's Club, *sanctus sanctorum* of the Establishment, is chosen by Steve Champion for his meeting with Charles Bonnard at the beginning of *Yesterday's Spy*; in *SS–GB*, Douglas Archer is dismissed by an uncooperative Sir Robert Benson in the courtyard of the Reform Club, as the King sits muffled in a wheelchair on the pavement outside; in *XPD* it is over luncheon at Boodles that Sir Sydney Ryden unwittingly determines the fate of Paul Bock; and in *Winter* the roof of the Travellers Club offers Cyrus and Glenn Rensselaer a commanding view of a Zeppelin air raid on London during World War I.

Less distinguished clubs provide the setting for Ross's attempt to suborn the narrator in *The IPCRESS File* and Giles Trent's clandestine meeting with Chlestakov in *Berlin Game*, while in *Mexico Set*, Erich Stinnes chooses to surface in Mexico City's Kronprinz Club—certain he can draw the attention of Werner and Zena Volkmann.

code-breaking. *See* cryptanalysis.

code-names. *See* cryptonyms.

codes. A code system substitutes plaintext (the intelligible text) units of *variable* length, such as words and phrases, whereas ciphers break up the plaintext into units of *regular* length. To transform a message using a code system is to encode it, the unintelligible message is known as the codetext, and to legitimately reverse the transformation is to decode it.

Cohen, Emmy. Thin white-haired mother of Simon Cohen in *Bomber*. A German emigré like her husband, she welcomes her son's RAF colleagues into their home, but can't help feeling a little afraid of 'these handsome boys who set fire to the towns she'd known when a girl'.

Cohen, Mr. Apprehensive, elderly father of Simon Cohen in *Bomber*, whose request that Sam Lambert look after his son, draws a promise that Lambert is powerless to fulfil.

Cohen, Sergeant Simon. Bright-eyed young RAF navigator, probably the best in the Lancaster squadron stationed at Warley Fen in *Bomber*. The youngest crew member of 'Creaking Door', he's fatally injured by flak on their homeward journey—a loss which hits skipper Sam Lambert hard.

Cohen, 'Spider'. Former Wormwood Scrubs cell-mate of Bob Appleyard, employed as a waiter at the Chester Hotel, who sets up the Honourable Gerald Spencer as a suitable mark for the trio of confidence tricksters in *Only When I Larf*.

the Cold War. The term originated in a speech given by Bernard Baruch in South Carolina on 16 April 1947, and describes the political and diplomatic conflict between the Western Powers and the Soviet-led Eastern bloc since World War II. The series of crises that marked the 1950s and early 1960s has been followed by a period of relative stability, but there is no point at which the Cold War can be said to have ended. It is the contemporary context for *The IPCRESS File*, *Funeral in Berlin*, *Billion-Dollar Brain*, *Spy Story*, *Twinkle, Twinkle, Little Spy*, *XPD*, *Berlin Game*, *Mexico Set* and *London Match*.

Colfax, Peter. Reg Hardcastle's replacement as butler at Thaxted Hall in *Goodbye Mickey Mouse*, whose 'accidental' encounter with Lieutenant Mickey Morse alerts the American pilot to the fact that his sweetheart, Vera Hardcastle, is a married woman.

collaborators. Award-winning designer (and lately novelist) Ray Hawkey has been responsible for almost all of the jackets for Deighton's English hardcover books, many of the paperbacks, and several of the American hardcover editions. He and Deighton were students together at London's Royal College of Art, and Hawkey's black-and-white photographic jackets for the first three novels, *The IPCRESS File*, *Horse Under Water* and *Funeral in Berlin*, were widely praised for so successfully catching the gritty, yet witty, flavour of the books. He was responsible for many of the celebrated promotional items, including the books of 1941 United Kingdom postage stamps bearing the head of Adolf Hitler, produced to promote the novel *SS–GB*. They were so authentic-looking, that five years later many philatelists believed them to have been produced during the war as either a German propaganda device, or, to quote *The Stamp Magazine*, 'for a more sinister purpose'. Hawkey also devised and designed the TOP SECRET wallet laid into the first English edition of *An Expensive Place to Die*, containing letters and documents purporting to have originated from the President of the United States, the US Secretary of Defense, the Central Intelligence Agency, and the British Prime Minister. They were so convincing that both the FBI and Britain's Special Branch carried out investigations into their provenance, and some years later they surfaced in a BBC2 television documentary about the spy Kim Philby—a fact which when revealed by the London *Evening Standard* caused the BBC considerable embarrassment. Ray Hawkey also designed the titles for Deighton's film *Oh! What a Lovely War*.

In 1967 Deighton collaborated with Michael Rand and Howard Loxton to produce *The Assassination of President Kennedy*, and that same year saw the publication of *Len Deighton's London Dossier*, with contributions from Adrian Bailey, Drusilla Beyfus, Eric Clark, Daniel Farson, Adrian Flowers, Spike Hughes, Steve Race, Milton Shulman, Godfrey Smith, Nick Tomalin, Frank Norman, John Marshall, Michael Wale and Jane Wilson.

Arnold Schwartzman, a noted graphic designer turned film-maker—he won an Oscar for Best Documentary Feature in the 1982 Academy Awards for *Genocide*, a film narrated by Elizabeth Taylor and Orson Welles about the Holocaust in World War II—collaborated with Deighton on *Airshipwreck*, and the well-known American airmail collector, Fred Blau, provided much of the basic material for *The Orient Flight L.Z.127-Graf Zeppelin* and *The Egypt Flight L.Z.127-Graf Zeppelin*.

Collins, Sergeant 'Tapper'. Veteran RAF bomb-aimer of nineteen, the only survivor of an earlier crash landing, who safely completes his twenty-ninth trip and his tour of duty aboard 'Joe for King' in *Bomber*.

Combined Services Information Clearing House (C-SICH). A footnote in *The IPCRESS File* reveals it to be a secret British agency responsible for industrial and commercial intelligence. Among its agents is Charlie Cavendish, whose murder panics Jay into making the fateful rendezvous with Dalby witnessed by the narrator. It also figures in *Horse Under Water*, passing to the narrator confidential files on the crypto-Fascist Cabinet Minister, Henry Smith.

'come to rest'. According to a footnote in *Billion-Dollar Brain*, a person who has 'come to rest' is no longer under surveillance, and can be safely contacted.

computers. Deighton's fascination with electronic hardware is reflected in the contemporary application of computers in his espionage novels. They are neither heroes, nor villains, and whether it is the primitive IBM collator ('the key to WOOC(P)'s reputation') in *The IPCRESS File*, the 'Brain' (which today, could probably be housed in a single room) in *Billion-Dollar Brain*, the war-gaming computers in *Spy Story*, General Shumuk's KGB computers in *XPD*, or those employed in 'the yellow submarine' in *Berlin Game*—they remain the tools of their often fallible operators.

Despite this it's often been said the computer is king in Deighton's world, and no doubt as a gentle riposte to his critics, the debate is satirised in 'Man From the Palace', Marshall Stone's ill-fated film in *Close-Up*.

See also: word processors.

'concens'. Carswell's term for the unusual concentration of S1s (i.e. persons considered vital to the national interest) at different sites across England, noted during a statistical analysis of

factors common to the disappearance of Raven and other top
biochemists in *The IPCRESS File*.

concentration camps. Originally established by the Nazis to
detain political, racial and social 'undesirables', the system was
expanded following the outbreak of World War II to include
extermination camps such as Auschwitz-Birkenau, Dachau,
Sobibar and Treblinka. More than eight million people are
believed to have perished in the camps, among them about six
million Jews.

The testimonies of Jewish survivors from Treblinka shed light on
the fate of Paul Louis Broum in *Funeral in Berlin*, while in
Bomber, the shamed reaction of Luftwaffe pilot Christian Himmel
on learning of experiments being conducted at Dachau, leads to his
arrest for treason and execution. Paul Winter sacrifices his father's
mistress to save Lottie Winter from the camps in *Winter*, and Boris
Somló makes a rare escape from the transport train taking him to
Auschwitz-Birkenau, but in the Nazi councils of Berlin the camps
are no more than names on the files of bureaucrats prepared to do
anything they are told without questioning it.

confidence tricks are the subject of Deighton's sixth novel,
Only When I Larf: 'I was attracted by the idea that the characters
are required to adopt all the traits of spies, building up their cover
stories and lying to their victims.'[11] This comic study emerged from
research for an abandoned non-fiction book, which had its origins
in his own innocent involvement with a Hong Kong gold-
smuggling organisation while working as a steward for BOAC.

A massive confidence trick also figures in *XPD*, when Peter
Friedman embezzles one hundred million dollars from the Swiss
bank owned by Charles Stein and the 'Kaiseroda Raiders', in the
hope of forcing Stein to part with the coveted Hitler Minutes.
  See also: mark.

consort watch. Monitoring a person's location without
necessarily maintaining direct surveillance (e.g. by bribing a
concierge), according to a footnote in *Funeral in Berlin*.

Continuum. Ambitious film investment company, whose haemorrhaging finances force actor Marshall Stone into a humbling reconciliation with Leo Koolman in *Close-Up*.

control. *See* case officer.

cookery. 'Cooking is the art of the possible,' observes Silas Gaunt in *Berlin Game*, an art at which Deighton is considerably skilled. Son of a professional cook, he spent vacations from the Royal College of Art working in restaurants, and the experience led to his innovative Cookstrips, and the publication of the three popular cookbooks, *Action Cook Book*, *Où est le garlic* and *Basic French Cooking*. His early novels put deliberate emphasis on the independent bachelor habits and culinary expertise of his heroes, and he couldn't resist setting the climax of *The IPCRESS File* in the kitchen, where the narrator finds Jay expertly basting a lobster with butter and champagne.

the Cookstrip. In 1961, the London *Daily Express* printed an innovative diagrammatic cookery strip devised by Deighton originally for his own use ('Why write the word "egg" when a simple oval drawing tells the story?'[12]). Subsequently he was invited to contribute a weekly feature to *The Observer*, and the series ran from 18 March 1962 until 7 August 1966. Deighton produced a total of 189 Cookstrips for the paper, and they proved so popular that readers demanded that the strips be printed on tea towels, laid in plastic tabletops, and turned into kitchen wallpaper. They were reprinted between covers in *Action Cook Book*, *Cookstrip Cook Book*, *Où est le garlic* and *Basic French Cooking*. Sharp-eyed viewers will spot one of the strips pinned to Harry Palmer's kitchen wall in the opening credits of the film, *The Ipcress File*.

COOKSTRIP COOK BOOK (Bernard Geis, New York, 9 September 1966; non-fiction). American edition of *Action Cook Book*, first published in England in March 1965.

Cooper, Dr Bernard. Ruddy-faced scholarly psychologist, father of Victoria Cooper in *Goodbye Mickey Mouse*, who despite a profound understanding of the difficulties faced by parents and their maturing children, finds himself ill-prepared for his daughter's love for Jamie Farebrother.

Cooper, Margaret. Mother of Victoria Cooper in *Goodbye Mickey Mouse*. A complex woman, unable to reconcile herself to her daughter's liberating love affair with Jamie Farebrother.

Cooper, Victoria. Elegant passionate English girl of twenty-five, private secretary to a Cambridgeshire newspaper owner, whose exhilarating and defiant love for American pilot Jamie Farebrother in *Goodbye Mickey Mouse*, has far-reaching consequences for her conventional parents and Jamie's pal, Mickey Morse.

Co-ordinator of Intelligence and Security. As the title suggests, he's the only man who can tell both MI6 and MI5 what he wants done, and his hand is seen behind the convening of the 'Rensselaer Committee' in *London Match*. Ostensibly set up to review the progress of the Stinnes debriefing, its hidden purpose is to consider evidence that Bret Rensselaer is a longtime KGB agent—sparing MI6 the humiliation of having MI5 investigate one of its senior staff.

Costa, Humberto. Ambitious revolutionary army officer, whose compelling need for weapons and assistance dramatically changes Albert Sampson's life in *Bonus for a Salesman*.

counter-espionage. The battle in the shadows—that depends on cunning entrapments, double- and triple-crosses, betrayals and deceptions—to penetrate the opposition's intelligence services while at the same time preventing them from penetrating your own. It is the stuff of *The IPCRESS File*, *Funeral in Berlin*, *Twinkle, Twinkle, Little Spy* and the *Game, Set & Match* trilogy.

counterfeit money provides the starting-point for Operation Alforreca in *Horse Under Water*, the underwater search for Allied money manufactured by the Nazis during World War II.
See also: 'Bernhard'.

counter-intelligence. The management of raw information received from counter-espionage activities.

countries used as backgrounds in the novels and short stories include Algiers, Austria, Czechoslovakia, Denmark, East Germany, England, Finland, France, Gibraltar, Holland, India, Ireland, Italy, Lebanon, Mexico, Morocco, Portugal, the Soviet Union, Spain, Switzerland, the United States of America, Vietnam and West Germany.

country drop. A hiding place in a secluded, and rarely frequented area, where an agent can deposit or collect messages and material.

couriers still play an essential role in espionage operations. Philippa Pike is identified as a courier for the Facts for Freedom network in *Billion-Dollar Brain*, and the narrator's first task after having been recruited by Harvey Newbegin is to smuggle viruses stolen from Porton MRE into Finland. Douglas Reid-Kennedy first comes to the attention of Marjorie Dean while working as a courier for her husband in postwar Berlin in *Twinkle, Twinkle, Little Spy*; Danny Barga is parachuted into Nazi-occupied Britain to deliver a crucial message from the American Government to the Resistance in *SS–GB*; Werner Volkmann is used by British Intelligence to bring out Brahms Four's material in *Berlin Game*; but Bret Rensselaer unsuccessfully poses as a KGB courier to trap members of the Cambridge Network in *London Match*. Business travel is known to provide ideal cover, and the KGB has no difficulty framing the hapless Paul Biedermann as one of their couriers in *Mexico Set*.

Couzins, Annie. Artist's model and part-time hostess at the scandalous Avenue Foch Clinic in *An Expensive Place to Die*. Murdered by Martin Langley Byrd after revealing her British Intelligence connections to Monsieur Datt.

cover is said to be 'official' or 'unofficial'. An intelligence officer holding a legal embassy post (and thus enjoying diplomatic immunity) has official cover—e.g. Harvey Newbegin in *Funeral in Berlin*, Yuriy Grechko in *XPD* and Henry Tiptree in *Mexico Set*. But when posing as a civilian he's operating with unofficial cover—e.g. the narrators of *An Expensive Place to Die* (travel agency director) and *Twinkle, Twinkle, Little Spy* (tourist), Boyd Stuart in *XPD* (film financier) and Brian Samson in *Winter* (aero-engine draughtsman).
See also: deep cover agents.

cover names. 'I heard a soft voice say "Hello Harry". Now my name isn't Harry, but in this business it's hard to remember if it ever had been', admits the narrator of *The IPCRESS File*. For those who find equal difficulty in such matters, here's a list of identities behind the cover names: Frederick Anthony (narrator, *Twinkle, Twinkle, Little Spy*), Patrick Armstrong (narrator, *Spy Story*), Mr Aristo (Christian Stakowski), Stanley Beamish (narrator, *The IPCRESS File*), Charles Bonnard (narrator, *Yesterday's Spy*), Elliot Castlebridge (Sir Sydney Ryden), Howard Craske (narrator, *Horse Under Water*), Liam Dempsey (narrator, *Billion-Dollar Brain*), Edmond Dorf (narrator, *Funeral in Berlin*), Captain Maylev (Colonel Stok), Lieutenant Montgomery (Barney Barnes), Sergeant Murray (Lieutenant-Colonel Harriman), Melodie Page (Helen Bishop), Samantha Steel (Hanna Stahl) and Erich Stinnes (Nikolai Sadoff).

covert operations. Individual entries can be found under the following cryptonyms: ALFORRECA, APOCALYPSE, BERNHARD, SIEGFRIED, TASK POGONI, TURNSTONE and VITAMIN.

Craske, Howard. Cover name used by the narrator during a brief London stopover, to evade Cabinet Minister Henry Smith's surveillance, in *Horse Under Water*.

'Creaking Door'. The battle-scarred RAF Lancaster whose last flight over Germany on the night of 31 June 1943 lies at the heart of *Bomber*. Skippered by Flight Sergeant Sam Lambert, its aircrew comprises Sergeant Battersby (flight engineer), Sergeant Cohen (navigator), Flight Sergeant Digby (bomb-aimer), Sergeant Gordon (gunner), Sergeant Grimm (wireless operator) and Sergeant Jones (gunner).

Criminal Records Office (CRO). Scotland Yard's registry of files identifying known and suspected criminals, which provides the narrator of *The IPCRESS File* with a lead to Housemartin, and through him to Jay's abandoned experiments at the 'haunted house' in Acacia Drive.

crossword puzzles are a cerebral diversion for the narrator in *The IPCRESS File* and *Horse Under Water*, but prove the undoing of Miss Trent in *Berlin Game*. Discerning readers of *Horse Under Water* will discover the chapter headings offer the clues to a crossword puzzle, the solution to which doubles as the table of contents.

Cruyer, Daphne. Dicky Cruyer's arty irrepressible wife in the *Game, Set & Match* trilogy. An energetic woman in her early thirties, 'with the loud voice and upper-class accent that go with weekends in large unheated country houses'.

Cruyer, Dicky. Trendy, excitable, thirty-eight-year-old MI6 German Stations Controller in the *Game, Set & Match* trilogy. A curious mixture of scholarship and ruthless ambition, he sees himself as the Department *Wunderkind* among the dark suits and Eton ties, but proves a mercurial boss as Bernard Samson confronts the multiple betrayals debilitating London Central.

cryptanalysis. The most ambitious organisations engaged in this work are America's National Security Agency (NSA) at Fort Meade, Maryland, and Britain's Government Communications Headquarters (GCHQ) at Cheltenham, Gloucestershire. Although silicon-chip technology has transformed their work—the NSA's Cray XMP supercomputer can perform 200 million computations *per second*, a speed 200,000 times faster than that of your IBM PC—computers have in no way conferred total victory in the unending struggle to render codes and ciphers intelligible.

However, the National Security Agency's giant ATLAS computer does break Moscow Centre's two-part radio message to its Washington legal in *XPD*, revealing the first recorded use of the cryptonym 'Task Pogoni'. In *Berlin Game* an abrupt change of Soviet military codes provides damning evidence of treachery within London Central, while Soviet success in breaking the MI6 station's codes in Mexico City is revealed by KGB defector Erich Stinnes in *Mexico Set*.

cryptonyms. At the risk of compromising security, here are the identities behind principal cryptonyms employed in the novels: BLUE-JACKET (King George VI), BOX FOUR (Christian Stakowski), BRAHMS FOUR (Dr Walter von Munte), DEATH'S-HEAD HAWK MOTH (Paul Louis Broum), FABIAN (Professor Andrei Bekuv), JAY (Christian Stakowski, again), KADAVER (narrator, *Funeral in Berlin*), KING (Johnnie Vulkan), PIG IRON (Fiona Samson), SARACEN (Mason) and SHOESHINE (Major Mickey Mann). Two further cryptonyms employed by WOOC(P) in *The IPCRESS File* refer to unnamed individuals, HOUSEMARTIN (Stakowski's assistant) and RAVEN (the missing Porton biochemist). JAKE in *London Match* is revealed to be no more than a nominal cryptonym employed by the KGB to sow confusion within London Central, and SIXPACK is the cryptonym for an Allied agent dropped into Nazi Germany in *Winter*.

da Cunha, Manuel. The Portuguese identity assumed by Fregattenkapitän Knobel, a former scientific officer of the wartime German Navy, in *Horse Under Water*.

Curtiss, Dr. Boyd Stuart's MI6 case officer during his assignment in California to secure the Hitler Minutes in *XPD*.

Czechoslovakia. Visited in autumn by the narrator of *Funeral in Berlin* ('the trees had just the last few tenacious leaves hanging on like jilted lovers'), in his quest to learn more about the fate of Paul Louis Broum.

D

Dalby, ———. Elegant, languid, public-school Englishman 'of a type that can usually reconcile his duty with comfort and luxury', with a leading role in *The IPCRESS File*. Head of WOOC(P), his responsibility is direct to the Cabinet, making him almost as powerful as anyone gets in the intelligence business. Admired by the narrator as 'one of the best bosses I ever had', he's later unmasked as a key member of Jay's treacherous IPCRESS Network.

'Daniel'. USAF P-51 Mustang piloted by Rube Wein in *Goodbye Mickey Mouse*, austerely decorated with only the carefully lettered name.

Danziger, Lottie. *See* Lottie Winter.

Danziger, Simon. American entrepreneur, father of Lottie Winter in *Winter*. A white-haired, rotund, somewhat cherubic little man, whose every spare cent is invested in the dizzying boom on Wall Street. Visiting Germany with his wife to see Lottie and their new son-in-law in October 1929, he learns of the greatest financial crash in history and steps out in front of a horse-drawn dray on Berlin's Potsdamer Platz.

Datt, Monsieur. Urbane blackmailer with a leading role in *An Expensive Place to Die* as the owner of a *maison de passe* on Paris's Avenue Foch, which he operates with the hidden purpose of compiling dossiers on influential clients from East and West. With friends among France's political elite he's seemingly immune from prosecution, until Chief Inspector Loiseau of the Sûreté Nationale secures the help of the British Intelligence officer narrator.

Davies, Alun. Ex-public-school RAF navigator aboard Lancaster 'Q for Queen' in *Bomber*, who replaces 'Jammy' Giles as bomb-aimer and is chastened to find that from four miles high a whole city block on fire is nothing more than a 'pimple of red' in a vast bowl of darkness.

Davis, Detective Sergeant. Jaundiced Met. officer in *Spy Story*, who grudgingly provides Patrick Armstrong with the name of Miss Sara Shaw—the only witness to Ben Toliver's near-fatal traffic accident.

Dawlish, George. Senior British Intelligence officer, who replaces Dalby as head of WOOC(P) in *Horse Under Water*, *Funeral in Berlin* and *Billion-Dollar Brain*. A tall, grey-haired Establishment figure of about fifty, for the most part depicted by the narrator as an obtuse, spinsterish and quaintly eccentric bureaucrat. Yet he adroitly defends the department against Whitehall's backbiting, and reveals a shrewd understanding of the complexities of modern espionage. ('You didn't understand your role, my boy . . . We didn't want you to *discover* anything. Somehow we knew that you would make them do something indiscreet.')

Dawlish makes a welcome return in *Spy Story*—exhibiting all his old cunning as he draws a reluctant Patrick Armstrong back into fieldwork, and again briefly figures in *Yesterday's Spy*.

dead drop, or **dead-letter box.** A hiding place where an agent can deposit or collect messages and material. The so-called 'live' drop is when people meet to pass material.

See also: city drop, country drop *and* moving drop.

Dean, Hank. Former CIA officer—once a rising star in the intelligence community, until cuckolded by his wife and compromised by the KGB—falsely implicated in the leak of classified American scientific data in *Twinkle, Twinkle, Little Spy*.

Dean, Henry Hope. Illegitimate son of Marjorie Dean and traitor Douglas Reid-Kennedy, who grows up believing his father to be Hank Dean, a fiction benevolently maintained by Major Mann in *Twinkle, Twinkle, Little Spy*.

Dean, Marjorie. Estranged wife of Hank Dean. A callous New Yorker of German extraction in her mid-forties, whose relationship with Douglas Reid-Kennedy leads to her complicity in the betrayal of first her husband, and then her country, in *Twinkle, Twinkle, Little Spy*.

'Death's-Head Hawk Moth'. WOOC(P)'s cryptonym for the enigmatic Paul Louis Broum in *Funeral in Berlin*.

DECLARATIONS OF WAR (Jonathan Cape, London, 21 October 1971/**Eleven Declarations of War**, Harcourt Brace Jovanovich, New York, 6 March 1975; fiction). Deighton's only book of short stories spans twenty-three centuries of warfare. From Hannibal's march on Rome—when strange, moving objects terrorise the troops of one of the toughest and most skilful armies in history, to war-torn Vietnam—where two lost American soldiers stumble across an abandoned military airfield.

Listed alphabetically, the thirteen short stories are: *Action, Adagio, Bonus for a Salesman, Brent's Deus Ex Machina, Discipline, First Base, It Must Have Been Two Other Fellows, Lord Nick Flies Again, Mission Control: Hannibal One, A New Way To Say Goodnight, Paper Casualty, Twelve Good Men and True* and *Winter's Morning*.

See also: short stories.

deep cover agents. Foreign agents posing as seemingly innocent citizens and accepted members of the community—e.g. Gerry Hart in *Twinkle, Twinkle, Little Spy*, and Willi Kleiber and Edward Parker in *XPD*.

defectors. Most defections are induced, and all are greeted with great caution since they may be enemy deceptions or provocations, such as the enrolment of Erich Stinnes in the *Game, Set & Match* trilogy. The offer of superior facilities and a chair at New York University persuades Professor Andrei Bekuv to defect to America in *Twinkle, Twinkle, Little Spy*, but his wife's subsequent arrival in New York is recognised as a KGB ploy. The possible defection of another Soviet scientist lures the narrator to East Berlin in *Funeral in Berlin*, only to find KGB Colonel Stok insisting it is *he* who wishes to settle in the West, while the British Intelligence operation to exfiltrate a high-level Soviet defector in *Spy Story* is later revealed to be a cunning provocation intended to sabotage German reunification talks.

Harvey Newbegin's decision to return to 'the land of his father' in *Billion-Dollar Brain* appears, like so much else he undertakes, to lack any real conviction, but worries British Intelligence sufficiently for the narrator to push him into the path of a bus on Leningrad's Nevsky Prospekt. And when Peter Winter claims in *Winter* that he was trapped in the USA by the outbreak of war, Glenn Rennselaer points out that he's wearing the uniform of a US Army Colonel, America is at war with Germany, and his countrymen will hardly accept that it's all a trick of fate . . .

Deighton, Leonard Cyril (1929–). Len Deighton was born in Marylebone, London, on 18 February 1929. His father was chauffeur and his mother cook to Campbell Dodgson, Keeper of Prints and Drawings at the British Museum. He was a ferociously inquisitive child, and despite his later claim to have been a poor scholar, passed his 11-plus exam in the top third of his class and went to Marylebone Grammar School. But in common with other children at the time, his education was considerably disturbed by the outbreak of war. Many of London's schools were evacuated to the country, and he found himself transferred to an emergency school in North London. He left before taking his matriculation, and at the age of seventeen was conscripted into the Royal Air Force.

Following his National Service discharge, Deighton studied at St Martin's School of Art on an ex-service grant, then in 1952 won a scholarship to that cradle of protean talent, the Royal College of Art. (Among the intake of other gifted students that year were John Bratby, Bruce Lacey, Bridget Riley and Joe Tilson.)

After graduating in 1955, Deighton joined BOAC as an air steward, then pursued a short, very successful career as a designer and illustrator. He worked on all kinds of advertising and publicity material in London and New York, did drawings for several magazines—among them *Esquire*—and illustrated over two hundred book jackets for various British publishers, including André Deutsch, William Heinemann, Secker & Warburg and Penguin Books.

In 1961, the *Daily Express* printed an innovative, diagrammatic cookery strip devised by Deighton originally for his own use. Subsequently, he was invited to contribute a weekly feature to *The Observer*, and the first Cookstrip in what was to become a long-running series, appeared in March 1962.

Len Deighton's first novel, *The IPCRESS File*, was published in November of the same year.

Delaney, Jerry. One of the 'Kaiseroda Raiders', now owner of a topless-bottomless club in the Los Angeles suburb of Lennox, whose underworld connections provide a false passport and papers for Charles Stein in *XPD*.

Delft, Suzy. Rootless, vivacious nineteen-year-old actress in *Close-Up*. One of a dozen girls that studio boss Leo Koolman describes as his 'discoveries', her tabloid romance with Hollywood star Marshall Stone successfully conceals the prosaic truth that she's Stone's illegitimate daughter.

Dempsey, Liam. Cover name used by the narrator of *Billion-Dollar Brain* to infiltrate General Midwinter's Facts for Freedom organisation.

See also: Sonny Sontag.

Dempsey, Percy. Former British 'Desert Rat' longtime resident in Algeria, whose hard-earned knowledge of the Sahara makes him an invaluable local asset in the CIA-MI6 operation to facilitate the defection of Andrei Bekuv in *Twinkle, Twinkle, Little Spy*.

denied areas. Important regions of target countries may be closed even to their own citizens, and although spy satellites now provide a global intelligence net, some objectives can only be achieved through conventional means—the so-called 'denied area' operations, involving border crossings and frequently the co-operation of emigré groups—e.g. Midwinter's private enterprise infiltration of Soviet Latvia in *Billion-Dollar Brain*.

Denmark. Neutral location chosen by KGB General Shumuk for a clandestine meeting with MI6 officer Boyd Stuart in *XPD*. The visit prompts Stuart to recall the day he fled Rostock, in East Germany: 'It had been a damned long sail to the Danish coast. Never since had he ever heard Danish without offering up a prayer of thanks.'

desk officer. A Resident's liaison officer back at head-quarters, who is very often being groomed to take over from him at the end of his tour of duty. For example, Bernard Samson in the *Game, Set & Match* trilogy, though his chances of replacing Frank Harrington seem remoter than ever by the end of *London Match*—'I said you should have Berlin . . . But the old man said that you were lucky not to be facing grave charges.'

detectives. The success of *SS–GB*, a novel set in a Nazi-occupied Britain of 1941, owes much to Deighton's choice of a Scotland Yard Murder Squad officer, Detective Superintendent Douglas Archer, as the protagonist. (The genesis of this character is revealed in the interview.) Elderly Detective Sergeant Harry Woods plays a crucial role alongside Archer, and a French detective, Chief Inspector Claude Loiseau of the Sûreté

Nationale, proves an unexpected ally for the narrator in *An Expensive Place to Die*.

Policemen with minor roles include Captain Keightley in *The IPCRESS File* and *Funeral in Berlin*, Chief Inspector Baix in *Horse Under Water*, Detective Sergeant Davis in *Spy Story*, Inspector Seymour in *Yesterday's Spy*, PC Jimmy Dunn in *SS–GB*, Los Angeles detective Lieutenant Harry Ramirez in *XPD*, Detective Sergeant Jenkins in *Goodbye Mickey Mouse*, Chief Inspector Nicol in *Mexico Set* and Theodor Steiner in *Winter*. The Renseignements Généraux Inspector, Fabre, encountered by Charles Bonnard in *Yesterday's Spy*, isn't a policeman at all; rather, an underworld hit-man hired by Steve Champion.

detention centres. London's Albert Hall, Wembley Stadium and Earls Court Exhibition Hall are all hurriedly requisitioned by the Nazis in *SS–GB* to house the thousands rounded up following the Highgate Cemetery explosion, but in *The IPCRESS File* less celebrated accommodation is found for the members of Jay's IPCRESS Network detained by British Intelligence. ('The last time we had seen anything on this sort of scale was when the Home Office pulled in all aliens during the war'.)

Digby, Flight Sergeant. Thirty-two-year-old Australian RAF bomb-aimer aboard 'Creaking Door' in *Bomber*. Elderly by combat aircrew standards, his balding head and weathered face single him out from the other crew members, as does his readiness to puncture the dignity of any officer.

dinner parties. After an absence of eight years (his previous appearance was in *Billion-Dollar Brain*), George Dawlish surfaces at a dinner party in *Spy Story* to persuade Patrick Armstrong to leave STUCEN and return to field intelligence work. (He declines, but is inevitably drawn into Dawlish's scheme.) A dinner party hosted by Frank Harrington brings together Bernard Samson and Poppy Biedermann in *Berlin Game*—an encounter which is to have dramatic consequences in *Mexico Set*. In *London Match*, a rare dinner invitation causes Samson to reflect on his social life (or rather, lack of it) since his wife's flight to East Berlin: 'I'd expected that all my friends and acquaintances would be inviting me out—I'd heard so many wives complaining how difficult it was to find that "extra man" for dinner. But it doesn't work like that; at least it didn't for me . . .' And Dr Isaac Volkmann engages in a tricky exercise in social engineering in *Winter*, throwing a dinner party in the hope of re-establishing the former close relationship between the two Winter brothers, who haven't taken a meal together since Peter and his wife visited the Obersalzburg at Christmas 1930.

Direction de la Surveillance du Territoire (DST).
France's counter-intelligence agency is controlled by the Ministry of the Interior on the rue de Saussaies, and freely employs the resources of the Renseignements Généraux. It was the DST which in late March 1987 rolled up the Soviet-bloc espionage network passing data on the HM-60 cryogenic rocket motor designed to launch the European Space Agency's *Hermes* space shuttle. West European progress in rocket technology is of singular interest to the Soviets, who are developing their own space shuttle at Baikonur.

Grenade is a member of the DST, and with the aid of the agency's amazing system of card indexes (now replaced by computers), he succeeds in identifying the enigmatic Paul Louis Broum as a former communist assassin in *Funeral in Berlin*.

Direction Générale de Sécurité Extérieur (DGSE).
Prior to President Mitterand's election in 1981, France's foreign intelligence and espionage agency was known as the Service de Documentation Extérieure et de Contre-Espionage (SDECE). Over the years it has been embroiled in any number of scandals (the Ben Barka affair, the Markevitch affair, etc.), the most recent of which concerned its operation in New Zealand waters to sink the Greenpeace ship leading the protest against France's Pacific nuclear tests.

In *An Expensive Place to Die*, Monsieur Datt deliberately encourages speculation that his Avenue Foch Clinic is owned by the SDECE, or the Ministry of the Interior, but neither rumour proves true.

DISCIPLINE. Short story in the collection *Declarations of War*. An émigré officer in the Union Army during the American Civil War finds an enemy ambush a convenient way to revenge himself on the soldiers who ridicule him.

Discipline (BBC Television, 18 December 1977). *exec.p.*: Bill Morton. *sc.*: Peter Prince. Based on the short story by Len Deighton. *d.*: Ben Rea. *l.p.*: Tony Maygarth (*Sergeant Winkelstein*), Bill Bailey (*Private Green*), William Hootkins (*Gray*), Norwich Duff (*Harvey*), Ray Jewers (*Private Ashton*), Bill J. Mitchell (*Soldier*), Blain Fairman (*Lieutenant Simms*), Bud Strait (*Captain*). 14 minutes.
See also: television adaptations.

disguises. 'The hair had been dyed but what was unusual about that?' observes the narrator after meeting Samantha Steel in *Funeral in Berlin*. Nothing, of course, unless you happen to operate in a world in which your enemies are as difficult to recognise as your friends, and a change of appearance more often than not signals a concealed identity: thus, Fernie Tomas in *Horse Under Water*, Max Breslow in *XPD* and Fiona Samson in *Mexico Set*. In *Billion-Dollar Brain*, Harvey Newbegin uses a chemical to simulate bad breath—an old trick to prevent people looking too closely at a hurried disguise, and Colonel Stok masquerades as a room-service waiter to waylay the narrator in his Riga hotel. Numerous guises are adopted by conmen Silas Lowther and Bob Appleyard in *Only When I Larf*, while at one point in *Horse Under Water* 'Tinkle Bell' is forced to don a gorilla mask—to maintain surveillance on Ivor Butcher.

Dodgson, Major Albert. Solitary British Army officer in the raiding party which hits Bringle Sands in *SS–GB*. Subsequently killed in Huth's carefully planned ambush, while leading a diversionary attack calculated to draw the Germans away from the Research Establishment.

Dorf, Edmond. Cover name used reluctantly by the narrator of *Funeral in Berlin*. ('You are always saying that foreign names are more convincingly English,' said my secretary. 'But not Dorf,' I said, 'especially not *Edmond* Dorf. I don't *feel* like an Edmond Dorf.' 'Now don't go metaphysical on me,' said Jean. 'Whom do you feel like?' . . . 'Flint McCrae,' I said.)

double-agents. Fiona Samson, the KGB's mole within London Central in the *Game, Set & Match* trilogy, is in no sense a double-agent; she is a British Intelligence officer, but an *agent* only to the Soviets. This is true also of Dalby in *The IPCRESS File* and Giles Trent in *Berlin Game*. However, notable examples include Johnnie Vulkan ('our friend changes his motive every time he comes through that East Berlin checkpoint'), Aziz, Helen Bishop, Gus and Mason, while Patrick Armstrong in *Spy Story* and Charles Bonnard in *Yesterday's Spy* both affect disenchantment with British Intelligence and join the 'opposition'. Two former double-agents are revealed in this latter novel: Steve Champion, whom it is said was run by British *and* Egyptian Intelligence until he exceeded London's brief and sold classified NATO wavelengths to Cairo; and Claude Winkler, who admits to having been an Abwehr agent while a member of the Guernica Network during World War II.

Dover, Air Marshal John. Much decorated RAF hero with a leading role in the short story *Action*. Thirty years after World War II, he recalls his days as a fear-ridden Pilot Officer but sees a very different portrayal unfold on a film set.

DRINKS-MAN-SHIP. *Edited by Len Deighton* (Haymarket Press, London, 21 November 1964; non-fiction). An illustrated guide to fine wines and spirits, assembled by the staff of the late *Town* magazine.

drugs figure largely in *Horse Under Water*, when traces of heroin ('horse') found in a canister retrieved from a sunken World War II U-boat establish the link between Kondit, Tomas, da Cunha and Henry Smith; and in *An Expensive Place to Die*, in which LSD is used by Monsieur Datt to manipulate the behaviour of clients at his Avenue Foch 'pleasuredrome'. Unidentified substances are used to knock out Raven and the narrator in *The IPCRESS File*, and Willi Kleiber in *XPD*, while drug-running provides Adem with additional income in the former novel and LSD expands neophyte director Richard Preston's 'frontiers of perception' in *Close-Up*. And to the narrator's astonishment, the desirable Charlotte Lucas-Mountford boldly identifies herself as an undercover agent for the US Federal Narcotics Bureau at the close of *Horse Under Water*.

Dunn, Detective Constable Jimmy. Enthusiastic young British policeman in *SS–GB*, whose slaying by the resistance following his identification of the Shepherd Market murder victim, is seen as a crude warning to Douglas Archer.

E

East German Intelligence. Foreign intelligence and espionage, counter-intelligence, domestic security and internal repression, are all the direct responsibility of the Ministerium für Staatssicherheit and the Minister for State Security, Armeegeneral Erich Mielke. At the same time, the Communist Party has its own Secretary for Security Affairs, Egon Krenz, who oversees the total security apparat—the Ministries of State Security, the Interior and and Defence. Both men are members of the ruling Politburo.

Frequently acting as a surrogate for the Soviet KGB, East Germany's intelligence services figure in *Funeral in Berlin* and the *Game, Set & Match* trilogy.

East Germany. *See* Germany, East.

Edwardes, Chief Petty Officer. Royal Navy officer based at H.M.S. *Vernon*, who joins the narrator of *Horse Under Water* in the helicopter search for Manuel da Cunha's elusive cylinder in the sea off Albufeira—said to contain the Weiss List and wartime letters from British Nazi sympathisers.

THE EGYPT FLIGHT L.Z.127-GRAF ZEPPELIN (Germany Philatelic Society, Maryland, September 1981; non-fiction). *Co-authored by Fred F. Blau and Cyril Deighton*. A collaboration between Len (Cyril) Deighton and a well-known American airmail collector, this philatelic handbook documents the airship's 1931 round trip to Cairo, and describes in detail the postal items associated with the flight.

See also: *The Orient Flight L.Z.127-Graf Zeppelin*.

Egyptian Intelligence. Intelligence and counter-intelligence are the responsibility of the Mukhabarat el-Aam, the general intelligence agency set up in the 1950s with the assistance of former Nazis employed by Reinhard Gehlen. The Mukhabarat is answerable only to the President and enjoys almost unlimited powers, bringing it into frequent conflict with the Mahabes el-Aam, which controls internal and political security.

In *Yesterday's Spy*, Bonnard foils a Mukhabarat-sponsored plan to radically alter the military balance of the Middle East, and also reveals Cairo's man in Geneva, Aziz, to have been on London's payroll for ten years; while in *Funeral in Berlin*, the narrator uncovers a crude Mukhabarat phone-tapping operation in London directed against Israeli agent, Samantha Steel.

Eichelberger, Dr. Taciturn guest at Foxwell's elegant soirée in *Spy Story*, about whom we learn only that his scientific papers are 'classified and circulated to a select few by the underwater weapons research department of the US Navy'.

EL ALAMEIN AND THE DESERT WAR, edited by Derek Jewell (Sphere Books, London, October 1967/Ballantine, New York, July 1968; non-fiction). Contains two essays by Deighton, which first appeared in *The Sunday Times Magazine* in September 1967. *Ironmongery in the Desert* examines the weaponry used in the North African campaign. *The Private Armies* recalls the work of the Long Range Desert Group and the Special Air Service.

ELEVEN DECLARATIONS OF WAR (Harcourt Brace Jovanovich, New York, 6 March 1975; fiction). American edition of *Declarations of War*, first published in Britain in October 1971. For reasons best known to the publisher, it omits the two stories *Mission Control: Hannibal One* and *A New Way To Say Goodnight*.
See also: short stories.

England is depicted at war in *Bomber*, *Goodbye Mickey Mouse*, *Winter*, in several of the short stories in *Declarations of War* and under Nazi occupation in *SS–GB*. It is, however, the postwar nation, fettered by rank and class and still adjusting to its declining status as a great power, that informs the greater part of Deighton's fiction.

The English are deadly, decides Johnnie Vulkan in *Funeral in Berlin*. 'A nation of inventive geniuses where there are forty different types of electrical plugs, none of which works efficiently. Milk is safe on the streets but young girls in danger, sex indecent but homosexuality acceptable, a land as far north as Labrador with unheated houses, where hospitality is so rare that "landlady" is a pejorative word, where the most boastful natives in the world tell foreigners that the only British shortcoming is modesty.' Seated among rich and powerful guests in Cyrus Rensselaer's London house in *Winter*, the little German banker Harald Winter reflects that no matter what one does, somehow the English always know how to make a foreigner feel a fool. And Lisl Hennig admits in *London Match* that she'll never understand them. 'If an Englishman says there's no hurry, that means it must be done immediately. If he says he doesn't mind, it means he minds very much. If he leaves any decision to you by saying "If you like" or "When you like", be on your guard—he means that he's made his requirements clear, and he expects them to be precisely met.'

enrolment v. recruitment. One *enrols* an enemy intelligence officer, especially one who might help to break his own networks (e.g. Erich Stinnes), but one *recruits* ordinary people to become spies (e.g. Dr Walter von Munte). It is a distinction patiently explained by Werner Volkmann in *Mexico Set*: 'When you recruit someone, and start them spying, you paint romantic pictures for them. You show them the glamour and make them feel courageous and important. But the agent you enrol knows all the answers already. Enrolment is tricky. You are telling lies to highly skilled liars. They're cynical and demanding. It's easy to start off but it usually goes sour some way along the line and everyone ends up mad at everyone else.'

Ercole, ———. French restaurateur in *Yesterday's Spy*,

whose endless stories about World War II and the glorious part he played in the liberation of France, inspire grandson Louis to partner Pina Baroni in a clumsy attempt on Steve Champion's life.

Erfurt Network. Former MI6 spy-ring operating in East Germany, whose collapse accounts for Brahms Four's unpopularity among the fieldmen in *Berlin Game*. Correct in their assumption that he blew the network, the fieldmen are unaware that it was a deliberate MI6 ploy to make Brahms Four *persona grata* with the KGB.

Erikson, ———. Enigmatic Soviet character in *Spy Story*, said to be ADC to Rear-Admiral Remoziva. At one point he clearly fears he's been identified by Patrick Armstrong, but he passes unrecognised.

Eriksson, ———. Swedish identity adopted by renegade American, Harvey Newbegin, as he enters Finland on the first leg of his journey to Leningrad at the end of *Billion-Dollar Brain*.

'Ermine'. Luftwaffe coastal radar station in Nazi-occupied Holland, commanded by Oberleutnant August Bach in *Bomber*. From the sea's edge the futuristic shape of the aerials is awesome. 'The metal graticule, as big as a large house, that swung gently from side to side was code-named Freya . . . Not far away were the two shorter-range, but more precise, giant Würzburgs. They were like electric bowl fires as big as windmills. They too swung gently around the horizon but always returned—like the Freya—to point westwards to where in East Anglia the Allied bomber airfields were but half an hour's flying-time away . . .'

espionage is often confused with 'intelligence', which is the collection and assimilation of raw information from a variety of sources. Espionage is a very specialised form of information procurement, generally undertaken when alternative means are inadequate. The classical form is the use of spies, but HUMINT now ranks considerably below satellites, cryptanalysis, and radio, electronic and radar intercepts, as a source of covertly acquired information.

Espionage agents encountered in the novels include Fiona Samson (for the Soviets), Gerry Hart, Douglas Reid-Kennedy, Willi Kleiber, Edward Parker, Brian Samson and Walter von Munte. Whereas the narrators of the early novels, and Colonel Stok, Colonel Schlegel, Major Mann, Hank Dean, Stuart Boyd, Yuriy Grechko, Erich Stinnes, Bernard Samson and Alan Piper are all intelligence officers—though at times required to carry out *acts* of espionage.

Esser, Fritz. The pig slaughterer's son in *Winter*, whose rise to Deputy Reichsminister of the Interior owes much to Paul Winter. Brimful of Marxist ideals at seventeen, he throws in his lot with the Spartakists until Paul Winter recruits him into the burgeoning Freikorps, where he shrewdly sees that the future lies with Hitler rather than Röhm and the SA. By the outbreak of war he's recognised as a power within the highest echelons of Nazi Germany, and it's said that when Hitler has a problem he often calls in Esser, who in turn summons his quick-witted friend. Arrested by the Allies in 1945, his choice of Paul as defence counsel at the Nuremberg war crimes trial has unforeseen consequences for both Winter brothers.

Eton. The renowned English private school has long been a natural forcing house for sons of the ruling class. 'How lucky you are not having the Party system working against you all the time,' observes KGB officer Erich Stinnes in *Berlin Game*. 'We have got it,' replies Bernard Samson. 'It's called Eton and Oxbridge.' A point of view shared by most of the protagonists, including the narrator of *Horse Under Water*: 'On Friday I took Charly Christmas shopping in the West End. She bought her father a subscription to *Playboy* and I sent Baix an Eton tie. I suppose we were each in our own way fighting the Establishment . . .'

EVEN ON CHRISTMAS DAY. Illuminating essay by Len Deighton, published in *Whodunit? A Guide to Crime, Suspense & Spy Fiction*, in which he discusses the process of writing and offers examples of his preparatory notes and sketches for the novel *Goodbye Mickey Mouse*. The title derives from Deighton's observation that once started on a new book, he's compelled to work seven days a week, usually doing an hour or so 'even on Christmas Day'.

exfiltrations are attempted by various means, and very often with unforseen consequences. A funeral cortège is laid on to covertly transfer Semitsa from East to West Berlin in *Funeral in Berlin*—leading to the exposure of Johnnie Vulkan's real identity. In *Spy Story*, a nuclear submarine is sent to bring Soviet Rear-Admiral Remoziva out of the Arctic—resulting in the collapse of German reunification talks. Dr Walter von Munte and his wife are smuggled out of East Berlin in a container truck in *Berlin Game*—at the cost of Bernard Samson's freedom and a confrontation with his treacherous wife. Douglas Archer discovers too late in *SS–GB* that the planned escape of King George VI from Nazi-occupied Britain was never intended to succeed. And in *Winter*, Peter Winter successfully crashes the Swiss frontier, though at some risk to his brother, but fails to persuade Paul to abandon Nazi Germany and join him in America.

AN EXPENSIVE PLACE TO DIE (G. P. Putnam's Sons, New York, 26 April 1967/Jonathan Cape, London, 11 May 1967; fiction). Deighton's fifth novel concerns a CIA operation to leak genuine classified nuclear fall-out data to the Chinese Embassy in Paris, using the British narrator as a cut-out to avoid compromising local CIA operatives. The conduit to the Chinese is Monsieur Datt, whose luxury bordello on the Avenue Foch caters for influential clients from East and West, and in the most macabre operation of his career, the narrator finds his job determined by hidden motives in a feud between Datt and Claude Loiseau of the Sûreté Nationale.

EXPLORING A NEW CITY. Essay in *Playboy* magazine, August 1968. Travel Editor Len Deighton offers a key to making the most of metropolitan vacationing.

ex-wives. The recollections of Mary Anson, Barbara Barga, Caty Baroni and Maria Chauvet scarcely flatter their former husbands, while Marjorie Reid-Kennedy's spurious claim to be divorced from Hank Dean conceals a dark secret from her own shameless past.

F

'Fabian'. CIA cryptonym for Soviet defector Professor Andrei Bekuv in *Twinkle, Twinkle, Little Spy*.

Fabré, Inspector. Alias assumed by 'The Corsican', an expensive hit-man from Zurich hired by Champion to snare Charles Bonnard in *Yesterday's Spy*.

Facts for Freedom. General Midwinter's fanatical anti-communist organisation in *Billion-Dollar Brain*, whose subversive activities in the Baltic States are masterminded from a giant computer complex in Texas, known as the Brain.

Fane, Lieutenant. Tall, elderly British Army officer, with a minor role in *Paper Casualty* as Major-General Parkstone's Camp Commandant.

Farebrother, Captain Jamie. Wealthy, well-educated twenty-five-year-old American pilot newly assigned to the 220th Fighter Group, with the leading role in *Goodbye Mickey Mouse*. Self-assured in battle, yet deeply affected by the conflict with his estranged father Alexander Bohnen, his tender love affair with Victoria Cooper has profound repercussions for his close friend, fellow pilot Mickey Morse.

Federal is Britain's central government telephone exchange. Housed in a network of secure tunnels, it was originally installed in the 1930s during the period of preparation against air raids, and today forms part of the government's secret underground infrastructure beneath metropolitan London.

In *The IPCRESS File*, 'Ghost' is identified as WOOC(P)'s exchange within the Federal system.

fictional settings, realised with such convincing detail that you'd be forgiven for believing them to be authentic: Altgarten, the Atelier, Berwick House, Café Leuschner, 'Ermine', H.M.S. Viking, Kroonsdijk, London Data Centre, Steeple Thaxted, STUCEN, Tokwe Atoll, the Valmy Complex, Warley Fen.

field agents sometimes become desk men, but they never lose their disdain for those career intelligence officers whose blood has been shed in committee rooms. 'Bret (Rensselaer) could never have been a field agent; he would never have been able to endure the squalor and discomfort,' observes Bernard Samson in *London Match*. 'And Bret could never have been a good field agent for the same reason that so many other Americans failed in that role: Bret liked to be seen. Bret was a social animal who wanted to be noticed. The self-effacing furtiveness that all Europeans have been taught, in a society still essentially feudal, does not come readily to Americans.'

FIGHTER: The True Story of the Battle of Britain (Jonathan Cape, London, 15 September 1977/Alfred A. Knopf, New York, 25 May 1978; non-fiction). The first published volume in Deighton's planned twelve-volume series examining important World War II battles and their technology. Describing the Battle of Britain as much from the German as from the British point of view, he considers the human factors that influenced the quality of aircraft, weapons and tactics, and explodes many of the myths that have collected around the events of those now distant days of August and September 1940. With an introduction by A. J. P. Taylor.

See also: *Battle of Britain*.

film adaptations. The autumn of 1962 saw the opening of the

first James Bond film *Dr No* and the publication of Deighton's first
novel *The IPCRESS File*. In his essay *Why Does My Art Go
Boom?*, Deighton recalls how Harry Saltzman, co-producer of the
Bond film, snapped up the film rights, telling him, 'A lot of people
are going to be after your book because of the success of *Dr No*,
and I'm the only producer who, you can be certain, won't make an
imitation Bond film from your book.' The resulting film (1965)
established Michael Caine as an international star (in the role
originally to be played by Christopher Plummer), and Saltzman
went on to produce *Funeral in Berlin* (1966) and *Billion-Dollar
Brain* (1967).

In 1968, while preparing the film of *Oh! What a Lovely War*,
Deighton and Brian Duffy produced *Only When I Larf*, directed
by Basil Dearden from a screenplay by John Salmon. Nicolas Roeg
was the original choice for director, in what would have been his
directing debut, and Terence Stamp and John Mills were to have
played the male leads. However, by the time the production
finance was secured, all three were committed elsewhere. A fifth
film to be adapted from Deighton's work, *Spy Story*, was produced
and directed by Lindsay Shonteff in 1976.

See also: television adaptations.

Finland. First stop in the narrator's investigation in *Billion-
Dollar Brain*, where he finds Harvey Newbegin fronting
subversive operations against the Soviet Baltic States for General
Midwinter's Facts for Freedom organisation.

FIRST BASE. Short story in *Declarations of War*, in which two
American soldiers lost in war-torn Vietnam recreate an urban
jungle in an abandoned SAC airbase.

first-person narratives. Eleven of Deighton's twelve
espionage novels employ a narrator (*XPD* is the exception), and
the critic George Grella has wisely suggested that they are the
same person, provided with a variety of names, pseudonyms and
aliases, 'as if identity itself were a shifting, unknowable, or
meaningless concept in the world of espionage'.[13] Much of the

entertainment value of *Only When I Larf* lies in the alternating and often conflicting accounts of the trio of confidence tricksters, and the jigsaw documentation of Marshall Stone's life in *Close-Up* is held together by the subjective narrative of his biographer Peter Anson.

The technique of having a narrator who never quite tells us the exact truth of events, just as none of the characters around him offer an unbiased view of the world, has been employed by Deighton ever since *The IPCRESS File*, and readers who accept the heroes' subjective accounts of events as the objective truth miss much of the intended content of these novels.

Fischer, SS-Sturmbannführer Adolf. Strident young officer in the 'Liebstandarte Adolf Hitler' temporarily billeted at Altgarten's Wald Hotel in *Bomber*, who cynically loots silver and antiques from Herr Voss's bomb-damaged house, assaulting Anna-Luisa as she tries to forestall his escape.

Fischer, Erwin. Business confidant and longtime friend of Harald Winter in *Winter*. A short, slight, jovial man, never afraid to speak his mind, he's forced into hiding with relatives outside Berlin after his son is arrested and the family holdings seized by the Nazis.

Fischer, Richard. Erwin Fischer's son in *Winter*. A big, confident, full-bearded fellow, arrested by the Berlin police and forced to sign over the family's considerable steel holdings to the Nazis. Although born a Catholic, his great-grandparents were Jews, and he disappears from Berlin without trace.

flashbacks. In a sense, both *The IPCRESS File* and *Goodbye Mickey Mouse* are told in flashback: past events framed between a contemporary prologue and epilogue. World War II is the most common experience which bears on the present situation of characters: Jan-im-Glück relives the evacuation of the Treblinka concentration camp in *Funeral in Berlin*; Silas Lowther, the Mediterranean campaign in *Only When I Larf*; Wool and Pelling, a tank battle during the Allied advance through Italy in *It Must Have Been Two Other Fellows*; and Charles Stein, the death of brother Aram in a landmine explosion in *XPD*. The most complex use of flashbacks occurs in *Close-Up*, in which Peter Anson embarks on a biography of actor Marshall Stone and concludes the story can only be written as a novel . . . which he'll call *Close-Up*.

Fleming, Pilot Officer Cornelius. Soft-spoken ex-medical student, newly commissioned skipper of the RAF Lancaster 'The Volkswagen' in *Bomber*. Shot down by Luftwaffe night-fighters over Holland, he's still strapped into his pilot's seat when he hits the ground at over 120 m.p.h.

Flugwachkommando (Fluko). The wartime German observer corps responsible for plotting Allied air raids and forewarning presumed target areas. As they monitor the incoming fleet of 700 RAF bombers in *Bomber*, cities, towns and villages across the Ruhr are told to prepare for an attack, and the small community of Altgarten unexpectedly finds itself included in the Alert Zone.

FLYING THE ATLANTIC. Article by Len Deighton published in *Elephanta* (Spring 1974), the journal of London's White Elephant Club. 'This dangerous expanse of water has always been the testing place of progress in the history of flight,' writes Deighton. The Zeppelin airships provided the first commercial transatlantic air service, and it was not until May 1939 that Pan American Airways introduced the first commercial aeroplane service connecting Europe and America. 'The war eventually saw the ferrying of aircraft across the Atlantic as an everyday event but it wasn't until the perfection of the jet engine that the Atlantic air was truly conquered.' Arnold Schwartzman was editor and art director of *Elephanta* at the time, and it was as a result of this article that he subsequently collaborated with Deighton on *Airshipwreck*.

Flynn, ———. Amiable guest at the Foxwell's intimate soirée in *Spy Story*, whose suggestion that German reunification could lead to the worst days of the Cold War being recalled with nostalgia, proves to be the line forcefully pursued by the Foreign Office and British Intelligence.

food. Difficult to imagine a Deighton novel *not* containing a reference to it! Ever since the hero of *The IPCRESS File* first went into battle for Queen and Country with a malleable lump of Normandy butter and garlic sausage wedged in his raincoat pocket, Deighton's narrators have enlightened aspiring gourmets on the world's culinary delights: ALGERIAN ('. . . the table was arrayed with the tiny dishes that the Arabs called *mezze*. There were miniature kebabs, sliced tomato, shiny black olives, stuffed vine leaves and bite sized pies of soft flaky pastry'—*Twinkle, Twinkle, Little Spy*); AMERICAN ('Signe had gone to a lot of trouble to make Harry feel he was back home . . . There was grapefruit, bacon, waffles, maple syrup, cinnamon toast and weak coffee'—*Billion-Dollar Brain*); FINNISH ('Lunch was open cold beef sandwiches, soup, cream cake, coffee and a glass of cold milk, which is practically the national drink'—*Billion-Dollar Brain*); FRENCH ('Through an open window came steam, and I heard Ercole telling someone that a meal was a conversation between diner and chef'—*Yesterday's Spy*); GERMAN ('Konrad brought our *Pinkel* and kale, a casserole dish of sausages and greens, with its wonderful smell of smoked bacon and onions. And having decided that I was a connoisseur of fine sausage, his mother sent a small extra plate with a sample of *Kochwürst* and *Bragenwürst*'—*Mexico Set*); INDIAN ('There was a smell of ginger, haldi and garlic. Near the cast-iron stove there was a row of freshly made chappatis. They were pale and flecked with meal, like unfired dinner plates awaiting the kiln'—*Twelve Good Men and True*); ITALIAN ('We ate the calamari and the chicken deep in which the garlic and butter had been artfully hidden to be struck like a vein of aromatic gold'—*The IPCRESS File*); LEBANESE ('The smell of Dgaj Muhshy—chicken stuffed with nutmeg, thyme, pine nuts, lamb and rice, and cooked with celery—taunted the nostrils'—*The IPCRESS File*); MEXICAN ('"Oh, I love chillies," said Dicky . . . as he reached for a plate on which many different ones were arranged . . . "It's the tiny, dark-coloured ones that blow your head off," Dicky explained. He took a large, pale-green cayenne and smiled at our doubting faces before biting a section from it. There was a silence after Dicky's mouth closed upon the chilli. Everyone except Dicky knew he'd mistaken the cayenne for one of the very mild *aji* chillies from the eastern province. And soon Dicky knew it too . . .'—*Mexico Set*); MOROCCAN ('The servant had brought pancakes with almonds and sugar inside . . . and we munched heartily into the plateful'—*Horse Under Water*); PORTUGUESE ('From the kitchen emerged a smell of olive oil, onion, pimento, cuttle-fish'—*Horse Under Water*); and RUSSIAN ('I helped myself to some more red caviare and that wonderful dark sour bread'—*Billion-Dollar Brain*).

Inevitably, it is the shortage of food and the banality of dishes resulting from wartime rationing that come in for comment in *Bomber*, *SS–GB*, *Goodbye Mickey Mouse* and *Winter*.

See also: cooking.

The Foreign Office. The nominal master of Britain's intelligence service, MI6, whose London headquarters south of the Thames is listed publicly as the Foreign Office 'Permanent Undersecretary's Department', the official title of the FO's liaison office with the service.

The FO's hand may be discerned behind several British Intelligence enterprises, notably Operation Alforreca in *Horse Under Water* and the cunning scheme to sabotage German reunification talks in *Spy Story*, but it comes in for scathing comment from Bernard Samson in *Mexico Set*: '. . . in 1914 the Foreign Office staff numbered a hundred and seventy-six people in London plus four hundred and fifty in the diplomatic service overseas. Now that we've lost the empire they need six thousand officials plus nearly eight thousand locally engaged staff.'

Foxwell, Ferdy. Genteel friend and colleague of the narrator of *Spy Story*, who runs the Soviet desk at STUCEN, assuming the role of the Red Admiral in war games designed to test NATO defence strategies. Misguidedly drawn into Ben Toliver's fated attempt to secure the defection of Rear-Admiral Remoziva, he's fatally injured in the Soviet ambush sprung at the Arctic rendezvous.

Foxwell, Teresa. Ferdy's socialite wife—on the wrong side of forty, but possessing the tranquil beauty that belongs to the very, very rich—whose musical soirée in *Spy Story* reunites Patrick Armstrong and his former boss, George Dawlish.

Fragoli, Signor. Hook-nosed Italian, employed as a cut-out by the Facts for Freedom network in *Billion-Dollar Brain*. First encountered posing as a girdle salesman in Leningrad, he's later found murdered (almost certainly by Signe Laine) in San Antonio, Texas.

France. Deighton wrote most of his first novel, *The IPCRESS File*, while living in the Dordogne, has written extensively on the subject of French cuisine and used France as the principal background for *An Expensive Place to Die* (Paris) and *Yesterday's Spy* (the Côte d'Azur). Other novels with a French setting, albeit brief scenes, are *Funeral in Berlin*, *Close-Up*, *Twinkle, Twinkle, Little Spy*, *XPD* and *Mexico Set*. A factual and detailed account of the German invasion in May and June 1940, is contained in *Blitzkrieg*, while the territorial advantage gained by the Luftwaffe is examined in *Fighter* and *Battle of Britain*.

Dr Frank. The mysterious Nazi Reichsbank Director who took delivery of Hitler's papers at the Kaiseroda Mine, recalled by Franz Wever in *XPD*. Despite dogged research, it is only later that Boyd Stuart identifies him as the former RSHA officer, Willi Kleiber.

Frankel, Serge. Arthritic Franco-Jewish stamp-dealer and former member of the Guernica Network in *Yesterday's Spy*, whose discovery that Steve Champion has promised to sell Egypt stolen atomic shells, leads to a clumsy attempt on Champion's life that results in his own murder.

Frazer, Lieutenant. British naval security officer, presumed to be reporting to Dawlish, in *Spy Story*.

Frederick, Brigadier 'Bunny'. Wartime British Army officer, required to show the deft touch of a diplomat when delivering his contested verdict on the war-game in *Paper Casualty*.

Freikorps. These volunteer bands of activists, mostly drawn from the armed forces, were raised to fight the red tide that swept Germany after World War I. Disciplined and armed, many wore the swastika emblem on their helmets to distinguish them from the regular army. Freikorps units later formed the nucleus of the Nazi SA.

In *Winter*, eighteen-year-old Paul Winter returns from the trenches to join a Berlin battalion under Captain Graf, then recruits disillusioned radical Fritz Esser during the 'Spartakist uprising', setting Esser on the path to high office in the Third Reich.

THE FRENCH FOREIGN LEGION by John Robert Young. *Introduced by Len Deighton* (Thames & Hudson, London and New York, September 1984). For 150 years, the French Foreign Legion kept its doors tightly closed to journalists and photographers, and in his introduction to this first picture documentary of the enigmatic fighting force, Deighton observes that '. . . it is remarkable that the man who finally got inside this secret world is an Englishman'.

French Intelligence. Foreign intelligence and espionage is the responsibility of the Direction Générale de Sécurité Extérieur (DGSE), formerly known as the Service de Documentation Extérieure et de Contre-Espionage (SDECE). Counter-intelligence and internal security are handled by the Direction de la Surveillance du Territoire (DST), which draws on the resources of the Renseignements Généraux (which keeps track of foreigners and union militants), and occasionally those of the Sûreté Nationale.

French Resistance. Three-fifths of France was surrendered by Marshal Pétain to Nazi Germany following the armistice of June 1940, and the remaining Vichy zone was occupied in the wake of the Allied landings in North Africa in November 1942. About 30,000 members of the Resistance are believed to have died fighting the occupiers, a further 20,000 to have been executed by the Nazi security forces, and upwards of 150,000 to have been deported to labour camps.

Wartime triumphs and betrayals are relived when surviving members of the anti-Nazi Guernica Network are reunited in *Yesterday's Spy*. Grenade's years in the Resistance are recalled by the narrator in *Funeral in Berlin* and the discovery that Paul Louis Broum was a member of the FTP—the network organised by the Communist Party and kept entirely separate from other resistance networks—unlocks the mystery of his subsequent fate in Treblinka.

Frenzel, Herr. Owner of Altgarten's best restaurant and finest wine cellar—scene of Mayor Walter Ryessman's birthday celebrations on the night of the RAF raid in *Bomber*.

Frick, Professor. Eminent elderly British physicist—whose reported death during the Nazi invasion of Britain in *SS–GB* is intended by the German Army to conceal his continuing work on atomic research—rescued in the American raid on Bringle Sands.

Friedman, Peter. Alias adopted by Willi Kleiber in *XPD*, when he embezzles one hundred million dollars from the Swiss bank owned by Charles Stein and the 'Kaiseroda Raiders', in the hope of forcing Stein to part with the coveted Hitler Minutes.

Friendly, Eric. Garrulous overweight *spieler* in *Only When I Larf*, who comes on like the owner of Ysobels gambling club after sizing up Silas Lowther as a possible mark!

Fryer, Pfc. Fred. Clerk in the USAF public relations office at Steeple Thaxted in *Goodbye Mickey Mouse*, who is well aware that even in wartime, the power of the press can outweigh that of the generals.

Fuller, ———. Hatchet-faced sociology graduate—who'd rather fiddle social security payments than 'ponce' off the capitalist system—who unwittingly plays a key role in Steve Champion's recruitment of Charles Bonnard in *Yesterday's Spy*.

FUNERAL IN BERLIN (Jonathan Cape, London, 17 September 1964/G. P. Putnam's Sons, New York, 11 January 1965; fiction). The hero of Deighton's third novel is the same anonymous, anti-public-school employee of WOOC(P) who appeared in *The IPCRESS File* and *Horse Under Water*. Sent to Berlin to arrange the covert transfer of a Soviet scientist whom Colonel Stok of the KGB is willing to sell to the West, he's drawn into a Byzantine plot whose key is a fortune stolen from Jews by the Nazis, that lies hidden in a Swiss bank.

Funeral in Berlin (GB 1966). *p.c.*: Lowndes Productions. A Harry Saltzman Production. *p.*: Charles Kasher. *d.*: Guy Hamilton. *sc.*: Evan Jones. Based on the novel by Len Deighton. *ph.*: Otto Heller. *2nd unit d.*: Peter Medak. *ed.*: John Bloom. *p.d.*: Ken Adam. *a.d.*: Peter Murton. *m.*: Konrad Elfers. *l.p.*: Michael Caine (*Harry Palmer*), Eva Renzi (*Samantha Steel*), Paul Hubschmid (*Johnnie Vulkan*), Oscar Homolka (*Colonel Stok*), Guy Doleman (*Colonel Ross*), Rachel Gurney (*Mrs Ross*), Hugh Burden (*Hallam*), Thomas Holtzmann (*Reinhart*), Gunter Meisner (*Kreutzmann*), Heinz Schubert (*Aaron Levine*), Wolfgang Völz (*Werner*), Klaus Jepsen (*Otto Rukel*), Herbert Fux (*Artur*), Rainer Brandt (*Benjamin*), Ira Hagen (*Monika*), Marte Keller (*Brigit*). 9,178 feet; 102 minutes.

Funfunn Novelty Company. The New York company owned by Karl Poster and Johnny Jones, relieved of a quarter of a million dollars by Silas Lowther, Liz Mason and Bob Appleyard in the opening chapters of *Only When I Larf*.

Furth, Doktor Hans. Medical Officer at the Luftwaffe's Kroonsdijk airfield in *Bomber*, from whose office Christian Himmel steals the horrifying report on Human Freezing Experiments being conducted at Dachau—leading Furth to suggest that the outstanding young pilot may be racially 'impure'.

G

Gallacher, Sergeant Ben. RAF flight engineer aboard 'Joe for King' in *Bomber*, whose reluctance to crew a reserve Lancaster is a measure of the superstitions adopted by men asked to face repeatedly the mathematical probability of death.

GAME, SET & MATCH (Hutchinson, London, 9 October 1986; fiction). The omnibus edition of *Berlin Game*, *Mexico Set* and *London Match*, published in the form that Deighton first conceived the trilogy—as an epic story of treachery played out in three acts. Contains a new preface by the author specially written for this edition.

Game, Set & Match (Granada Television, 1988). *p.*: Brian Armstrong. *sc.*: John Howlett. Based on the novels *Berlin Game*, *Mexico Set* and *London Match* by Len Deighton. *d.*: Ken Grieve and Patrick Lau. *l.p.*: Ian Holm (*Bernard Samson*), Mel Martin (*Fiona Samson*), Michael Degen (*Werner Volkmann*), Brigitte Karner (*Zena Volkmann*), Gottfried John (*Erich Stinnes*), Bruno Dietrich (*Paul Biedermann*), Anthony Bate (*Bret Rensselaer*), Michael Culver (*Dicky Cruyer*), Hugh Fraser (*Giles Trent*), Frederick Treves (*Frank Harrington*). Thirteen episodes of 52 minutes each, filmed on location in Mexico, West Berlin and the United Kingdom, for transmission in the UK and US, autumn 1988.

games. 'A voyage of destruction' is Madame Tastevin's terse description of Monopoly in *An Expensive Place to Die*, and an invitation to join the game provides the narrator with his first close look at the enigmatic Monsieur Datt. Chess is a unifying motif in *Funeral in Berlin*, and Colonel Stok, Johnnie Vulkan and SS-Gruppenführer Kellerman in *SS–GB* are all portrayed as excellent players. Red Bancroft plays an impressive high-stakes game of backgammon, winning the British narrator's approval, in *Twinkle, Twinkle, Little Spy*. And in *Impressions of New York*, Deighton describes how he was accosted by a little white-haired old lady wielding a Scrabble game on his arrival in the city, an incident he put to use eleven years later in the novel *Billion-Dollar Brain*.

Garin, Sydney. Sleek Armenian art dealer, who while prospering financially and socially from the Nazi occupation of Britain in *SS–GB*, shrewdly maintains a link with the underground and makes his country house available for Mayhew's clandestine meeting with American emissary Danny Barga.

Garrard, Flight Lieutenant John. Snobbish forty-year-old Medical Officer at RAF Brimington, whose stiff and unyielding practice drives Flying Officer Brent to reckless heroism in *Brent's Deus Ex Machina*.

Gaunt, Silas. Formidable retired MI6 officer, distantly related to Fiona Samson, in the *Game, Set & Match* trilogy. A Falstaffian figure, he still wields considerable influence within London Central, and is not averse to banging heads together during weekend house parties at which departmental staff, both past and present, are represented.

Gehlen, Reinhard (1902–1979). For three years during World War II, Gehlen ran the Abwehr's Foreign Armies East department, and his reports on the Soviet front revolutionised German military intelligence. Relieved of his duties close to the end of the war, he went to the Abwehr archives at Zossen and burned every document there—but not before microfilming them and locking the microfilms in steel canisters. He then allowed himself to be captured by the Americans who subsequently set him up as the head of a new intelligence outfit directed against the

Soviets, encouraging him to call upon many old comrades of the Sicherheitsdienst and the Abwehr. Energetic and hard-working, he served his new masters well. In 1956, control of the so-called Gehlen Bureau was transferred to the West German Government, who renamed it the Bundesnachrichtendienst, retaining Gehlen as its first chief.

In *XPD*, Willi Kleiber is identified as one of those former Abwehr officers who went to work for Gehlen after the war, while the new clean-cut generation of agents plays an important role in *Funeral in Berlin*.

Geneva. Muted setting in *Yesterday's Spy*, briefly visited by Bonnard in the course of his investigation of Steve Champion. 'Calvin's great citadel is perched precariously between the grey mountains of France and the grey waters of Lake Geneva. The city, too, is grey: grey stone buildings, grey-uniformed cops, even its money and its politics are grey. Especially its politics . . .' Geneva is also home for Colonel Pitman, Madame Mauring and the private detective Hugo Koch, in *XPD*.

George VI (1895–1952). Imprisoned in the Tower of London following the Nazi occupation of Britain in the novel *SS–GB*, the King's planned escape to Washington is deliberately foiled by George Mayhew to ensure he falls in battle alongside his American allies.

German Desk. The intelligence department within London Central headed by Dicky Cruyer, to which Bernard Samson is attached in the *Game, Set & Match* trilogy. It provides the essential link between the Berlin Station and the headquarters directorate. 'The German desk is senior to Berlin Resident in certain respects, but has to defer to it in others,' explains Samson in *London Match*. 'There is no hard-and-fast rule. Everything depends upon the seniority of the person holding the job. When my dad was Berlin Resident, he was expected to do as he was told. But when Frank Harrington went there, from a senior position in London Central, he wasn't going to be taking orders from Dicky who'd spent a lot of his departmental career attached to the Army.'

German reunification. The Allied victory of 1945 destroyed not only Nazi fascism, but the German Reich itself—the state which had existed since 1871 and had proved impossible for Europe to live with. The prospect of a reunited Germany between the Rhine and the Oder remains a provocative issue, and Stalin's Note of 1952 (in which he offered the reunification of Germany in return for the withdrawal of all foreign troops and neutral status) and the Foreign Ministers Conference of May 1959, both failed to suggest an acceptable solution.

The subject lies at the heart of *Spy Story*, in which British Intelligence frames Rear-Admiral Remoziva as a defector to bring about the collapse of new Soviet-sponsored talks being held in Copenhagen. 'They've got an analogue computer at the Foreign Office,' explains Dawlish. 'They put the German reunification on it and didn't like the scenario one little bit.'

Germans. Deighton's fascination with the complicated soul of the twentieth-century German lies at the heart of his epic story of a Berlin family, *Winter*, and is evident in several earlier novels, particularly *Funeral in Berlin*, *Bomber*, *SS–GB* and the *Game, Set & Match* trilogy. 'We Germans find reassurance in tyranny. That's always been our downfall,' observes Walter von Munte in *Berlin Game*, going on to suggest in *London Match* that it was the occupation zones that created the archetype postwar German. 'The French think all Germans are chattering Rhinelanders, the Americans think we are all beer-swilling Bavarians, the British think we are all icy Westphalians, and the Russians think we are all cloddish Saxons . . .'

Germany, East (German Democratic Republic). The Soviet occupation zone was formally established as an independent state on 7 October 1949, one month after the first assembly of the West German Parliament in Bonn. Although the communists achieved total control more quickly than in other East European countries, Soviet reparation policies and harsh living conditions led to a general strike and mass demonstrations in June 1953, and in the period up to the building of the Berlin Wall, approximately one-sixth of the population defected to the West.

The real centre of power is the Politburo of the Central Committee of the (communist) Socialist Unity Party, but the party leadership makes no major decisions without first having come to an agreement with Moscow.

East Germany, and its *de facto* capital East Berlin, figure largely in *Funeral in Berlin* and in the *Game, Set & Match* trilogy, while the vexed question of German reunification is the centre of attention in *Spy Story*.

Germany, West (German Federal Republic). Created out of the American, British and French zones of occupation, it was formally established as an independent state in 1949, and assumed full sovereignty on admission to NATO in 1955. The Allied powers, however, retain certain residual rights and responsibilities, including the maintenance of Berlin's special status.

West Berlin is a major setting in *Funeral in Berlin* and the *Game, Set & Match* trilogy, while the Federal Republic ('the high-density Mecca of espionage') figures briefly in *Yesterday's Spy*, *XPD* and *Mexico Set*.

Gestapo (Geheime Staatspolizei). The Third Reich's secret police force exercised unlimited powers and was one of the principal instruments of Nazi terror. Set up by Göring in 1933, it was taken over by Reichsführer-SS Himmler in 1939 to become Branch IV of the Reich Central Security Office (RSHA). The site of its notorious Prinz-Albrecht-Palais headquarters lies beside the Wall near Checkpoint Charlie in West Berlin, next to the Martin-Gropius-Bau museum.

At the heart of Deighton's family saga *Winter* is the story of Paul Winter's rise to a senior administrative role in the Gestapo, smoothing the way for the Nazi tyranny and earning for himself a minor celebrity status as one of the regime's elite. In *SS–GB*, Scotland Yard detective Douglas Archer is careful to distance himself from its activities in Nazi-occupied Britain, but Leutnant Kokke is unperturbed by rumours in *Bomber* that he's an agent provocateur in its pay, so long as it continues to provide an excuse for his constant criticism of the regime and its methods.

Ghost. *See* Federal.

GH7 'non stopped'. The security clearance enjoyed by the narrator's new assistant Jean Tonnesen in *The IPCRESS File*, meaning that nothing has been found to prevent her having a higher clearance should WOOC(P) wish to classify her higher.

Gibraltar. Very briefly visited by the narrator in *Horse Under Water*. 'It was still the same squalid town that I remembered from wartime . . . The secret of enjoying Gibraltar, a ship's doctor had once told me, is not to get off the boat.'

Giles, Flight Lieutenant 'Jammy'. Balding thirty-three-year-old Bombing Leader at RAF Warley Fen in *Bomber*, whose meticulously planned raid on Krefeld goes terribly wrong from the moment Alan Hill's Mosquito is shot down by a Luftwaffe night-fighter, and the target indicators are jettisoned over the south-east edge of Altgarten.

Gill, Sergeant 'Tex'. Veteran USAF crew chief in *Goodbye Mickey Mouse*, whose repeated pre-flight checks on 'Kibitzer' fail to reveal the faulty tyre that leads to Jamie Farebrother's fatal accident on 'Bad Monday'.

Glavnoye Razvedyvatelnoye Upravleniye (GRU). The Chief Intelligence Directorate of the Soviet General Staff engages primarily in the collection of strategic, tactical and technical military intelligence, and oversees the massive Soviet effort to acquire items of militarily significant Western technology (computers, cryogenics, superconductors, lasers, fibre optics) subject to COCOM controls. Famous spies once run by the GRU include Rudolf Abel, Klaus Fuchs, Gordon Lonsdale, the Rosenbergs, Richard Sorge, Henry Whalen and Eric Winnerstrom, while one of the most valuable agents the West ever had—Oleg Penkovsky—was a colonel in the service, until unmasked by the KGB.

Despite contributing effectively to the overall Soviet intelligence effort, the GRU remains subordinate to the KGB and may not employ anyone or assign personnel abroad without prior clearance. It rarely figures in the novels, with the notable exception of *Billion-Dollar Brain*, in which a Baltic Military District team led by Major Nogin ('a nice fellow for a GRU officer', dryly observes KGB Colonel Stok) intercepts Midwinter's subversive agents entering Latvia and arrests the hapless Ralph Pike in Riga's Luna Café.

Glover, Otis. The 'young executive' identity adopted by Bob Appleyard in *Only When I Larf* as the trio of confidence tricksters brazenly lift a quarter of a million dollars from New York marks, Karl Poster and Johnny Jones.

————, Glynn. Welsh narcotics expert on a small retainer from WOOC(P), consulted by the narrator in *Horse Under Water* after a canister containing traces of crude morphine is recovered from the sunken U-boat off Albufeira.

Goebbels, Dr Josef (1897–1945). One of the evil geniuses of the Third Reich, he possessed a cynical understanding of mass psychology. As Minister of 'Enlightenment and Propaganda' he was renowned for his virulent anti-Semitism and exercised a pervasive influence on the formation of opinion in Nazi Germany. Appointed Reich Chancellor in Hitler's testament, he poisoned his six children before shooting his wife and himself as the Red Army overran Berlin in 1945.

Mastermind behind the German–Soviet Friendship Week in the novel *SS–GB*, he escapes with superficial injuries in the resistance bombing of Highgate Cemetery during the disinterment of Karl Marx.

Goldman, Milton ('Doc'). Short, bespectacled USAF Flight Surgeon at Steeple Thaxted in *Goodbye Mickey Mouse*. An honours graduate from Johns Hopkins, who turned down a chief surgeon's post and a fat salary to get into the war, he draws on all his acknowledged skills to save the life of Jamie Farebrother following the freak accident on 'Bad Monday', but to no avail.

goodbye codes. According to Bernard Samson in *Berlin Game*, they are the emergency phone numbers and contact procedures used by an agent when his or her cover is blown. It's the *failure* of the KGB to supply any to Giles Trent, that convinces him that Trent is a mere pawn in a skilful gambit to protect the KGB's real mole within London Central.

GOODBYE MICKEY MOUSE (Hutchinson, London, 20 September 1982/**Goodbye, Mickey Mouse**, Alfred A. Knopf, New York, 28 October 1982; fiction). Deighton's fourteenth novel is a vivid evocation of wartime England, the story of a group of American fighter pilots flying escort missions over Germany in the winter of 1943–4. At the centre of the novel are two young men: the deeply reserved Captain Jamie Farebrother, estranged son of a deskbound colonel, and the cocky Lieutenant Mickey Morse, well on his way to becoming America's Number One Flying Ace. Alike only in their courage, they forge a bond of friendship in battle with far-reaching consequences for themselves, and for the future of those they love.

Gordon, Sergeant 'Flash'. Gap-toothed rear-turret gunner aboard the Lancaster 'Creaking Door' in *Bomber*. A former Nottingham miner, who joined the RAF on his twenty-first birthday despite being exempt from military service, his only ambition is to survive the war and never return to the mines.

Göring, Hermann (1893–1946). The ostentatious commander of the Luftwaffe was Hitler's successor designate until stripped of all offices following his attempt to form a government while the Führer was besieged in Berlin in April 1945. Arrested by the Americans in Austria at the war's end, he received the death sentence at the Nuremberg war crimes trial but succeeded in committing suicide on the eve of his execution in October 1946.

The principal character in the short story *A New Way To Say Goodnight*, he is among the Nazi elite encountered by Paul Winter in *Winter*, and is briefly recalled by Franz Wever in *XPD*. A factual account of his career, particularly his role as commander of the Luftwaffe, is found in *Fighter*, *Blitzkrieg* and *Battle of Britain*.

Government Communications Headquarters (GCHQ). Britain's highly secret signals intelligence organisation, based at Cheltenham, Gloucestershire, works closely with America's National Security Agency. GCHQ's tasks include producing the codes and cipher machines used by the British Government, breaking foreign codes and ciphers, and intercepting communications worldwide. Its principal interest is in diplomatic and military traffic, but commercial signals are also intercepted from stations such as that at Morwenstow, Cornwall, which allegedly taps the Intelsat commercial communications satellites over the Atlantic and Indian oceans. Major overseas feeding stations include those in Berlin and Cyprus, and perhaps the most important and most secret is that on Chung Hom Kok peninsula on the south side of Hong Kong island, which monitors the Soviet north Pacific military satellites, the Vladivostok naval HQ, the strategic rocket bases on Sakhalin Island, and provided much of the 'US intelligence' on the Soviet shooting down of the Korean 747 airliner in 1984.

GCHQ produces about eighty-five per cent of the secret intelligence available to the British government, and its director is an important member of the Joint Intelligence Committee. However, its close relationship with the NSA occasionally precludes its participation in British Intelligence operations—such as the clandestine acquisition of the Hitler Minutes in *XPD*: 'The chief of GCHQ had departed early. He always did when the agenda included as a last item "non-electronic systems". It was a polite way of asking him to leave the room. It was better that he did not know what was discussed, rather than to feign ignorance to his American colleagues.'

Graf, Captain. Diminutive homosexual Freikorps commander, with whom Paul Winter and Fritz Esser at times make common cause in *Winter*. A mercurial, violent and unforgiving man, he joins the burgeoning Nazi brownshirts and rises to a senior position under Röhm. Following Hitler's bloody purge of the SA during the 'Night of the Long Knives', his execution is witnessed by a dispassionate Paul Winter, who reminds himself that better men died alongside him in the trenches on the Western Front.

Graf Zeppelin. Every reader of Deighton's work must by now have noted his enthusiasm for airships! Following his factual accounts of the *Graf Zeppelin* in *Airshipwreck*, *The Orient Flight L.Z.127-Graf Zeppelin*, *The Egypt Flight L.Z.127-Graf Zeppelin* and *Flying the Atlantic*, he vividly realises the exhilaration of a transatlantic crossing in *Winter*, when Glenn Rensselaer and the Danzigers fly from New York to Germany to visit the Winter family in 1929.

Graham, Dorothy. Faded theatrical star in *Close-Up*, with 'that glazed look that actors get when they have to look for work instead of work looking for them'.

Grechko, Yuriy. The KGB's 'legal resident' in America in *XPD*, operating out of the Soviet embassy in Washington under the cover of Assistant Naval Attaché. A man who exemplifies the Soviets' infinite capacity for melancholy, his failure to secure the Hitler Minutes leads to a ruthless betrayal by his Moscow Centre enemy General Shumuk—and as a consequence, his suicide at the Rousillon Beach Motel.

Green, Private. Insolent twenty-eight-year-old conscript in

the Union Army in *Discipline*. A member of the advance party
ambushed by the Rebs, he's the only one who lives long enough to
return the rifle-fire.

Greenwood, Harvey Kane. Vainglorious American Senator
in *Twinkle, Twinkle, Little Spy*, whose stubborn refusal to accept
evidence linking his assistant Gerry Hart to the KGB, leads to his
kidnapping and bloody death at Washington-Dulles airport.

'Grenade'. Former French resistance worker who, after being
mixed up with the Perrier gang in 1947, settled down to a career
with the French counter-intelligence agency, the DST. A constant
friend to the narrator in *The IPCRESS File*, he plays a critical role
in *Funeral in Berlin*, identifying the mysterious Paul Louis Broum
as a former Communist Party assassin.

Grepos (Grenzpolizei). East Germany's 50,000 border
troops were detached from the National People's Army in
1974—to artificially reduce the size of the Army ahead of the
East–West Mutual & Balanced Force Reduction talks—and
formed into an independent body commanded by Generaloberst
Klaus-Dieter Baumgarten, deputy to the Minister of Defence.
They are conspicuously deployed along the 'inner frontier' with
West Germany and on the sector boundary in Berlin, where six
regiments from Command Mitte man the watch towers and
crossing points in the Wall. During the past quarter century
they've shot and killed 185 people attempting to escape to the
West, including 58 at the Wall.
   Under scrutiny from both sides of the frontier, they are an
inevitable presence in *Funeral in Berlin* and in the *Game, Set &
Match* trilogy.
   See also: Oberstabsmeister Nagel.

Grey, Guthrie. Artless young public relations man full of
careless bonhomie, who unwittingly sets up Ibo Awawa as a
suitable mark for the trio of confidence tricksters in *Only When I
Larf*—leading to a bruising encounter with agents of Ali Lin.

Grimm, Sergeant Jimmy. Cheerful twenty-three-year-old RAF wireless operator aboard 'Creaking Door' in *Bomber*. Fatally torn apart by flak on their homeward journey, he's survived by a widow and a two-year-old child.

Grimsdyke, Miss. Secretarial guise assumed by Liz Mason in *Only When I Larf*, when the trio of confidence tricksters embezzle a quarter of a million dollars from New York marks, Karl Poster and Johnny Jones.

Gruinard. The Scottish island mentioned but never named in *Spy Story*, on which biological warfare experiments were carried out during World War II and which to this day remains closed to the public.

Guderian, Heinz (1888–1954). The legendary German tactician commanded the world's first armoured corps and was the leading exponent of the radical 'lightning war', or blitzkrieg. After playing a decisive role in the victory over France in 1940, he was dismissed by Hitler in March 1945 for his failure to check the Soviet advance on Berlin.

The subject of Deighton's military history *Blitzkrieg* (which includes a foreword by Guderian's former Chief of Staff, General W. K. Nehring, a.D.), he is briefly recalled by Franz Wever in the novel *XPD*.

Guernica Network. The Allied Intelligence network set up by Steve Champion in occupied France during World War II, whose surviving members are reunited in adverse circumstances in *Yesterday's Spy*.

GUILT-EDGED by Merlin Minshall. *Foreword by Len Deighton* (Bachman & Turner, London, October 1975). Merlin Minshall's autobiography—his name is not assumed—presents a life more packed with experience than that of whole regiments of ordinary men! A professional photographer whose most notorious sitter was Hermann Göring, he took up motor racing and was presented with the Foreign Challenge Trophy by Mussolini, then worked with Ian Fleming in British Naval Intelligence before becoming the first agent to be sent into Nazi-occupied France by submarine.

————, **Gus.** Former member of the International Brigade during the Spanish Civil War, who acts as Steve Champion's informant at France's Atelier testing range in *Yesterday's Spy*. Later revealed to be working for fellow Brigade veteran Serge Frankel against Champion—an alliance for which both are murdered.

H

Hallam, James. Gaunt-faced Home Office civil servant of about forty-five well-preserved years in *Funeral in Berlin*, whose imminent dismissal for his homosexuality leads him to accept Johnnie Vulkan's bribe to issue Semitsa with identity papers in the name of Paul Louis Broum.

Hamburg. Meeting place for the trustees of Operation Siegfried in *XPD*. A city much liked by Willi Kleiber, for its 'ever-changing weather, its bars and its restaurants, the smell of the sea and the fine clear German that its inhabitants spoke'.

Hamid, ———. Lebanese identity forced upon Silas Lowther, as Bob Appleyard masterminds the scheme to gull the Honourable Gerald Spencer in *Only When I Larf*.

Hammet, Archibald. Identity assumed by Silas Lowther in Beirut—deliberately and easily mistaken for 'Hamid' over the phone—in *Only When I Larf*.

Hanratty, Bert. Veteran film director in *Close-Up*, who after many years in the business is well aware that power lies with the money and succumbs to a four-picture deal with the Koolman Studio—in exchange for surrendering control of Stone's ill-fated film 'Man From the Palace'.

'Happy Daze'. The USAF P-51 Mustang 'with a lightly clad girl and a bottle of whiskey painted on its nose', piloted by Earl Koenige in *Goodbye Mickey Mouse*.

'Happy Valley'. The RAF bomber crews' ironic nickname for the Ruhr—the industrial heartland of Nazi Germany and best defended target zone in Europe—the intended target for the routine heavy raid in *Bomber*.

Hardcastle, Sergeant Major Reg. Muscular hard-eyed British Army officer cuckolded by his wife Vera in *Goodbye Mickey Mouse*. Home on leave from Burma, he mistakenly identifies Vince Madigan as her Yank lover and murders both of them before turning a gun on himself.

Hardcastle, Vera. Trim, vivacious woman of thirty-two, whose freckles and snub nose give her a youthful tomboy look that ensnares American pilot Mickey Morse in *Goodbye Mickey Mouse*. Ruthlessly ignoring the existence of her soldier-husband in Burma, she encourages Morse's advances until murdered in a bloody *crime passionnel* on 'Bad Monday'.

Harmon, Corporal Steve. American soldier electrocuted by Dalby on Tokwe Atoll in *The IPCRESS File*, leading to the narrator's arrest and his subsequent abduction by members of Jay's IPCRESS Network.

Harriman, Lieutenant-Colonel. Officer in Special Field Intelligence seconded by Ross to work with the narrator in *The IPCRESS File* under the cover name of Sergeant Murray. Taken in by the deception, the narrator is subsequently saved by Harriman from precipitous action that would have wrecked Ross's carefully laid plan to expose Dalby as a traitor. Four years later, Harriman makes a brief reappearance in *Billion-Dollar Brain*.

Harrington, Frank. Willowy sixty-year-old Berlin Resident, who plays vulnerable ancient to Bernard Samson's role of bellicose son in the *Game, Set & Match* trilogy. Close to retirement, he's in line for a Knighthood until drawn into Samson's efforts to convince their London masters that Erich Stinnes is a KGB provocateur. He also makes a brief appearance as a young man in *Winter*, serving as Sir Alan Piper's special assistant in MI6 during World War II.

Harrington, Mrs. Frank Harrington's formidable wife in *Berlin Game*, who hosts the Berlin dinner party at which Bernard Samson has a timely encounter with CIA intelligence officer Joe Brody.

Harrison, J. B. D. American passenger on the narrator's flight to Beirut in *The IPCRESS File*, who shows unwelcome interest in the missing British biochemist Raven. Assassinated by the narrator during Raven's rescue, he's subsequently identified as a US Naval Intelligence officer.

Hart, Gerry. Lean thirty-one-year-old American lawyer, serving as Senator Greenwood's assistant on the Senate Scientific Development Sub-Committee in *Twinkle, Twinkle, Little Spy*. Exposed as a KGB agent, he's shot dead by the narrator at Washington-Dulles airport after taking the Senator hostage and demanding custody of Soviet defector Andrei Bekuv.

Hauptverwaltung Aufklärung (HVA). Thirty-one years after establishing the foreign intelligence and espionage arm of East Germany's Ministerium für Staatssicherheit, legendary spymaster Markus 'Misha' Wolf unexpectedly departed the HVA in early February 1987. (Informed sources believe his successor to be Generalleutnant Werner Grossmann.) Whether he was removed, or retired because of ill-health, his departure must have been welcomed by the hard-pressed officers of West Germany's counter-intelligence agency, the BfV. For 'Misha' Wolf, brother of the late film director Konrad Wolf, set the pace for European espionage operations. From 22 Normannenstrasse, the HVA runs at least 5,000 highly-placed agents, some 3,000 of whom are thought to operate in West Berlin and West Germany. Of the many spy scandals Bonn has had to weather over the past three decades, few have had the political impact of the case of Gunther Guillaume—a close aide and longtime personal friend of

Chancellor Willy Brandt—whose unmasking as an HVA agent in 1974 resulted in Brandt's resignation and plunged the Federal Republic into crisis. More recently, Hans Joachim Tiedge, head of the BfV's national department for East German counter-intelligence, himself turned up in East Berlin.

West German intelligence sources also report that East German special-purpose forces working with the HVA regularly infiltrate the country disguised as truck drivers—over 350,000 trucks from Warsaw Pact countries enter Western Europe each year—to familiarise themselves with the terrain and reconnoitre strategic targets. In a pre-war situation, they would return to disrupt lines of communications, assassinate or kidnap political leaders, and carry out acts of sabotage. (Measures undertaken by the West German government to defend the state against external attack reveal a high degree of contingency planning. In addition to fortified government citadels and food stores, all major bridges are constructed in such a way that they can be collapsed with a single explosive charge, and twenty-two sections of the country's motorway network are designed for rapid conversion to aircraft runways, complete with hidden fuel dumps and servicing areas.)

The HVA's Central American operations come under scrutiny in *Mexico Set*, when Erich Stinnes—the KGB officer encountered by Bernard Samson in Normannenstrasse at the close of *Berlin Game*—unexpectedly surfaces in Mexico City.

Hauser, ———. Harald Winter's trusted valet in *Winter*. An intelligent fellow from a village near Rostock, he's the only member of the domestic household who unfailingly travels with his master.

HAWAIIAN AYE! Essay in *Playboy* magazine, June 1968. Travel Editor Len Deighton counsels the traveller to escape the sometimes madding hordes of Honolulu and explore the less-frequented and unspoiled outer islands.

helicopters have diverse fly-on roles: Aziz is reported in *The IPCRESS File* as having drawn London's wrath after cheekily running drugs in an Alouette 2 supplied by British Intelligence ('in the long run it was beneficial . . . people never trust a completely honest individual'); the narrator of *Horse Under Water* finally locates da Cunha's elusive cylinder off the coast of Portugal using one laid on by the Royal Navy; a staged crash-landing of a Soviet Ka-26 is planned to cover the exfiltration of Rear-Admiral Remoziva in *Spy Story*; and Schlegel and Charles Bonnard hedge-hop across Europe after Champion's decoy convoy in one supplied by the West German police in *Yesterday's Spy*.

Helsinki. Keen, snow-bound location briefly visited by the narrator in *Billion-Dollar Brain*. 'Helsinki is a well-ordered provincial town where it never ceases to be winter. It smells of wood-sap and oil-heating, like a village shop. Fancy restaurants put smoked reindeer tongue on the menu next to the *tournedos Rossini* and pretend that they have come to terms with the endless lakes and forests that are buried silent and deep out there under the snow and ice. But Helsinki is just the appendix of Finland, an urban afterthought where half a million people try to forget that thousand upon thousand square miles of desolation and Arctic wasteland begin only a bus-stop away.'

Hendaye-plage. French Atlantic coastal resort close to the Spanish border, to which the narrator traces Johnnie Vulkan and his unexpected companion Samantha Steel in *Funeral in Berlin*.

Henderson, Major 'Skip'. Tough CIA officer and longtime friend of the narrator of *The IPCRESS File*—whom he suspects is being set up to take a fall on Tokwe Atoll. Shipped back to the States, it's left to his assistant Barney Barnes to deliver the warning.

Hennig, Erich. Talented pianist and protégé of Frau Wisliceny in *Winter*, who to Peter Winter's dismay marries Lisl Wisliceny and becomes a celebrity in the Third Reich after performing before Hitler at the Bach Festival in Leipzig. Later crippled by arthritis, he ends his days playing in the wartime tea-room that Lisl opens in their house off Kantstrasse.

Hennig, Lisl. Radiant Berlin matriarch in the *Game, Set & Match* trilogy, animated by memories of late friends among the artists and celebrities of a Berlin now gone forever. Fading photos evoking the heady days of the twenties and early thirties cover the walls of her shabby hotel off Kantstrasse, a house which has served Bernard Samson as a second home and bolt-hole virtually since the cradle. In the subsequent novel *Winter* we see her as a young girl in that cosmopolitan Berlin, marrying her mother's musical protégé Erich Hennig, but never establishing a close relationship with the Winter family as her brother-in-law Paul Winter rises to a senior position in the Third Reich.

'Henry'. Jay's highly-placed collaborator who remains unidentified at the conclusion of *The IPCRESS File*, and thus escapes the net. Curiously, in the following novel *Horse Under Water*, the narrator encounters a traitorous British Cabinet Minister named Henry Smith, and one may speculate . . .

Hesse, Captain Hans. Young German artillery officer, employed as assistant adjutant in the Little Wittenham prison camp in *SS–GB*. Later revealed to be a member of the Abwehr, after passing a cyanide capsule to murder suspect John Spode to prevent the Sicherheitsdienst from learning of the Abwehr's co-operation with Mayhew and his resistance people.

Highgate Cemetery. Historic London cemetery, where a resistance bomb explodes during the ritualistic disinterment of the bones of Karl Marx in the final ceremony of German–Soviet Friendship Week in *SS–GB*.

Hildmann, Oberleutnant. Veteran observation officer aboard Peter Winter's Zeppelin in *Winter*, who takes command when they're crippled by gunfire over England. Only after he is killed during their crash-landing in Germany does Winter realise how much he owed to the older man's guidance and tutelage.

Hill, Pilot Officer Alan. Pilot of the RAF Mosquito pathfinder shot down by a Luftwaffe Ju88S night-fighter two minutes short of Krefeld in *Bomber*—the key incident leading to the mistaken bombing of Altgarten.

Himmel, Unteroffizier Christian. Cherubic twenty-two-year-old Luftwaffe night-fighter pilot stationed at Kroonsdijk in *Bomber*. An outstanding and popular airman with the novel reputation of having more victories to his credit than claimed, his shamed response to a report on Human Freezing Experiments conducted at Dachau results in his arrest for treason, and subsequent execution.

Himmler, Heinrich (1900–1945). An early supporter of Hitler, the onetime Bavarian poultry farmer rose to become Nazi Germany's Chief of Police, Supreme Commander of the SS, and Reich Minister of the Interior. Arrested in hiding by British troops at the end of World War II, he committed suicide on 27 May 1945.

Fritz Esser serves as his Deputy Minister in *Winter*, and he's briefly encountered in London by Douglas Archer in *SS–GB*, as the SS attempt to wrest control of Britain's atomic research secrets.

Hinkelburg, Frau. One of Altgarten's smart *Hausfrauen* in *Bomber*. Her ears attuned to chance remarks and innuendo, she's held spellbound by the rumour that the town's Wald Hotel has been turned into a stud farm—where carefully chosen young Aryan girls are sent to have children by selected SS officers.

history as hypothesis. As T. J. Binyon has pointed out, 'history and fiction have always run parallel in Deighton's work',[14] and they merge in two of his novels constructed around counter-factual events. The battle for control of Britain's atomic research secrets in *SS–GB* is set amid a defeated Britain under Nazi occupation in 1941, while *XPD* concerns the bloody pursuit of the minutes of a clandestine meeting between Winston Churchill and Adolf Hitler in June 1940, at which Churchill allegedly considered handing over most of the British Empire to bring an end to the war. According to Deighton, the actual whereabouts of both leaders on 11 June 1940 are unknown. However, the outrage with which his fictional scenario was greeted in certain quarters surprised him. It was, said his critics, written in such a way that readers would believe it. 'Did they expect me to write a story that no one could believe?' he asks.[15]

hitch-hiking. Penetrating an unrelated organisation to obtain espionage material. For example, the KGB's use of the 1924 Society to procure secret American scientific data in *Twinkle, Twinkle, Little Spy*, and the KGB's manipulation of the Trust to acquire the Hitler Minutes in *XPD*.

Hitler, Adolf (1889–1945). The Austrian-born demagogue's rise to power in the aftermath of Versailles, the rapid growth of Nazism and Germany's headlong plunge into war overshadow the lives of the characters in Deighton's epic family saga *Winter*. And in the earlier novel *XPD*, Franz Wever vividly recalls a summons to the Führer Bunker in Berlin only weeks before Hitler took his life and that of Eva Braun. 'Der Chef . . . was a shocking sight. His face seemed to have aged forty years, his eye sockets were deeply sunken and the skin of his cheeks dark, as if bruised. He was stooped and seemed to have lost the use of his left arm, which trembled constantly. His voice was very low and hoarse and almost unrecognizable to anyone who had heard his speeches of earlier years—and which of us had not!'

Hitler's rise to power and conduct of the early years of World War II are examined at length in *Blitzkrieg*, and briefly in *Fighter* and *Battle of Britain*.

The Hitler Minutes. The sensational wartime document simultaneously sought by British Intelligence, the Soviet KGB and the Trust, in the novel *XPD*. The only record of an alleged secret meeting between Winston Churchill and Adolf Hitler on 11 June 1940, to discuss a negotiated settlement between Great Britain and Nazi Germany.

H.M.S. Vernon. The Royal Navy diving school in Portsmouth, reluctantly attended by the narrator in preparation for Operation Alforreca in *Horse Under Water*. (The Navy cleared Deighton to visit the school to gather material for the novel. It was only halfway through the diving course that he admitted he couldn't swim.)

H.M.S. Viking. Fictional deep-water anchorage for NATO submarines in Western Scotland, visited by Patrick Armstrong in *Spy Story*.

Hogarth, Mabel. Attractive red-haired secretary in the Downing Street Whips Office in *London Match*, who identifies the 'Vitamin' memo which reached Moscow as a photocopy of the one issued to London Central—the one Bret Rensselaer had been given for action. ('. . . when sensitive material like this is circulated, the word processor is used so that the actual wording of its text is changed. Just the syntax, you understand; the meaning is not affected. It's just a precaution . . . so that if a newspaper prints a quote from it, the actual copy can be identified.')
See also: 'Posh Harry'.

Holland under Nazi occupation in World War II is the setting for Redenbacher's Luftwaffe night-fighter airfield and Bach's coastal radar station 'Ermine' in *Bomber*. And in *London Match*, Tessa Kosinski stuns Bernard Samson by disclosing that she secretly met Fiona near Eindhoven to celebrate their aunt's birthday—and passes on the ominous message that Fiona wants the children in East Berlin.

A factual analysis of the German invasion of May 1940 is to be found in *Blitzkrieg*.

Holländer, Herr. Altgarten's registrar of marriages, with a minor role in *Bomber*. Despised by his neighbours as a rodent-faced bureaucrat who uses his job as air-raid warden to interfere and pry into their lives, he nevertheless risks his life touring the shelters and checking their empty apartments for fire-bombs during the RAF raid.

Hollywood. The American film capital, and the movie industry from the early talkies to the present day, are coolly portrayed in *Close-Up*. It serves as a backdrop to the relentless quest for the Hitler Minutes in *XPD*, and thanks to a lucky investment by his father-in-law provides Peter Winter with employment on his arrival in America in *Winter*.

Holroyd, Section Officer Maisie. Plump thirty-eight-year-old WAAF officer at Warley Fen in *Bomber*, who overlooks Ruth Lambert's continued use of her maiden name for WAAF records, rather than subject her to a posting and separation from her husband of three months.

homicides are generally committed to silence characters, sometimes to remove them, only rarely for revenge. The majority of victims are shot, including Monsieur Datt, Serge Frankel, Gus, Miles MacIver, Julian MacKenzie, Vince Madigan, Jean-Paul Pascal, William Spode, Fernie Tomas, Topaz and Giles Trent. Paul Bock, Annie Couzins, Vera Hardcastle and Bernie Lustig are brutally stabbed to death. Steve Harmon is electrocuted, bombs kill Joe MacIntosh and Franz Wever, a hairpin is used to murder Olaf Kaarna and Signor Fragoli, and poison to kill Paul Biedermann. Ingrid Rainbow, a British diplomat mistaken for Boyd Stuart, and an unidentified East German selected by the Gehlen Bureau, are all killed in car 'accidents'. Unidentified means are used to silence Charlie Cavendish, Jimmy Dunn, Housemartin and Melodie Page, while Dalby, Willi Kleiber, Paul Moskvin and Harvey Newbegin all have their lives 'terminated with extreme prejudice'.

Horner, Alex. Son of an East Prussian landowner in *Winter*, whose rise from cadet to general with a key role in the

Bendlerblock is a career his close friend Paul Winter might have matched but for one isolated piece of bad judgement. An honourable Prussian of the old-fashioned kind, Horner valiantly serves his country through two World Wars, but disillusioned with Hitler he joins dissident officers in an attempt to overthrow the Nazi regime and secure a negotiated peace.

HORSE UNDER WATER (Jonathan Cape, London, 21 October 1963/G. P. Putnam's Sons, New York, 5 January 1968; fiction). The dead hand of a long-defeated Nazi Third Reich reaches out to Portugal, London and Marrakech in Deighton's second novel, which features the same anonymous narrator and milieu of *The IPCRESS File*, but finds Dawlish now head of the secret British Intelligence unit, WOOC(P).

hotels. Almost present as a character in its own right is Lisl Hennig's faded establishment in the *Game, Set & Match* trilogy, which has served Bernard Samson as second home and bolt-hole virtually since the cradle. (The house was formerly owned by Lisl's parents, and is frequently depicted in *Winter*.)

They are the setting for incidents in *Funeral in Berlin*, when the narrator traces Johnnie Vulkan to a deserted French hotel in Hendaye-plage; in *Billion-Dollar Brain*, when Colonel Stok waylays the narrator in the Hotel Riga; in *Yesterday's Spy*, when Charles Bonnard returns to the shabby 'hotel' in Nice once used as a safe house by the Guernica Network; in *SS–GB*, when Douglas Archer interrupts a secret meeting between George Mayhew and members of the Abwehr in London's Hotel Lübeck; in *XPD*, when Boyd Stuart snatches Billy Stein from a London hotel, and the CIA stake out the Rousillon Beach Motel to trap the KGB's North American *rezident*; and in *London Match*, when Erich Stinnes is handed back to the KGB in the penthouse suite of West Berlin's luxury Steigenberger Hotel. In *Winter*, Simon Danziger first learns of the Wall Street crash while staying in Berlin's fashionable Adlon Hotel (model for Vicki Baum's *Grand Hotel*) at No. 1 Unter den Linden, from where he walks to Potsdamer Platz and steps out in front of a horse-drawn dray.

'Housemartin'. WOOC(P)'s cryptonym for Jay's assistant in *The IPCRESS File*, murdered by Jay's own people after having been arrested in Acacia Drive for impersonating a Metropolitan Police Chief Inspector.

HOW TO BE A PREGNANT FATHER by Peter Mayle. Illustrated by Arthur Robins. *Recipes by Len Deighton* (Lyle Stuart, Secaucus, October 1977/Macmillan, London, March 1980). A humorous and sensible guide for that oft-forgotten race of human beings—pregnant fathers. Advice on the secrets of mother's cravings, labour pains, hospitals and an admirable cookery section with simple recipes by Deighton.

Hudson, ———. American hydrogen researcher, despatched to Paris by the CIA to pass classified fall-out data to Kuang-t'ien in *An Expensive Place to Die*.

HUMINT (Human Intelligence). While ELINT (electronic), PHOTINT (photographic), RADINT (radar) and SIGINT (signals) intelligence today absorb the greater part of intelligence budgets, they have limitations. 'You can't explain to the Minister about electronic intelligence gathering, or show him pictures taken by spy satellites. It's too complicated, and he knows that all that technological hardware belongs to the Americans,' explains Fiona Samson in *Berlin Game*. 'But tell the Minister that we have a man inside the Moscow Narodny and on their Economic Intelligence Committee, and he'll get excited.' Thus human intelligence—the use of spies, sleepers, agents of influence—continues to play an important if evolving role, and the battle in the shadows between the Samsons and Stinnes of the espionage world retains a contemporary authenticity.

Hungary. A carefully executed charade convinces the narrator that he is imprisoned in Hungary, following his abduction from Tokwe Atoll in *The IPCRESS File*. KGB fieldman Chlestakov plays an unconvincing Hungarian émigré in *Berlin Game*, while Gloria Kent—the daughter of Hungarian émigrés—reveals in

London Match that her father spied for British Intelligence in Hungary before her parents fled to Britain.

Hutchinson, Peter. RAF observer aboard Alan Hill's Mosquito pathfinder in *Bomber*, killed by a Luftwaffe Ju88S night-fighter moments after arming the 250-lb target indicator bombs intended for Krefeld.

Huth, SS-Standartenführer Oskar. Handsome ambitious thirty-five-year-old SD officer attached to Himmler's personal staff, whose arrival in Nazi-occupied London has dramatic consequences for Douglas Archer in *SS–GB*. Determined to wrest Britain's atomic secrets for the SS's own research programme, he is outflanked by SS-Gruppenführer Kellerman and obstructed by the Abwehr, before being sentenced to death for his role in the events at Bringle Sands.

I

Ilfa, Johannes. Battle-scarred German fireman of twenty-six, with a minor role in *Bomber*. Repelled by the Nazis, he works selflessly for the fire service as a way of fighting the evils of Hitler's war, only to die in the holocaust that consumes Altgarten.

'illegals'. Deep cover agents infiltrated into hostile countries posing as seemingly innocent citizens—e.g. Edward Parker in *XPD* and Carol Miller in *London Match*.

'Import Licences'. The Home Office's chaste name for official requests for false documents—such as the Broum papers issued by James Hallam for the covert transfer of Semitsa in *Funeral in Berlin*.

IMPRESSIONS OF NEW YORK. Deighton's second published piece is a lively report on his first visit to the city, which appeared in Issue 13 of *Ark* (1955), the journal of the Royal College of Art.

India under British rule in 1920, specifically the Northwest Frontier region, is the setting for the short story *Twelve Good Men and True*. 'Between the shimmering white peaks of the western Himalayas and the equally white and even more shimmering desert that stretches to the Arabian sea, there is the Punjab. To cool stations in its lush green foothills, favoured units of the British Army retired each May. After that, life on the plains became so unbearably hot that even the natives sat quite still all day, waiting for the movement of air that sometimes came with dusk.'

Very recently, Deighton has said he's attracted to the idea of writing more fiction about India, particularly the period under British rule.

infiltrations. Ralph Pike endures a contour-hugging flight and a drop into the snow drifts to covertly enter Soviet Latvia in *Billion-Dollar Brain*, while Danny Barga survives an equally hazardous parachute drop into Nazi-occupied Britain in *SS–GB*. (Both infiltrations are detected.) Charles Bonnard recalls in *Yesterday's Spy* the night in 1940 when a submarine landed him in occupied France—where he was met by Steve Champion 'with a girl on each arm and an open bottle of champagne'. Bernard Samson infiltrates East Berlin via the underground railway tunnel linking the divided city to reach London Central's beleaguered spy Walter von Munte in *Berlin Game* (the same U-Bahn tunnel in which a group of East German army conscripts were allegedly shot dead while trying to escape to the West in 1986), and Peter Winter is dropped into Nazi Germany with orders to link up with Brian Samson and assist the anti-Hitler conspirators in *Winter*.

informants. Maria Chauvet acts for her ex-husband, Chief Inspector Claude Loiseau, as he strives to destroy her father's blackmailing operation centred on the Avenue Foch 'pleasuredrome' in *An Expensive Place to Die*. Mason is revealed as Dawlish's source within Ben Toliver's cabal in *Spy Story*, reporting on their eager pursuit of Rear-Admiral Remoziva. Claude Winkler admits to having been reporting to the Abwehr while a member of the wartime Guernica Network, and Gus is revealed as Champion's man at the Valmy Complex, in *Yesterday's Spy*. And in *SS–GB*, Douglas Archer is devastated to find that Harry Woods has been acting as an informant for SS-Gruppenführer Kellerman, but chastened to learn he struck the deal to save Douggie Archer from being sent to a Hitler Youth unit in Nazi Germany.

intelligence. The collection and management of information obtained from a variety of sources. Not to be confused with 'espionage', which is a very specialised form of information procurement.

interrogation. 'Promise the interviewee anything. Promise him freedom. Promise him the moon. He'll be in no position to argue with you afterwards,' suggests the London Central training manual penned by Giles Trent. Advice ironically taken to heart by Bernard Samson as he detains Trent at Berwick House in *Berlin Game*. However, Monsieur Datt prefers to use LSD to weaken the narrator's resistance in *An Expensive Place to Die*, and Professor Bekuv remains stubbornly uncooperative until joined by his wife in *Twinkle, Twinkle, Little Spy*. Willi Kleiber opens up to his CIA interrogators only after having been confronted with evidence of his ruthless blood-letting in *XPD*, while Erich Stinnes's mercurial behaviour in *London Match* is only later recognised as a carefully planned KGB ploy to debilitate London Central.

THE IPCRESS FILE (Hodder & Stoughton, London, 12 November 1962/Simon & Schuster, New York, 29 October 1963; fiction). 'There has been no brighter arrival on the shady scene since Graham Greene started entertaining,' observed the *New Statesman* on the publication of Deighton's first acclaimed novel. Its nameless narrator, resolutely working-class in background and point-of-view, is transferred from British Military Intelligence to a small but important civilian department known only by the initials WOOC(P), and an apparently straightforward operation to trace a missing biochemist leads him to confront a massive conspiracy to brainwash the entire framework of the nation.

The Ipcress File (GB 1965). *p.c.*: Steven/Lowndes Productions. *exec.p.*: Charles Kasher. *p.*: Harry Saltzman. *d.*: Sidney J. Furie. *sc.*: Bill Canaway, James Doran. Based on the novel by Len Deighton. *ph.*: Otto Heller. *ed.*: Peter Hunt. *p.d.*: Kenneth Adam. *a.d.*: Peter Murton. *m.*: John Barry. *l.p.*: Michael Caine (*Harry Palmer*), Nigel Green (*Dalby*), Guy Doleman (*Colonel Ross*), Sue Lloyd (*Jean*), Gordon Jackson (*Carswell*), Aubrey Richards (*Radcliffe*), Frank Gatliff (*Bluejay*), Thomas Baptiste (*Barney*), Oliver Macgreevy (*Housemartin*), Freda Bamford (*Alice*), Pauline Winter (*Charlady*), Anthony Blackshaw (*Edwards*), Barry Raymond (*Gray*), David Glover (*Chilcott-Oakes*), Stanley Meadows (*Inspector Keightley*), Peter Ashmore

(*Sir Robert*), Michael Murray (*Raid Inspector*), Antony Baird (*Raid Sergeant*), Tony Caunter (*ONI Officer*), Charles Rea (*Taylor*), Ric Hutton (*Records Officer*), Douglas Blackwell (*Murray*), Richard Burrell (*Telephone Operator*), Glynn Edwards (*Police Sergeant*), Zsolt Vadaszffy (*Prison Doctor*), Joseph Behrmann, Max Faulkner, Paul S. Chapman (*Prison Guards*). 9,810 feet; 109 minutes.

'**Ipcress Man**' seems the most appropriate name by which to refer to the anonymous narrator of *The IPCRESS File*, and the three subsequent novels *Horse Under Water*, *Funeral in Berlin* and *Billion-Dollar Brain*. Described by critic Julian Symons as 'the first anti-hero in spy fiction',[16] the wise-cracking, anti-public-school upstart from Burnley is regarded as one of Deighton's most original contributions to the genre, although his creator is the first to admit to feeling great sympathy for the people who have to put up with this intractable character.

The path that led Ipcress Man to be working for British Military Intelligence, before his posting to the civilian unit WOOC(P), is deliberately obscured, though Harvey Newbegin offers a tantalising early portrait of him in *Billion-Dollar Brain*. 'The first time I ever saw him was in Frankfurt. He was sitting in a new white Jensen sports car that was covered in mud, with a sensational blonde, sensational. He was wearing very old clothes, smoking a Gauloise cigarette and listening to a Beethoven quartet on the car radio, and I thought, "Oh boy, just how many ways can you be a snob simultaneously".'

IPCRESS Network. Broken by Colonel Ross and the narrator of *The IPCRESS File*, its members include Jay, Dalby, Housemartin, Swainson, two unidentified employees of the United States Medical Department, an undisclosed number of S1s and the elusive 'Henry'.

Ireland. Briefly visited by Major Mann and the narrator in *Twinkle, Twinkle, Little Spy*, where they unearth the gruesome remains of a German family hacked to death by Douglas Reid-Kennedy and find further evidence of his treachery.

'Ironfoot'. Bernard Samson's mistranslation of *Gusseisen*, meaning 'Pig Iron', the Moscow Centre assignment code for their deep penetration agent within London Central in the *Game, Set & Match* trilogy.

IRONMONGERY OF THE DESERT. Illustrated essay by Len Deighton, first published in *The Sunday Times Magazine*, 24 September 1967, in which he examines the weaponry used in the North African campaigns during World War II. One of two essays by Deighton published in *El Alamein and the Desert War*.

islands. The Pacific island of Tokwe Atoll is the setting for the American nuclear test, Dalby's final act of treachery, and the narrator's abduction by members of Jay's IPCRESS Network in *The IPCRESS File*. Gruinard is the unnamed Scottish island in *Spy Story* where biological warfare experiments were carried out during World War II. The Danish island of Sjaelland is chosen by the KGB's General Shumuk for a clandestine meeting with MI6 officer Boyd Stuart in *XPD*, and daydreaming of California's Catalina island provides Jamie Farebrother with a momentary respite from the bleakness of wartime Britain in *Goodbye Mickey Mouse*.

Italy. Recalled in wartime by Pelling and Wool in *It Must Have Been Two Other Fellows*, and the sun-lit location for Marshall Stone's ill-fated film 'Man From the Palace' in *Close-Up*.

IT HAPPENS IN MONTEREY. Essay in *Playboy* magazine, July 1968. Travel Editor Len Deighton reports on the spectacular scenery of California's Monterey Peninsula, and recalls the rich tradition of eccentrics with which it has been blessed in history and in literature.

IT MUST HAVE BEEN TWO OTHER FELLOWS. Short story in the collection *Declarations of War*. Some twenty-five years after World War II, a salesman and his former commanding officer discover lost ambitions and misremember past exploits.

It Must Have Been Two Other Fellows (BBC Television, 18 December 1977). *exec.p.*: Bill Morton. *sc.*: Peter Prince. Based on the short story by Len Deighton. *d.*: Ben Rea. *l.p.*: William Lucas (*James Pelling*), Victor Winding (*Wool*), Graham Weston (*Steeple*), Jay Neill (*Sergeant*), Richard Kates (*Sloan*), John Dallimore (*Keats*).   17 minutes.

See also: television adaptations.

J

'Jake'. Fabricated KGB assignment code purposely leaked to Bernard Samson in *London Match* to suggest a second KGB mole remains undetected within London Central.

Jan-im-Glück ('Lucky Jan'). Wizened orthodox Jew, a survivor of the Treblinka concentration camp, whose recollection of the murder of fellow prisoner Paul Louis Broum proves misleading evidence for the narrator in *Funeral in Berlin*.

Jarman, Group Captain. Patronising, blimpish commander of RAF Warley Fen in *Bomber*, who spitefully threatens to ground Flight Sergeant Sam Lambert, in response to Lambert's disinterest in his beloved station cricket team.

'Jay'. WOOC(P)'s cryptonym for Christian Stakowski, a leading character in *The IPCRESS File*. (All people under long-term surveillance by WOOC(P) are designated by bird names—e.g. 'Housemartin', 'Raven'.)

'J.B.F.'. Readers tempted to take at face value the dedication of *The IPCRESS File* to 'the late J.B.F. upon whom the character of Cavendish was based' (and for that matter, the very convincing Acknowledgements in *Spy Story*), would be well advised to note the review of Deighton's work in the French journal *L'Express*: 'Instead of bringing light he leaves us in the dark. Never were shadows more dazzling.' Deighton has never dedicated books except to fictional people.

Jews. Their horrific plight in Europe during World War II is movingly realised in *Winter* through the lives of Lottie Winter, Dr and Lily Volkmann, Martha and Boris Somló and Erwin and Richard Fischer. It is further personified by the Cohen family and Hans-Willy Meyer in *Bomber*, by Rube Wein in *Goodbye Mickey Mouse*, and is painfully recalled by Jan-im-Glück and Josef-the-Gun in *Funeral in Berlin* and by Werner Volkmann in the *Game, Set & Match* trilogy. The catastrophe to European Jewry and the interests of the modern state of Israel impel both Samantha Steel in *Funeral in Berlin* and Serge Frankel in *Yesterday's Spy*.

'Joe for King'. RAF Lancaster skippered by Flight Sergeant Carter in *Bomber*. Other named crew members are Sergeant 'Tapper' Collins (bomb-aimer), Sergeant Ben Gallacher (flight engineer) and Roland Pembroke (navigator).

Johnson, Private. Member of the Royal Fusiliers firing squad despatched to Pooglui Camp in *Twelve Good Men and True*. A merciful man, who in France during World War I 'had milked cows into the ground rather than see them in discomfort'.

jokes. The laughs in the novels almost always arise from the characterisation and situations, but there are some set-piece jokes worth retelling . . .
socialism: 'Capitalism is the exploitation of man by man. Yes? Well socialism is exactly the reverse.' (Stok, *Funeral in Berlin*)
socialism: 'The factory workers say that it's impossible to do anything right. If you arrive five minutes early you are a saboteur; if you arrive five minutes late you are betraying socialism; if you arrive on time they say, "Where did you get that watch?"' (Stok, *Funeral in Berlin*)
wartime rationing: 'A fellow drives into a service station. The driver has only got coupons for half a gallon. He says, "A good show Monty's boys are putting on, eh?" "Who?" says the bloke in the service station, very puzzled. "General Montgomery and the Eighth Army." "What army?" "The Eighth Army. It's given old Rommel's panzers a nasty shock." "Rommel? Who's Rommel?"

"O.K.," says the bloke in the car, putting away his coupons. "Never mind all that crap. Fill her up with petrol and give me two hundred Players cigarettes and two bottles of whisky." ' (Sweet, *Bomber*)

movies: Two goats in the Mojave desert. They find a tin of film. One of them nuzzles it until the lid comes off. The film leader loosens around the spool and the goat eats a few frames. The second goat eats some too, and they pull all the film off the reel until they have eaten the whole of it. There is nothing left except the can and the spool. The first goat says, "Wasn't that great?" and the second goat says, "The book was better." ' (Stone, *Close-Up*)

theory of relativity: 'A chap spending three minutes in a dentist's chair thinks it's an hour. A chap spending an hour in bed with the blonde WAAF from Met. thinks it's three minutes—And for this they made Einstein a professor!' (Woodhall, *Adagio*)

sociologists: 'A civil service candidate made an official complaint: he had missed promotion because at the civil service selection board he had admitted to being a socialist. The commissioner apologised profusely—he had thought the candidate had admitted to being a sociologist.' (Ryden, *XPD*)

Jones, Sergeant 'Binty'. Twenty-one-year-old RAF gunner aboard 'Creaking Door' in *Bomber*. Fatally injured in a motor cycle accident, minutes after returning unscathed from the night's raid over Germany.

Jones, Private Des. Slim pale twenty-one-year-old American GI in *First Base*, who on finding himself lost in war-torn Vietnam, recreates an urban jungle in an eerily abandoned SAC airbase.

Jones, Johnny. Short, middle-aged New York businessman, overweight 'but attractive like a teddy bear in his soft overcoat', who with his partner in the Funfunn Novelty Company, proves an easy mark for the trio of confidence tricksters in *Only When I Larf*.

Josef-the-Gun. A survivor of the Treblinka concentration camp like his brother Jan-im-Glück, his sceptical testimony of Paul

Louis Broum's murder persuades the narrator of *Funeral in Berlin* to continue his investigation into Broum's fate.

'Jouster'. The USAF P-51 Mustang sporting a garishly painted knight in armour on its nose, piloted by Spurrier Tucker in *Goodbye Mickey Mouse*.

Joyce, Colonel. Plump little British Army officer 'dark skinned from a quarter-century of Indian sun', with a minor role in *Paper Casualty* as Major-General Parkstone's GSO1.

K

Kaarna, Olaf. Freelance Finnish journalist, murdered by Signe Laine early in *Billion-Dollar Brain* after stumbling across the Facts for Freedom network's anti-Soviet operations run out of Finland.

'Kadavar'. Cryptonym assigned to the narrator by the Gehlen Bureau in *Funeral in Berlin*, during the operation to covertly transfer Semitsa from East to West Berlin.

Kaiseroda Mine. Very deep and extensive German potassium mine at Merkers in Thuringia, some 200 miles south-west of Berlin, where in April 1945 the American Third Army discovered a substantial part of the gold and monetary reserves of the Third Reich, over 400 tons of looted art treasures and thousands of secret Nazi records. The hoard was immediately transported to the safety of the former Reichsbank building in Frankfurt, which now lay in American hands, but the rumour has persisted for years that at least one truckload disappeared in transit.

This incident lies at the heart of *XPD*, in which the Hitler Minutes are among the documents stolen along with gold and other valuables from the military convoy by the 'Kaiseroda Raiders'.

the 'Kaiseroda Raiders'. Conspiratorial group of US Third Army soldiers led by Charles Stein in *XPD*, who in April 1945 plundered gold and papers from the American military convoy transporting the contents of the Kaiseroda Mine to Frankfurt. For thirty-five years, surviving members have lived comfortably from the proceeds of the robbery, most of which was used to found a small Swiss bank, but the whole artful structure is threatened when MI6, the KGB and the Trust simultaneously battle to acquire the most secret of the stolen Nazi documents: the Hitler Minutes.

Kalkhoven, Melvin. Tall, thin, thirty-five-year-old CIA field agent, nicknamed the 'Bible-basher' by his Langley colleagues for his habit of underscoring his comments with biblical quotations, who masterminds the abduction of Willi Kleiber from Switzerland in *XPD*.

Kar, Jan. White-haired Polish emigré acquaintance of Bernard Samson in *Berlin Game*. The owner of 'Kar's Club'—which he opened at the war's end when he realised he'd never return to his homeland again.

Kar's Club. Smokey basement chess and drinking club in London's Soho, where KGB fieldman Chlestakov stages an incriminating rendezvous with Giles Trent in *Berlin Game* as part of a carefully planned ploy to protect the KGB's real mole within London Central.

Keating, Alf. London cockney ('teeth like rusty railings') into whose vegetable garden the narrator of *The IPCRESS File* stumbles, after escaping from his cell in the 'Hungarian' prison.

Keightley, Captain. Military Liaison Officer in Scotland Yard's Criminal Records Office, dressed down by the narrator in *The IPCRESS File* for passing evidence to Ross at Military Intelligence, then praised for his sterling work in *Horse Under Water* and *Funeral in Berlin*.

Kellerman, SS-Gruppenführer Fritz. Senior SS and Police Chief in Nazi-occupied Britain, with a leading role as Douglas Archer's overlord in *SS–GB*. A genial Prussian in his late fifties, his expert imitation of an absent-minded old buffer who likes English tweeds, house parties and *la dolce vita*, hides a ruthless ambition. Recognising newly-arrived SS-Standartenführer Oskar Huth as a threat to his future, he cunningly manipulates both Archer and Harry Woods, then has Huth arrested for treason following the raid on Bringle Sands.

Kent, Gloria. Sharp, romantic nineteen-year-old 'Executive Officer' in London Central, who provides Bernard Samson with love, understanding and not a few insights in *Mexico Set* and *London Match* following the defection of his wife, Fiona.

Kersten, Frau. Minor German character in *Bomber*. The subject of much gossip in Altgarten, she dies in the arms of a French prisoner-of-war as Sweet's flak-damaged Lancaster spins out of control and demolishes her farmhouse.

'Kibitzer'. The USAF P-51 Mustang decorated with a beautifully painted nude girl hiding behind playing cards, piloted by Jamie Farebrother in *Goodbye Mickey Mouse*.

kidnapping. *See* abduction.

kill file. Opened by Helen Bishop's MI6 desk officer, following her anomalous disappearance and presumed murder in *Yesterday's Spy*.

Kimber-Hutchinson, David. Autocratic, bigoted tycoon father of Fiona Samson and Tessa Kosinski in the *Game, Set & Match* trilogy, whose custodial challenge for the grandchildren following Fiona's flight east, leads to an inevitable clash of wills with his son-in-law Bernard Samson.

Kimon, 'Papa'. Languid, overweight Lebanese whom Silas Lowther has known since the war, in whose shabby Beirut hotel the trio of confidence tricksters pass the final hours before swindling the Honourable Gerald Spencer in *Only When I Larf*.

'King'. Cryptonym assigned to Johnnie Vulkan by the Gehlen Bureau in *Funeral in Berlin*, during the operation to covertly transfer Semitsa from East to West Berlin.

King, Kitty. Blonde secretary to MI6's Deputy Chief of Operations (Region Three) and current girl-friend of Boyd Stuart in *XPD*, who unwittingly provides the key to Sir Sydney Ryden's personal interest in the fate of the Hitler Minutes.

Kinzelberg, Sergeant. Duke Scroll's clerk at Steeple Thaxted in *Goodbye Mickey Mouse*. A hard-eyed former bookies' runner, who 'wouldn't give you the time of day unless he checked it back with records'.

———, Klara. Lisl Hennig's devoted housekeeper in *Mexico Set* and *London Match*, whom she habitually refers to as her 'girl', though at sixty she's only marginally younger than Lisl herself.

Kleiber, Willi. Cynical ruthless German with a quick eye for other men's weaknesses, who leads the KGB's relentless search for the Hitler Minutes in *XPD*. A wartime Abwehr officer, he not only witnessed the secret Hitler–Churchill meeting of 1940, but was present as Nazi assets and documents were hidden in the Kaiseroda Mine in 1945. Two generations later, and now a Moscow Centre agent, he cunningly manipulates the Trust to support his hunt for the document revealing Britain's greatest wartime secret.

von Kleindorf, Rudolf. Son of a Prussian noble family, a careerist Wehrmacht officer, battle-hardened in combat, serving under General Horner in *Winter*. Captured in France following the D-Day landings, he's repatriated in time to rally support for Horner, who faces trial accused of responsibility for the execution of Allied POWs.

Klimke, Leutnant. Kokke's radar man aboard his Ju88 night-fighter, killed in the bird-strike which sends the plane into the waters of the IJsselmeer shortly after scrambling to engage the RAF bombers in *Bomber*.

'Knee-Jerk'. Pass-code prefix, known to only a handful of British Intelligence personnel, which accesses the London Data Centre's automatic computer link to CIA files. Bernard Samson's late discovery in *Berlin Game* that the KGB mole is cleared to use the prefix, establishes that the traitor is very senior, very close to Operations.

Knobel, Fregattenkapitän. Former wartime scientific officer in the German Navy, living in Portugal under the assumed name of Manuel da Cunha in *Horse Under Water*. Having fled Nazi Germany in 1945 aboard a U-boat, carrying surefire 'insurance' in the form of heroin and the Weiss List, he successfully blackmails the influential Nazi sympathisers named on the List, until forced to flee to Marrakech following the narrator's investigations in Albufeira.

Koby, Gerda. John Koby's withdrawn German wife in *London Match*. Self-conscious among her husband's American and British friends, she continues to shoulder the blame for her brother's role in his fall from grace after the war.

Koby, John. Embittered, disingenuous American in *London Match*, who ran the Berlin System for British Intelligence until implicated in early postwar black marketeering. Nearly forty years later, he blames Bret Rensselaer for his downfall, offering this as evidence of Rensselaer's longtime allegiance to Moscow.

Koch, Hugo. Desiccated-looking Zurich private detective, who earns every penny of his MI6 retainer in *XPD* when he retrieves the Hitler Minutes from Pitman's wrecked Jaguar following the Colonel's heart attack on a Swiss autoroute.

Koch, Lothar. Portrayed as a harmless little Berliner in his mid-eighties, content to while away his days partnering Lisl

Hennig at bridge in *Mexico Set* and *London Match*, he is revealed to have been an early recruit to Heydrich's burgeoning Sicherheitsdienst and a longtime associate of Paul Winter in *Winter*. The story that he was a clerk at Berlin's Kaiserhof hotel prior to 1933—passed on by Bernard Samson in *Mexico Set*—can now be seen as a fiction intended to obscure the dark corners of his Nazi past.

Koenige, Lieutenant Earl. Blond-haired farmer's son from Georgia, painfully aware of having relatives still living in Magdeburg, as he flies escort missions over Germany in *Goodbye Mickey Mouse*. Shot down whilst strafing a Luftwaffe airfield, his Mustang cartwheels into a spectacular explosion.

(One perceptive American critic pointed out that his name resembles 'Erlkönig'—the evil spirit of German mythology who abducted children to the land of death. The novel is about parents who kill the 'thing they love'.)

Kokke, Leutnant. Young Luftwaffe night-fighter pilot, noted for his devastating sarcasm and polished flying skill, killed by a bird-strike as he takes off from Kroonsdijk to engage the RAF Lancasters in *Bomber*.

Komitet Gosudarstvennoi Bezopastnosti (KGB). The Soviet Union's all-pervasive Committee for State Security is the linear descendant of the Cheka, the terror organisation formed in 1917 to liquidate opponents of communism, and was described by the late CIA director Allen Dulles as 'a multipurpose, clandestine arm of power . . . an instrument for subversion, manipulation and violence'. The KGB is a major power within the Soviet establishment and was reportedly a key supporter of Mikhail Gorbachev when he was elected Soviet leader in March 1985. It is a prime agent of political repression at home, but in an unprecedented public admission in January 1987, Viktor Chebrikov—current head of the KGB—announced in *Pravda* that a senior officer stationed in the Ukraine had been dismissed for falsifying charges against a Soviet citizen. Whether this marked the beginning of a genuine reform of domestic practices, or was a nominal move to pacify Gorbachev, only time will tell.

Overseas, the KGB operates chiefly through an extensive network of officers placed in Soviet embassies and missions, and under the official cover of such organisations as Aeroflot, Tass, Intourist, Amtorg, the Moscow Narodny Bank, Morflot Shipping and the United Nations. Formerly run from Dzerzhinsky Square—named after the first head of the Cheka—several of its Directorates have now moved to modern new offices in Moscow linked by an extensive computer and telex network.

Western intelligence officials give the KGB high marks for its professionalism and discipline, and the endless war between the foot soldiers of both sides figures largely in *Funeral in Berlin*, *Twinkle, Twinkle, Little Spy*, *XPD* and the *Game, Set & Match* trilogy, while the KGB's efforts to counter Western operations directed against the Soviet Union are portrayed in *Billion-Dollar Brain* and *Spy Story*. KGB officers encountered in the novels include the very human Colonel Alexeyevitch Stok, Major Nikolai Sadoff, General Stanislav Shumuk, Yuriy Grechko, Colonel Pavel Moskvin and Chlestakov.

Kondit, Harry. Garrulous American expatriate in *Horse Under Water*, whose interest in the narrator's activities in Albufeira is hastened by the need to protect his narcotics operation run in partnership with Fernie Tomas.

———, Konrad. Solicitous teenage son of the proprietor of the 'Golden Bear'—the inn by the Elbe on the inner-German border, where an apprehensive Bernard Samson awaits Werner Volkmann's return from the East in *Mexico Set*.

Koolman, Leo. Thick-necked balding film mogul in *Close-Up*, who remains an anachronism in a Hollywood run by a procession of ex-agents and accountants, after inheriting the Koolman Studio from his uncle and staying at the helm for over twenty years.

Koolman, Max. Pioneering American film mogul in the tradition of Cohn, Goldwyn and Mayer in *Close-Up*, who founded the Koolman Pictures Corporation in 1921 and built it into a major studio, securing his place in Hollywood mythology on his death in 1956.

Kosinski, George. Energetic thirty-six-year-old London cockney, wealthy car trader and cuckold in the *Game, Set & Match* trilogy. Seemingly resigned to his wife Tessa's infidelites, he shares with Bernard Samson a blighted relationship with his father-in-law David Kimber-Hutchinson.

Kosinski, Tessa. Affluent, promiscuous thirty-three-year-old sister of Fiona Samson in the *Game, Set & Match* trilogy. Although the antithesis of her sister, they are very close—'the result perhaps of having suffered together the childhood miseries that their pompous, autocratic father thought character forming'—and Fiona's flight east in *Berlin Game* removes one of the few sources of continuity in her directionless life.

Krebs, Helmut. Prominent West German businessman who lends his name to the cunning CIA deception in *XPD* that persuades Willi Kleiber to embark on a private jet in Geneva, expecting to be flown to a business meeting in Venice.

Krefeld. German industrial town chosen as the primary target for the RAF raid in *Bomber*, whose fate is ironically spared as the TI markers fall short and the 700 bombers mistakenly unleash their high explosives and incendiaries on Altgarten.

Kronprinz Club. Social club patronised by Mexico City's large German community, where Erich Stinnes deliberately mistakes Zena Volkmann for Poppy Biedermann in *Mexico Set*, and sets in motion his enrolment by London Central.

Kroonsdijk. The Luftwaffe night-fighter airfield in occupied Holland, lying upon the direct route from the bomber airfields in eastern England to the heart of industrial Germany, where Major Peter Redenbacher commands three Staffeln of aircraft in *Bomber*. Set close to the IJsselmeer, the great inland sea that opens the heart of Holland to the northern storms, the airfield is designed to appear from the air like a Dutch farm, with herds of pantomime cows made from lath and plaster installed near the runways to complete the illusion.

Krugelheim, Oberfeldwebel. Elderly chief Luftwaffe mechanic, whose misanthropy keeps the night-fighters flying from Kroonsdijk in *Bomber*.

Kuang-t'ien. The nuclear expert at the Chinese Embassy in Paris, safely conducted out of France by the narrator in *An Expensive Place to Die* after having received classified American fall-out data leaked by the CIA.

Kupka, Count. The Austrian Emperor's feared secret police chief, whose Machiavellian scheming in the opening of *Winter* gains Harald Winter the plot of land on the Obersalzburg fraught with destiny for his son Paul.

L

Laine, Signe. Strikingly pretty Finnish teenager, a trained assassin for the Facts for Freedom organisation and Harvey Newbegin's lover in *Billion-Dollar Brain*. 'Signe was a born infiltrator; it was almost impossible not to be in love with her, but you'd need a guileless mind to believe half the things she said. When he was with her Harvey had a guileless mind.'

Lambert, Corporal Ruth. Sam Lambert's beautiful childlike wife, a serving WAAF officer at Warley Fen in *Bomber*. Nineteen, twenty at most, she's calmly supportive of her husband, sharing his distaste of those who liken war to a 'glorified cricket match'.

Lambert, Flight Sergeant Sam. Thoughtful twenty-six-year-old RAF Lancaster pilot, with the leading role in *Bomber*. A pre-war recruit, acknowledged as one of the best skippers at Warley Fen, his enlightened command of 'Creaking Door' earns him the respect and loyalty of the aircrews. But when after forty-five missions he starts to question the strategy of bombing German city centres (for few factories ever lie in this target area), he's stripped of his rank and assigned to sanitation duties.

'Lange', John. *Also known as* John Koby.

'The Last Vaquero'. The fictional smash-hit Western in *Close-Up*, scripted by Peter Anson, produced by Kagan Bookbinder and directed by Laurence Pastor, which launched unknown English actor Marshall Stone to stardom in 1948.

Latimer, Sir Stephen. Urbane identity assumed by Silas Lowther as the trio of confidence tricksters embezzle a quarter of a million dollars from the Funfunn Novelty Company in *Only When I Larf*.

Latvia. One of fifteen Federal Republics that make up the Soviet Union. The birthplace of Felix and Ralph Pike, and target for the Facts for Freedom organisation's subversive activities in *Billion-Dollar Brain*.

laundered money. 'Money is to espionage what petrol is to the motor-car,' observes the narrator of *The IPCRESS File*, after admitting to having learned every legal and illegal way of moving funds about the globe. An antiques business provides the perfect cover for raising and laundering money to help the resistance fight the Nazi occupation forces in *SS–GB*; a series of back-to-back transactions between the Bayerische Vereinsbank, a Luxembourg holding company and Brazil's Banco Nacional are used by Walter von Munte to disguise his payments from London Central in *Berlin Game*; while Paul Biedermann confesses to having assisted the KGB by laundering their donations to trade unions and peace groups in *Mexico Set*.

Fiscal games are played for personal gain by Harvey Newbegin in *Billion-Dollar Brain*, as he pockets the salaries of his largely fictional network of agents; by SS-Gruppenführer Kellerman in *SS–GB*, who manages to tuck away over fifteen million Reichsmarks in numbered Swiss accounts; and by Charles Stein and the 'Kaiseroda Raiders' in *XPD*, who chose to start a small Swiss bank to launder the Nazi gold stolen from the American military convoy in 1945.

Lebanon. The pre-civil war setting for Raven's last minute rescue in *The IPCRESS File* and for the surprise triple-cross in *Only When I Larf*.

Leds. The Soho coffee-house to which the narrator traces Jay in the opening of *The IPCRESS File*, and where he has a clandestine rendezvous with Ossie Butterworth in *Horse Under Water*. 'Leds is one of those continental style coffee-houses where coffee comes in a glass. The customers, who mostly think of themselves as clientele, are those smooth-rugged characters with sun-lamp complexions, half a dozen $10'' \times 8''$ glossies, an agent and more time than money on their hands.'

Lee, Colonel. Commander of an armoured regiment during the war-game in *Paper Casualty*, who has smelled the scent of victory in the North African campaign and breathes it proudly among colleagues who have 'tasted the sand of Dunkirk'.

'legals'. Intelligence officers working overseas under diplomatic or other legitimate cover, such as Harvey Newbegin (State Department) in *Funeral in Berlin*, Aziz (World Meteorological Organisation) in *Yesterday's Spy* and Yuriy Grechko (Assistant Naval Attaché) in *XPD*.
See also: 'illegals'.

legend. A false biography created for an agent infiltrated into a hostile country—e.g. Edward Parker in *XPD*, planted in North America as an importer of electronic components, after serving for three years with the KGB First Main Directorate's Scientific and Technical Section.

LEN DEIGHTON'S CONTINENTAL DOSSIER: A Collection of Cultural, Culinary, Historical, Spooky, Grim and Preposterous Fact. Compiled by Victor and Margaret Pettitt. *Introduced by Len Deighton* (Michael Joseph in association with Wylton Dickson Publishing, London, 11 November 1968; non-fiction). In his introduction, Deighton tells how the Pettitts had been fellow students at St Martin's School of Art, and over the years had compiled copious travel notes. When he first opened one of their notebooks, all his own work 'went to pot' because their material made such compulsive reading, and he felt sure it could be assembled into an original travel guide.

LEN DEIGHTON'S LONDON DOSSIER. *Compiled and annotated by Len Deighton* (Jonathan Cape in association with Penguin Books, London, 27 April 1967; non-fiction). With contributions from Adrian Bailey, Drusilla Beyfus, Eric Clark, Daniel Farson, Adrian Flowers, Spike Hughes, Steve Race, Milton Shulman, Godfrey Smith, Nick Tomalin, Frank Norman, John Marshall, Michael Wale and Jane Wilson.

Deighton writes in his foreword: 'A couple of years ago I opened my big mouth at lunch and instead of putting food into it I spoke. I suggested that Cape and Penguin publish a "real London guidebook". Choose a dozen or so residents who really know the town and let them be biased and contradictory on their own subject . . .' Read today, the dossier presents a lively, and for many, nostalgic, portrait of the city in the mid-1960s.

Lenin, V. I. (1870–1924). Founder of the Bolshevik Party and leader of the Soviet state which emerged from the October revolution. 'I touched Lenin. I stood beside him in Vosstaniye Square in July 1920—the second congress,' proudly confides Colonel Stok to the narrator in *Billion-Dollar Brain*.

Leningrad, 'the halfway house between Asia and the Arctic', is the setting for the narrator's unexpected encounter with Colonel Stok, and Harvey Newbegin's surprising XPD, in *Billion-Dollar Brain*. 'When it's daylight in Leningrad and the buses and lorries are roaring along the wide Nevsky, and African delegates are being toasted at multi-course lunches at the Astoria, then it's easy to see Leningrad as the birthplace of Communism. But when it's dark and the moon glints on the Peter and Paul Fortress, and two out of every three street lights are extinguished for economy so that the puddles and newly fallen snow are discovered only by an errant foot, then it is once again St Petersburg, and Dostoevsky is hump-backed in a slum . . . and Pushkin is dying after his duel and saying "Goodbye, my friends" to his rows of books.'

Lichterfelde Barracks. The leading Prussian military academy in Berlin where Paul Winter and Alex Horner first meet as cadets in 1914 in *Winter*. Within a couple of decades of this fictional encounter, the blue tunics of the Prussian army were relics of a dead era, replaced by the asphalt uniforms of Hitler's SS bodyguard, the 'Liebstandarte Adolf Hitler' (the SS division to which Gerda Koby's brother is said to have been attached, in *London Match*).

Liebknecht, Karl (1871–1919). Twice jailed for high treason, he led with Rosa Luxemburg the revolutionary Spartakist movement, and marched into the Imperial Palace in the final days of World War I to proclaim a 'free Socialist Republic of Germany'. Both were murdered in Berlin after days of street fighting.

Liebknecht's Marxist rhetoric galvanises pig slaughterer's son Fritz Esser into radical action in *Winter*, and only Paul Winter's timely intervention saves Esser from sharing his hero's fate at the hands of the Freikorps.

Lightfoot, Dennis. Sycophantic film executive in charge of the Koolman Studio's European productions in *Close-Up*.

Lin, Ali. Courteous Chief of Security at Magazaria's London embassy in *Only When I Larf*, who foils Silas Lowther's scheme to sell scrap metal as armaments to War Minister Awawa.

LITERARY AGENTS by Anthony Masters. *Introduced by Len Deighton* (Basil Blackwell, Oxford, October 1987). A non-fiction account of writers who have served with the security services, from Erskine Childers and John Buchan to Le Carré, Howard Hunt and Ian Fleming. The author quotes from interviews with the living and the writings of the dead.

'Little Friends'. Affectionate nickname given the Mustang fighter escorts by the American bomber crews in *Goodbye Mickey Mouse*.

Loden, Erich. Colonel Pitman's devoted chauffeur, servant and general factotum in *XPD*. Had he been driving when Pitman suffers his fatal heart attack, the Hitler Minutes might well never have reached MI6.

Loiseau, Chief Inspector Claude. Tenacious fifty-year-old senior officer of the French Sûreté Nationale, who shrewdly engages the narrator of *An Expensive Place to Die* in his efforts to destroy Monsieur Datt's blackmailing operation centred on the Avenue Foch 'pleasuredrome', and to break Datt's puppet-like hold over his former wife, Maria Chauvet.

Lombardo, Sal. Melodramatic Italian–American identity assumed by Silas Lowther as the trio of confidence tricksters depart New York with their ill-earned gains in *Only When I Larf*.

London is a constant presence in Deighton's novels. In much of the spy fiction it is a metropolis of anonymous offices from which British Intelligence pursues the clandestine interests of the state, a province of accommodation addresses, dead-letter boxes and safe houses. *Winter* offers a portrait of the city at war, under attack from Zeppelin air raids in 1917 and host to Allied intrigues in 1942–4. *Close-Up* presents an actor's London, a world of green rooms and proscenium arches, dubbing theatres and glittering premieres. But it is *SS–GB* that offers the most original view of the capital; a fictional portrait of the city under the rule of Nazi occupation forces in 1941, with the Dorchester in ruins but able to open a few rooms for American visitors, Wehrmacht personnel on leave buying antiques at knock-down prices and senior civil servants still lunching at the Reform Club.

See also: *Len Deighton's London Dossier*.

London Central. The British Intelligence department, headed by a nearly senile Director General and debilitated by betrayal and endless internecine office warfare, at the centre of the *Game, Set & Match* trilogy. Senior staff include Sir Henry Clevemore, Bret Rensselaer, Dicky Cruyer, Morgan, Bernard and Fiona Samson.

London Data Centre. British Intelligence's secret computer centre nicknamed 'the yellow submarine' in *Berlin Game*, which occupies three floors below Whitehall: one for the big computers, one for the software and its servicing staff, and the lowest and most secure, housing the data. Access is through the Foreign Office, since its entrance is used by so many others that it makes it difficult for enemy agents to identify and target the Centre's staff.

London Debriefing Centre. *See* Berwick House.

LONDON MATCH (Hutchinson, London, 10 October 1985/ Alfred A. Knopf, New York, 3 January 1986; fiction). Deighton's concluding novel in the *Game, Set & Match* trilogy, anchored in London and Berlin, finds Bernard Samson harbouring increasing doubts about prize defector Erich Stinnes and forced to follow a trail that may lead to a second Soviet mole within London Central.

Long Past Glory (ABC Television, 17 November 1963). *p.*: Leonard White. *sc.*: Len Deighton. *d.*: Charles Jarrott. *l.p.*: Maurice Denham (*Charles*), John le Mesurier (*Harry*), David Andrews (*Roy*). 52 minutes.

Rats and running water . . . a cold, dark underground hideout. Two men who make it their home. And a talkative young stranger who comes to share the damp and the discomfort. Why are they there? What is the hidden menace that binds them together? Deighton's only original play for television expresses his views about those people in modern society who pay lip service to liberal ideas, but do little to put them into practice.

Longbottom, Simon. The role of Bob Appleyard's clerk reluctantly assumed by Silas Lowther, as the trio of confidence tricksters set up the Hon. Gerald Spencer in *Only When I Larf*.

Longfellow, Flying Officer. Cultured thirty-eight-year-old Intelligence Officer at RAF Warley Fen in *Bomber* who, when asked by Lambert during the crew briefing to justify the bombing of Krefeld city centre, hurriedly suggests they'll be hitting "a

Gestapo headquarters and poison gas factory'—a reminder that truth is too often the first casualty of war.

LORD NICK FLIES AGAIN. Short story in the collection *Declarations of War*, in which a young World War I airman piloting a flimsy biplane across the English Channel enacts the heady exploits of a comic book hero.

Los Angeles. The city, and its famous suburbs of Hollywood and Beverly Hills, are the dazzling background for the film world portrayed in *Close-Up*, and provide an unexpected setting for the intrigues in *XPD*.

Loveless, Graham. Henry Smith's late nephew, whose court-martial for wartime treason and subsequent hanging are recalled by Fernie Tomas in *Horse Under Water*. The inevitable result, claims Tomas, of Loveless's threat to name every Englishman on the Weiss List.

von Löwenherz, Oberleutnant Victor. Fastidious Prussian aristocrat, an experienced pilot and Staffelkapitän at the Luftwaffe night-fighter station at Kroonsdijk in *Bomber*. After successfully engaging the force of RAF Lancaster bombers over Holland, he is himself fatally shot down by his own countrymen manning the coastal flak-ship *Held*.

Lowther, Silas. Classy British conman in his late forties, one of three leading characters in *Only When I Larf*. Capable of imitating anyone from a British Army officer to a Lebanese banker (most of his aliases have to have the initials S.L., because he has so many shirts, hair brushes, suitcases, studs and handkerchiefs bearing that monogram), he masterminds the trio's not always successful scams until ousted as leader of the group by an ambitious Bob Appleyard. His revenge is bitter-sweet.

Lowther, Brigadier S. British Army alias adopted by Silas Lowther as the trio of confidence tricksters in *Only When I Larf* conspire to sell Ibo Awawa scrap metal disguised as armaments for his planned African putsch.

Lucas-Mountford, Charlotte ('Charly'). Sexy, vivacious British Admiral's daughter assigned by WOOC(P) as housekeeper for Operation Alforreca in *Horse Under Water*. Her presence in Albufeira certainly lifts the narrator's spirits, but she proves something of an enigma, for 'among the several articles in Charly's room that a young single girl shouldn't know how to buy were twenty-five rounds of 7.65 parabellum ammunition . . .' A mystery solved when she tries to detain Harry Kondit, identifying herself as an undercover agent for the US Federal Narcotics Bureau.

Ludlow, Flight Lieutenant. Shy RAF Navigation Leader on his third tour of duty at Warley Fen in *Bomber*. Killed in the night's raid over Germany, he fails to beat the actuarial odds that give only two per cent of airmen a chance of surviving three tours.

The Luftwaffe. Created by General Hans von Seeckt in a memo of 1923, the Luftwaffe played a major role in the German 'blitzkrieg' victories of the first months of World War II. It failed however to gain air supremacy over the English Channel in the Battle of Britain in 1940, largely due to Göring's disastrous inability to plan or direct the Battle; and because he enjoyed a powerful political position within the Third Reich, there was no possibility of calling him to account. 'For the rest of the war,' writes Deighton in *Battle of Britain*, 'the Luftwaffe suffered the consequences of being commanded by this indolent sybarite, broken in energy and purpose for anything except retaining his own offices and power.'

The men, the machines, the strategies and blunders of the Luftwaffe, are factually examined in *Fighter*, *Blitzkrieg* and the previously mentioned *Battle of Britain*, and are fictionally portrayed in *Bomber*—which also offers an Allied point of view, similarly found in *Adagio* and *Goodbye Mickey Mouse*.

Lustig, Bernie. American film producer slaughtered by Willi Kleiber in *XPD* to make way for Max Breslow to take over the proposed film about the Kaiseroda gold robbery. However, what was intended to appear a simple disappearance turns into a homicide investigation with the chance discovery of Lustig's dismembered body in the trunk of a parked car—leading to the formal identification of KGB 'illegal', Edward Parker.

MacGregor, ———. Burly Scottish landlord encountered by Patrick Armstrong in *Spy Story*, shortly after disembarking from a nuclear submarine at H.M.S. *Viking*. Almost certainly employed by British Intelligence to monitor from his pub the approach road to the deep water anchorage.

MacIntosh, Flying Officer. Pilot of one of the two P.F.F. Mosquito aircraft sent to mark the target for the very first RAF bombers in *Bomber*. Forced to turn back twenty-five miles short of Krefeld when his Oboe direction-finding set goes dead, he abandons the task to the second Mosquito piloted by Alan Hill—which itself is being tracked by a specially modified Ju88S Luftwaffe night-fighter.

MacIntosh, Joe. WOOC(P)'s man in Iberia in *Horse Under Water*. After alerting the narrator to the fact that copies of all signals traffic are being redirected to someone at the House of Commons (Cabinet Minister Henry Smith), he's killed by a car-bomb planted by Harry Kondit at London-Heathrow.

MacIver, Miles ('Miles the Mouth'). Former military policeman attached to Patton's Third Army, whose decision early in *XPD* to confide to Billy Stein details of Lustig's planned film about the Kaiseroda robbery, changes the lives of many people, and ends the lives of several, including his own.

MacKenzie, Julian. Keen young London Central probationer first encountered in *Berlin Game*, subsequently mistaken for

Bernard Samson in *Mexico Set* and murdered by Colonel Moskvin in the department's West Sussex safe house.

Madigan, Captain Vince. Burly amiable-looking thirty-two-year-old Public Relations Officer for the 220th Fighter Group in *Goodbye Mickey Mouse*. Everything a girl's mother warns her about—but who by his own account has always been unlucky in love—he's murdered by Reg Hardcastle on 'Bad Monday' after having been mistakenly identified as Vera's Yank lover.

Madjicka, Second Lieutenant Stefan. Hard-nosed young co-pilot at the USAF's 280th Bombardment Squadron in *Goodbye Mickey Mouse*, to whom falls the task of writing to Jamie Farebrother with news of Charlie Stigg's suicide.

Madrid. Briefly visited by the narrator of *Horse Under Water*, from where he traces the fugitive Manuel da Cunha to Marrakech. 'If you ever get clear away from a difficult situation by abandoning a large part of your personal belongings, you may feel an urgent need of certain articles you have left behind, like a Locarte fluorimeter that has an eight-month delivery time. Don't *send* for them; because that's how we traced da Cunha.'

MAMISTA! Unpublished Deighton novel, quite unlike anything else he has written, about a group of South American guerillas and three foreigners who join them.

Other novels he has put aside when almost complete include a story of USAF fighter pilots flying Phantom F-4s during the Vietnam War, and another concerning a mining company which attempts to restore a tribal chief to his African throne by financing a military coup. He also intended writing a non-fiction book about confidence tricksters, and spoke with dozens of conmen and their victims. He abandoned the project, but subsequently used the research to write the novel *Only When I Larf*.

'Man From the Palace'. Fictional film with an important role in *Close-Up*. A satire about a contemporary prince who succeeds to the throne of a mythical European country, and whose decision to purchase a computer to discover an answer to many of the problems of Western urban life has far-reaching consequences for his country and its citizens.

Backed by a new style of finance company, the film promises to be a milestone in the business, and Marshall Stone leaps headlong into the project. But as its increasingly troubled finances become apparent, the wheeler-dealer politics and back-stabbing tactics of the richest industry in the world force Stone into a humbling reconciliation with cunning movie mogul Leo Koolman.

See also: computers.

Mann, Bessie. Tall, slim wife of Major Mickey Mann, who acts as matchmaker to the narrator and Red Bancroft in *Twinkle, Twinkle, Little Spy*.

Mann, Major Mickey. Feisty American CIA officer and the narrator's temporary boss in *Twinkle, Twinkle, Little Spy*, who's not averse to bending the rules when he doesn't like them, for otherwise 'you end up as the kind of dispassionate robotic bastard that communism breeds'. Leads the joint CIA/MI6 operation to secure the defection of Soviet scientist Andrei Bekuv, though it becomes apparent that his real interest is in capping a major KGB source of classified American scientific data on Capitol Hill.

Manning, Sylvia. Malcontented young Scotland Yard clerk and passionless former girl-friend of Douglas Archer in *SS–GB*. Held by the Nazis following the Highgate Cemetery explosion, she's shot dead helping Harry Woods to escape from the Caledonian Market detention camp.

———, Marjorie. Patrick Armstrong's stoical girl-friend in *Spy Story*, who unknowingly supplies key evidence of Ben Toliver's conspiracy, before walking out of Armstrong's life to take up a new job in Los Angeles.

mark. The target or intended victim of a confidence trick—e.g. Karl Poster, Johnny Jones, Ibo Awawa and the Honourable Gerald Spencer in *Only When I Larf*. 'The mark must be in a state of hypnosis, he has to be entranced, but frantic,' explains Silas Lowther. 'It's his own speed that makes him tumble. And that speed and momentum must be avarice. A man who isn't greedy can never fall prey to a con trick.'

Marrakech. North African city visited by the narrator in *Horse Under Water*, first to negotiate with the VNV, and later to confront the fugitive Manuel da Cunha. 'Marrakech is just what the guide-books say it is. Marrakech is an ancient walled city surrounded with olive groves and palm trees. Behind it rise the mountains of the high Atlas and in the city the market place at Djemaa-el-Fna is alive with jugglers, dancers, magicians, story-tellers, snake-charmers and music.'

Marsh, Rita. Bright-eyed English good-time-girl, companion of the Honourable Gerald Spencer in *Only When I Larf*, who surprisingly teams up with Silas Lowther to double-cross his partners after they've successfully conned Spencer in Beirut.

masers. Acronym for Microwave Amplification Stimulated Emission Radiation. 'A crystal gimmick that gets pumped up with electronic energy so that it amplifies the weakest of incoming radio signals', explains Major Mann to the narrator in *Twinkle, Twinkle, Little Spy*. And it's Soviet Professor Andrei Bekuv's leading expertise in this field that seems to make him such a valuable defector to American and British Intelligence: until they reveal they have more worldly plans for him.

Mason, Liz. Vivacious colonel's daughter in her late twenties, one of the trio of confidence tricksters in *Only When I Larf*, whose fluctuating affections for Silas Lowther and Bob Appleyard mirror their battle for leadership of the team.

Mason, ———. Former STUCEN employee, assigned by

Dawlish in *Spy Story* to infiltrate Ben Toliver's cabal and monitor his attempts to secure the defection of Soviet Rear-Admiral Remoziva.

Master File. According to the narrator of *Yesterday's Spy*, a subject's Central Registry file containing full biography, known associates, interests, assets, year-by-year summaries, etc. Released only in exceptional circumstances (such as the investigation of Steve Champion), since Action Abstracts usually satisfy departmental enquiries.

Mauring, Madame. Elderly owner of the popular Geneva tea room and confiserie, where Charles Stein conceals the Hitler Minutes in *XPD*.

Mauser, Axel. A senior clerk in the Berlin Polizeipräsidium records office, who assists boyhood friend Bernard Samson to unlock the identity of Frank Harrington's mistress in *Berlin Game*.

Mauser, Rolf. Wily sixty-year-old father of Axel Mauser, a resident of East Berlin and member of the Brahms Network in *Berlin Game*. After murdering Giles Trent in the mistaken belief he is about to blow the Network, he's arrested by MfS officers in East Berlin as Bernard Samson prepares to bring Brahms Four to safety in the Western Sector. Mauser is also glimpsed as a young man in *Winter*, heading a flying tribunal that briefly detains Dr Isaac Volkmann as the Soviet Red Army sweeps into Berlin in April 1945.

Mayhew, George. Former army colonel and enigmatic leading figure in the British resistance movement, with a key role in *SS–GB*. Ruthlessly determined to write the future history books, he murders physicist Dr William Spode and destroys his papers to force the Americans to fight for Britain's wartime atomic research secrets, then ensures the King falls in battle alongside his allies during the US Marine raid on the Bringle Sands Research Establishment.

Maylev, Captain. The name on the Soviet identity card Colonel Stok presents to the narrator at their first meeting in *Funeral in Berlin*. 'And your passport says that you are Edmond Dorf . . . we are both victims of circumstance.'

McDonald, Aircraftman. The first victim of the Krefeld raid in *Bomber*. An RAF armourer at Warley Fen, he's crushed to death when a 1,000-lb medium capacity bomb falls from the bay of Tommy Carter's Lancaster.

Mebarki, ———. Steve Champion's Arab secretary in *Yesterday's Spy*. Most certainly employed by the Egyptians to mind Champion, he executes Topaz during the final evacuation of the Tix mansion.

Meyer, Hans-Willy. Twenty-one-year-old Altgarten farm-worker in *Bomber*, who bypasses the heinous Nazi racial laws forbidding marriage between persons of one-third Jewish blood by insisting he be 'downgraded' to two-thirds Jewish.

Mexico. Sultry location in *Mexico Set*, where Bernard Samson approaches and successfully enrols KGB officer, Erich Stinnes. 'In the world of real-life spying,' writes Deighton, 'the Russian embassy in Mexico City is one of the most active and most troublesome in the western world. From here the Soviet networks throughout the USA are controlled.'[17]

MEXICO! Essay by Travel Editor Len Deighton in *Playboy* magazine, October 1968. He first visited the country in the mid-1950s, and returned a quarter century later when researching *Mexico Set* 'determined not to fall prey to its attractions'.[18]

Mexico City. Briefly visited by Edward Parker, General Shumuk and Yuriy Grechko for a crash meeting at the Soviet embassy in *XPD*. And of course a major setting in *Mexico Set*: 'It was like stepping into a sauna bath to get off the plane into the heat of Mexico City,' complains Bernard Samson. 'I arrived on a particularly bad day, when the humidity and temperature had reached a record-breaking high . . . such weather played upon the nerves of even the most acclimatized inhabitants, and the police statistics show a pattern of otherwise unaccountable violence that peaks at this time of year.'

MEXICO SET (Hutchinson, London, 22 October 1984/Alfred A. Knopf, New York, 28 February 1985; fiction). The second novel in Deighton's *Game, Set & Match* trilogy finds Bernard Samson travelling to the steamy heat of Mexico to shadow a passed-over KGB major whom British Intelligence wishes to coax to the West. With doubts cast on his own loyalty following his wife's earlier treachery, Samson moves on to London, Berlin and Paris, before returning to Mexico to orchestrate the defection which will restore his credibility within London Central.

MI5: the Security Service. Britain's counter-intelligence and domestic security agency owes its foundation to the delusion that Edwardian Britain was overrun with German spies. It acquired its modern name in the War Office reorganisation of 1916 and since 1952 has been responsible to the Home Office rather than, as previously, to the War Office. Having no powers of arrest, it works closely with the Special Branch which also presents its evidence in court. Its activities, like so much else concerning British Intelligence, are shrouded in secrecy. The British Government's intense efforts to suppress publication of *Spycatcher*, the memoirs of retired MI5 officer Peter Wright, is the most recent example of its efforts to dampen public discussion of MI5's activities, for as Lord Denning's official report on the Profumo scandal explained: 'The Security Service in this country is not established by Statute nor is it recognised by Common Law. Even the Official Secrets Acts do not acknowledge its existence.'

MI5 completed the move to its new London headquarters at Curzon Street House in the early 1970s. It continues to maintain a number of discreet offices in South Audley Street, Grosvenor Street and Gower Street, and operates a joint electronic surveillance and bugging facility with MI6 and the police at Camberwell, South London.

It is divided into six branches scattered throughout these buildings: 'A' Branch handles operations and resources, 'B' Branch is responsible for personnel matters, 'C' Branch is charged with the protective security of government staff and buildings, 'E' Branch monitors international communists and political activists, 'F' Branch is responsible for countering domestic subversion and 'K' Branch for keeping track of hostile agents.

Almost inevitably, the service lives in the shadow of its more glamorous sister organisation MI6, and when on occasion it steps in to investigate one of its staff, the latent rivalry between the two can turn to outright hostility.

Dalby deflects American suspicions in *The IPCRESS File* by letting it be known MI5 suspects that the narrator may be working for the KGB—an idea the CIA is keen to believe since he killed a couple of ONI people during Raven's rescue in the Lebanon. In *Horse Under Water* Jean Tonnesen suggests the watchers shadowing the narrator on his return from H.M.S. Vernon may be from MI5 (it's soon established they're employed by Cabinet Minister Henry Smith), but it's in *London Match* that the battle lines between these two arms of British Intelligence are drawn in earnest—when Bret Rensselaer crosses the demarcation line which confines MI6 to foreign soil and sends Bernard Samson with Ted Riley up to Cambridge to break into the Cambridge Network's safe house. And when MI5's repeated requests for access to defector Erich Stinnes are stonewalled by London Central, the hardening suspicion that Bret Rensselaer may be a KGB mole leads MI5 to despatch a team from K7 to his Berkshire mansion.

See also: breaking and entering.

MI6: the Secret Intelligence Service. Despite the ancient pretence that officially it doesn't exist in peacetime (a fiction abandoned in the wake of Anthony Blunt's public unmasking in 1979), the agency has been around in its modern form since 1909, when it was established as the foreign section of the Secret Service

Bureau with responsibility for overseas intelligence and espionage. Its nominal master is the Foreign Office and the head of the agency is an important member of the Joint Intelligence Committee. Since the late 1960s its headquarters have been at Century House, a twenty-storey tower block near Waterloo Station on the south bank of the Thames, but it continues to maintain a number of other discreet facilities in central London and an undercover training establishment at Fort Monkton, near Gosport.

Broadly speaking, its headquarters staff are organised into area divisions and the so-called regional 'desks', which provide the essential link between London and the overseas stations staffed by MI6 personnel operating under 'legal' cover.

Historically, the agency has enjoyed a high reputation within the global intelligence community, but given the necessary cloak of secrecy drawn over its affairs, it is difficult to make a balanced assessment of its operational record: its successes are rewarded in private, its failures only revealed when a major scandal reaches print.

Clearly the activities of MI6 inform much of Deighton's spy fiction but only recently has the agency been directly portrayed in the novels. In *The IPCRESS File*, *Horse Under Water*, *Funeral in Berlin* and *Billion-Dollar Brain* he succeeds in creating a highly authentic department ('envied, criticised and opposed by other intelligence units') known only by the initials WOOC(P). *An Expensive Place to Die*, *Spy Story*, *Yesterday's Spy* and *Twinkle, Twinkle, Little Spy* merely place the narrator within 'British Intelligence', without reference to MI6. However, *XPD* firmly establishes the agency at the centre of affairs, and the *Game, Set & Match* trilogy focuses attention on a department within MI6 that Deighton chooses to call 'London Central'.

See also: Berlin Station.

Miami. Briefly visited by Major Mann and the narrator of *Twinkle, Twinkle, Little Spy* to interview Hank Dean's estranged wife, Marjorie Reid-Kennedy. 'From the air it looks like a clutter of fancy boxes, washed up on to a tropical shore. But Miami's ocean was blue and inviting and its sky cloudless. Regardless of all those jokes about the Bahamas being where Florida's rich people spend the winter, arrive in Miami straight from an Irish January and you begin to realize that the oranges are not so stupid.'

'Mickey Mouse II'. The USAF P-51 Mustang—its nose painted with the cartoon rodent toting six guns and a ten gallon hat—piloted by Mickey Morse in *Goodbye Mickey Mouse*.

Midwinter, General. Reactionary Texan billionaire who dreams of launching a private assault on the Soviet Union in *Billion-Dollar Brain*. 'A tiny man, dapper and neat like most small men. His flesh was soft; a badly-fitting mask that around the eyes showed a moist pink edge'. Having poured his fortune into the Facts for Freedom organisation, his absurd plans to liberate the Soviet Baltic States are finally subverted by Harvey Newbegin's betrayal and attempted defection in Leningrad.

'Mikado'. The NATO codeword for secret documents that alerts Bernard Samson to Paul Biedermann's arrest as a KGB courier at Paris-Charles de Gaulle, in *Mexico Set*.

Miller, Carol. Thin drawn Englishwoman in her mid-fifties, resident in East Berlin, with a key role in the KGB's deception plans in *London Match*. Detained in West Berlin, she confesses to having worked for the KGB in London and claims to have handled items for shortwave transmission to Moscow from *two* agents, code-named 'Pig Iron' and 'Jake'.

Ministerium für Staatssicherheit (MfS). Some 1500 staff work in East Germany's Ministry for State Security at 22 Normannenstrasse, in Berlin-Lichtenberg, and a further 60,000–80,000 are directly or indirectly employed throughout the country to maintain the multiple layers of internal controls. In common with other communist regimes ultimate power rests with the Party, and while the Minister for State Security, Armeegeneral Erich Mielke, is a member of the ruling Politburo, the MfS is also answerable to the Party through its Secretary for Security Affairs Egon Krenz—widely tipped to succeed Erich Honeker as First Secretary.

Foreign intelligence and espionage are the exclusive preserve of the Hauptverwaltung Aufklärung, headed for thirty-one years by the legendary spymaster Generaloberst Markus 'Misha' Wolf. The domestic guardians of the regime—the Security Police (Stasis) and the Wachregiment Felix Dzerzhinsky—come under the centralised command of Generalleutnant Rudolf Mittig. A third department, Verwaltung 2000, headed by Generalmajor Dr Gerhard Neiber, monitors the 'political reliability' of soldiers in the National People's Army in conjunction with the Party's own department for Security Affairs run by Dr Wolfgang Herger. A KGB bureau within the Ministry is responsible for liaison between the two services, at the same time keeping a watchful eye on the staff on behalf of Moscow Centre. (Readers still left wondering who is watching whom within this oppressive apparat could do worse than telephone 'Normannenstrasse' direct—on East Berlin 590.)

Very often the cat's paw for the KGB, the Ministry's activities come under scrutiny in *Funeral in Berlin*, *Berlin Game* and *London Match*.

MISSION CONTROL: HANNIBAL ONE. Short story in *Declarations of War*, first published in the London *Evening Standard*. Set in the third century BC, strange moving objects terrorise the troops of the mighty Roman army as the brilliant Carthaginian commander, Hannibal, marches on Rome.

Mitchell, Brigadier. Blond thirty-seven-year-old British Army officer, who seems certain to inherit command of Major-General Parkstone's division following the surprise outcome of the World War II war-game in *Paper Casualty*.

Mohr, Dr Ernst. Former Treblinka SS-Medical Officer with a minor off-stage role in *Funeral in Berlin*. Having helped Paul Louis Broum to escape and assume the identity of murdered camp guard

Johnnie Vulkan back in 1945, he's coerced by Vulkan/Broum to testify to his real identity, so that he can collect the family fortune deposited in a Swiss Bank.

mole. A hostile spy who penetrates an intelligence organisation—e.g. Fiona Samson in the *Game, Set & Match* trilogy.

Moncrieff, Michael. Charles Bonnard's shyster defence lawyer in *Yesterday's Spy*. Despite the fact that three QCs from the Public Prosecutor's department have worked a holiday weekend to build mistakes into the case that puts Bonnard into Wormwood Scrubs prison, Moncrieff needs ten days, the advice of two consultants and a substantial fee to spring his release.

————, Monique. Sad young Parisienne in her mid-twenties, a close friend of Annie Couzins and occasional hostess at the Avenue Foch Clinic in *An Expensive Place to Die*. Interviewed by the narrator after Annie's death, she admits their task was to get the Clinic's influential clients to talk about their work while bedside microphones relayed every word to banks of tape recorders in another part of the building. 'So boring, men talking about their work, but are they ready to do it? My God they are.'

Morgan, ————. Brazenly ambitious hatchet-man and assistant to the ailing Sir Henry Clevemore in *Mexico Set* and *London Match*. Although his only qualifications for being in London Central are an honours degree in biology and an uncle in the Foreign Office, he skilfully exploits his position to become a formidable power within the department—'the Martin Bormann of London South West One', wryly jokes Frank Harrington.

Morocco. Exotic location twice visited by the narrator of *Horse Under Water*: first to negotiate with the VNV, and later to confront the fugitive Manuel da Cunha. 'Let me welcome you to our beautiful country,' announces Chief Inspector Baix of the Sûreté

Nationale. 'The oranges are plump on the trees. The date is moist and the snow is crisp and firm on our mountain slopes.'

Morse, Jamie. The son borne by Victoria Cooper several months after the tragic accident which kills his natural father, Jamie Farebrother, at the close of *Goodbye Mickey Mouse*.

Morse, Lieutenant Mickey. Turbulent, cocky, twenty-four-year-old pilot on his way to becoming America's Number One Flying Ace, with a leading role in *Goodbye Mickey Mouse*. Utterly dissimilar in background and character from freshman Jamie Farebrother, the two forge a bond of friendship in battle that has far-reaching consequences for themselves and for the future of those they love.

Moscow is portrayed in *XPD* as a grim, cheerless city. As its citizens go about their daily business, General Stanislav Shumuk idly studies them from his KGB office high in the new SEV building on Kalinina Prospekt: 'The Red Square bus arrived, and the line of passengers began to board. There was not enough room for everyone. One woman stepped out to hail a passing taxi and a man in a bright-blue woollen hat shouted angrily at the bus driver as the bus pulled away. It was unseemly and un-Russian, and the others, although equally angry, turned away to pretend it had not happened . . .'

Moscow Centre. Figurative name for the KGB headquarters in Moscow. Formerly at 2 Dzerzhinsky Square, the Directorates are today spread throughout the city, linked by a new computer and telex network.

Moskvin, Colonel Pavel. Saturnine KGB officer of about fifty, 'a great bull of a man, with a big peasant frame upon which years of manual labour had layered hard muscle' in *Mexico Set* and *London Match*. After attempting to foil Erich Stinnes's defection in Mexico, he is later gunned down by a KGB hit-team in West Berlin in an act of mystifying cold-blooded expediency.

moving drop. A hiding place in an aircraft, bus, train, etc., where an agent can deposit and collect messages and material. *See also*: dead drop.

Mrosek, Leutnant. Löwenherz's nineteen-year-old observer aboard his Ju88 night-fighter in *Bomber*. Ordered to bail out when the aircraft is accidentally holed by the German flak-ship *Held*, he suffers several broken ribs and falls 3,000 feet before regaining consciousness in time to deploy his chute over occupied Holland.

Müller, Carol. *Also known as* Carol Miller.

Munich. Adolf Hitler and the Nazi Party were for a long time dismissed as 'Bavarian' phenomena by the Prussian burgers of Berlin. The NSDAP was spawned in Munich, and following Hitler's abortive 1923 putsch, the city—and the bierkeller used as headquarters by the conspirators—became the legendary shrine of Nazism. Fritz Esser follows Captain Graf to Munich to join the SA in *Winter*, and as Paul Winter becomes preoccupied with the Party's affairs he finds himself frequently summoned to the Bavarian capital.

Munro, Group Captain John. Thirty-five-year-old commanding officer of the RAF bombers and their crews at Warley Fen in *Bomber*. Whilst not among the most popular of officers on the station, he is nevertheless widely respected for listening to all ranks with the same degree of attention. A good deskman and experienced skipper, he returns from the raid over Germany, his sixtieth and final trip of the tour, only to die riding pillion on a motor-bike taking him home on leave.

Munte, Klaus. Franz Pawlak's loader aboard the German coastal flak-ship *Held* in *Bomber*. A plump butcher's delivery boy from Königsberg, he fails to tame Pawlak's frenzied pursuit of anything that comes within range of their radar-controlled gun.

von Munte, Dr Walter. Lugubrious sixty-year-old senior

official of East Germany's Deutsche Notenbank, one of British Intelligence's most reliable, most valuable agents behind the Iron Curtain, with a key role in *Berlin Game*. Reluctant to share his growing suspicion that a KGB mole is at work within London Central, his decision to cut and run sends a ripple of panic through the German Desk, and only when brought out to the West by Bernard Samson does he provide the evidence identifying the traitor. He resurfaces in *London Match* as Samson follows a trail that may lead to a second KGB agent within British Intelligence, and briefly appears as a young man in *Winter*, living with his ailing father and his own motherless baby son in the Russian occupation zone of Germany.

von Munte, Baron Wilhelm. Elderly Prussian landowner, father of Walter von Munte, in *Winter*. An influential member of one of the anti-Hitler cabals, he uses General Horner to canvass Paul Winter's support for their attempt to overthrow the regime and secure a negotiated peace with the Allies.

von Munte, Frau Doktor. Walter von Munte's staid second wife, who after fearlessly accompanying her husband westwards in *Berlin Game*, keenly feels the social disadvantage she suffers as a refugee in *London Match*.

Murphy, Flight Sergeant Mickey. Ox-like RAF flight engineer, with a minor role in *Bomber*. Reassigned from 'Creaking Door' to Sweet's crew, he bails out over Altgarten, only to be killed by two Teno men wielding spades.

Murray, Sergeant. Cover name used by Lieutenant-Colonel Harriman of Special Field Intelligence in *The IPCRESS File*.

music. Deighton spends a lot of time and effort ('too much time and effort',[19] he suggests) getting the music right in the novels.

Mozart receives special attention. On hearing the second movement of Mozart's 41st, the narrator of *The IPCRESS File* recalls the evening early in the novel when he sat with Adem listening to the song of the blacktop in Lebanon. Teresa Foxwell's protégé stills her guests with selections of Mozart, and Albert Dodgson confesses one of his secret pleasures is to lie back in the leather of Bret Rensselaer's Bentley and play Mozart on the car's superb stereo system ('I'd just as soon listen to Mozart here in an underground garage as anywhere in the world'). Both Bernard Samson and Patrick Armstrong are revealed as collectors of Ingrid Haebler's recordings, and Chief Inspector Claude Loiseau is moved to claim that the composer is the only person who understands him!

Bach and Beethoven are included in the repertoire at the Foxwell's soirée and form a major part of Charlie Cavendish's record collection. Lisl Hennig's mother uncovers a rare talent in Erich Hennig in *Winter*, who wins acclaim throughout Germany after performing before Hitler at the Bach Festival in Leipzig.

Johnnie Vulkan/Paul Louis Broum is the surprise author of an analysis of Bartok's string quartets 'which will shatter the music world when published'. Soviet defector Andrei Bekuv spends considerable time on his arrival in New York purchasing expensive stereo equipment on which to play recordings of his beloved Shostakovich. James Hallam's pride and joy is his pristine collection of recordings of the finest composers of the twentieth century, Berg, Stravinsky, Schönberg, Ives—a collection that would meet with the approval of the narrator of *Funeral in Berlin*, who invites Samantha Steel to a London concert to allow Ossie Butterworth to turn over her apartment ('Sam was right about the Schönberg "Variations for wind band". I'd wanted to go on account of the Charles Ives "Three Places in New England", because I liked the crazy military band sequence, but the Schönberg was something else again').

A passion for opera is shared by several characters. Finding himself alone in Leningrad, the narrator of *Billion-Dollar Brain* visits the Maly Opera Theatre to see Verdi's *Otello*. Vince Madigan proves to be an enthusiastic Mozart buff, and Giles Trent a frequent visitor to Covent Garden—a source of regret after he becomes embroiled in the KGB ploy to safeguard their mole within London Central. And Bernard Samson is reminded that Gerda Koby was once a famous opera singer throughout Germany as he inspects her collection of ancient posters that give her billing above the title: Wagner in Bayreuth, *Fidelio* at the Berlin State Opera, and in Munich a performance of *Mongol Fury*—the Nazi's 'Aryanised' version of Handel's *Israel in Egypt*.

Patriotic songs and rousing dance bands lift the spirits of characters plunged into war in *Bomber* and *Goodbye Mickey Mouse*, and in *SS–GB* exhausted and defeated Londoners pack the Edgware Road's Metropolitan Music Hall to see Flanagan and Allen, and to hear Vera Lynn ('By the summer of 1941 the lyrics of her songs had become a motif of the repression felt by the people of Occupied Great Britain . . . "We'll meet again, don't know where, don't know when", was a promise cherished by the thousands of men and women who had their loved ones in some distant German prison camp').

Popular music also plays a role in *Funeral in Berlin*, when Colonel Stok instructs the narrator to arrange for band-leader Victor Sylvester to play 'There's a small Hotel' on the BBC Overseas Service to signal the British Government's agreement to purchase Semitsa ('I'm not sure I can do that'. 'Not sure if you can make this man Sylvester play "There's a small Hotel"?' says Stok incredulously. 'Not sure if I can stop him . . .'). Peter Winter develops a taste for popular music and jazz after meeting and marrying Lottie Danziger in *Winter*, and goes on to write several movie scores during his exile in America. And in the *Game, Set & Match* trilogy, the only leisure activity that Frank Harrington permits himself—apart from sporadic love affairs with unsuitable young women—is to sit in the large drawing room of the Department's Grunewald mansion and listen to his unique collection of Duke Ellington recordings.

See also: *Oh! What a Lovely War*.

MY FILE ON SURPRISING PLACES. Article by Len Deighton, published in the London *Daily Express*, February 1964. Light-hearted advice for travellers to Portugal ('yesterday's spy centre'), Athens ('the first thing you see at Athens airport isn't the blue neon sign "Athinai", it's the big red neon sign advertising instant coffee'), Beirut ('one of the most active of espionage centres'), Czechoslovakia and Vienna.

Nagel, Oberstabsmeister. Ill-humoured young West German border guard encountered by Bernard Samson as he awaits Werner Volkmann's return from East Germany in *Mexico Set*. Unimpressed by Samson's cover story, he reels off a depressing list of measures employed by the communist regime to prevent its citizens crashing the frontier: mine-fields, contact fences, acoustic warning devices, free running dogs, raked control tracts, searchlights and observation towers manned by machine-gunners—'You might as well understand that your friend will not be coming,' he adds.

See also: Grepos.

National Security Agency (NSA). The American Defense Department's huge organisation responsible for signals and electronic espionage has the world's greatest concentration of computers at its Fort Meade headquarters, and delivers over 200 tons of classified material every week to its intelligence masters.

It works closely with Britain's security watchdog, the Government Communications Headquarters, intercepting traffic via a network of hundreds of listening posts around the globe, many operated by other government departments such as the Army, Navy and Air Force's Security Services.

Yet despite these resources, the Agency still has difficulty cryptanalysing the high-grade ciphers and codes used by the Soviets and Warsaw Pact countries, though it registers a notable success in *XPD*, when its giant Atlas computer breaks Moscow Centre's two-part radio message to Yuriy Grechko in Washington, revealing the first recorded use of the cryptonym 'Task Pogoni'.

Nazi Intelligence. The Nazi Party had its own intelligence service, the Sicherheitsdienst (SD), which was established in 1932 as the intelligence arm of the SS and headed by Himmler's ruthless protégé, Reinhard Heydrich. With Hitler's assumption of power the Party was effectively merged with the state, and Heydrich schemed to win total control of the Third Reich's intelligence services.

In September 1939, the organs of the state (SIPO) and the Party (the SD) were combined in a new security agency, the Reichssicherheitshauptamt (RSHA). Then two years after Heydrich's assassination in 1942, Ernst Kaltenbrunner seized the Abwehr from the military, leading to the realisation of Heydrich's ambition of a unified German intelligence service under SS control.

Characters employed at one time or another by these agencies include Feldwebel Blessing, Captain Hans Hesse, SS-Standartenführer Oskar Huth, Willi Kleiber, Lothar Koch, General von Ruff, Dr Hans Starkhof, Theodor Steiner, Claude Winkler and Paul Winter.

necrology. Anna-Luisa, Private Joshua Ashton, Hansl Bach, Colonel Dan Badger, Barbara Barga, Danny Barga, Barney Barnes, Professor Andrei Bekuv, Elena Bekuv, Paul Biedermann, Helen Bishop, Paul Bock, Gerd Böll, Heinrich Brand, Paul Louis Broum, Charlie Cavendish, Steve Champion, Sergeant Simon Cohen, Annie Couzins, Dalby, Simon Danziger, Monsieur Datt, Major Albert Dodgson, Detective Constable Jimmy Dunn, 'Inspector Fabre', Captain Jamie Farebrother, Pilot Officer Cornelius Fleming, Ferdy Foxwell, Signor Fragoli, Serge Frankel, Captain Graf, Yuriy Grechko, Private Green, Harvey Greenwood, Sergeant Jimmy Grimm, Gus, James Hallam, Sergeant Major Reg Hardcastle, Vera Hardcastle, Corporal Steve Harmon, J. B. D. Harrison, Gerry Hart, Oberleutnant Hildmann, Unteroffizier Christian Himmel, 'Housemartin', Peter Hutchinson, SS-Standartenführer Oskar Huth, Johannes Ilfa, Sergeant 'Binty' Jones, Olaf Kaarna, Frau Kersten, Willi Kleiber, Leutnant Klimke, Lieutenant Earl Koenige, Leutnant Kokke,

Max Koolman, Oberleutnant Victor von Löwenherz, Flight-Lieutenant Ludlow, Bernie Lustig, Aircraftman McDonald, Joe MacIntosh, Miles MacIver, Julian MacKenzie, Captain Vince Madigan, Sylvia Manning, Colonel Pavel Moskvin, Group Captain John Munro, Flight Sergeant Mickey Murphy, Harvey Newbegin, Andi Niels, Jean-Paul Pascal, Kit Pepper, Bernard Thomas Peterson, Petzval, John Elroy Pitman, Karl Poster, Ingrid Rainbow, Douglas Reid-Kennedy, Dutch Relay, Cyrus Rensselaer, Ted Riley, Boris Somló, Sergeant 'Pip' Speke, Dr John Spode, Dr William Spode, Professor Max Springer, Charles Stein, Captain Charles Stigg, Flight Lieutenant Sweet, Topaz, Giles Trent, Herr Voss, Captain Waley, Lieutenant Rube Wein, Franz Wever, Harald Winter, Lottie Winter, Paul Winter, Peter Winter, Frau Wisliceny, SS-Standartenführer Wörth.

neo-Nazism, is uncovered in *Horse Under Water*, when the narrator establishes the link between Manuel da Cunha, Fernie Tomas, Henry Smith and the Young Europe Movement, while in *Funeral in Berlin* a pensive Colonel Stok observes—'They know how to look after themselves, Vaclav, these Germans. Sometimes I wonder how we managed to beat them.' 'The Nazis?' 'Oh we still haven't beaten *them*. The Germans I mean.' And in *XPD*, the economic consequences of rewriting the history books to make Hitler into a hero unite members of the Trust behind Dr Böttger's efforts to suppress the Hitler Minutes—'All of us have given a great part of our life to making Germany prosperous, strong and a good place to live. What we have built from the ashes of 1945 could be quickly destroyed by neo-Nazi madmen . . . Hitler is dead. Let him remain dead.'

networks. See individual entries for the Berlin Network, Berlin System, Brahms Network, Cambridge Network, Erfurt Network, Guernica Network and the IPCRESS Network.

A NEW WAY TO SAY GOODNIGHT. Short story in the collection *Declarations of War*. An eminent former fighter pilot visits a young doctor of philosophy in his university chambers, and convincingly argues the cause of a new political movement which will restore the country's fortunes. Not until the end do we learn that the country is Germany, the celebrity is Captain Hermann Göring, and that the movement is the Nazi Party.

New York. Londoner Len Deighton recalls his first visit in *Impressions of New York*, and uses the city as a setting in *Only When I Larf*, *Twinkle, Twinkle, Little Spy*, *XPD*, only briefly in *Winter*, but notably in *Billion-Dollar Brain*: 'Five o'clock in the morning . . . I was moving through mid-town Manhattan in General Midwinter's chauffeur-driven Cadillac—the one with the leopard skin seats. Just for one hour the city is inert . . . The only movement is compressed steam roaring along at three hundred miles an hour under the roadways, escaping now and again with a spectral puff, and the shuffle of wet newspapers as far as the eye can see down the long, long streets to the bloodshot dawn.'

Newbegin, Harvey. Neurotic, opportunistic American intelligence officer, with 'that soft Boston accent that Americans acquire when they work for the State Department', first encountered in *Funeral in Berlin* operating out of the US Embassy in Prague. In *Billion-Dollar Brain*, he assumes a major role freelancing as General Midwinter's agent on the Soviet border, controlling a largely fictional network of agents whose salaries he gratefully pockets, until his decision to defect to the Soviets obliges the narrator to shoulder him under a bus on Leningrad's Nevsky Prospekt.

Newbegin, Mercy. Avaricious wife of Harvey Newbegin in *Billion-Dollar Brain*, whose betrayal of General Midwinter is revealed when it becomes known that Harvey has been laundering the salaries of his fictional agents through her San Antonio bank account.

'Newmarket Tony'. West End wide-boy and pal of Spider Cohen, encountered by Bob Appleyard during a night on the town in *Only When I Larf*. Working one of Soho's oldest pavement cons—gulling wide-eyed tourists into parting with an entrance fee to a basement blue-movie theatre—his convincing patter nearly pulls in Bob, until Spider explains the place is a billiards club.

Nice, and the Côte d'Azur, are revisited by Charles Bonnard in *Yesterday's Spy*, bringing back memories of the days when he and Steve Champion operated an anti-Nazi intelligence network out of Villefranche during World War II.

Nicholson, Edgar. Inscrutable forty-eight-year-old English film producer in *Close-Up*, who in 1948 traded an uncertain acting career for the Koolman Studio's payoff and accepted paternity of Marshall Stone's illegitimate daughter by Ingrid Rainbow.

Nicol, Chief Inspector Gérard. A well-known personality of the Sûreté Nationale, 'senior enough to have his own well-furnished office in the Ministry building on the rue des Saussaies', unwittingly drawn into the KGB ploy to frame Bernard Samson for Paul Biedermann's murder in *Mexico Set.*

Niels, Andi. Solemn young clerk to Altgarten's Mayor in *Bomber*, with a reputation for trading extra clothing coupons for favours from the town's girls. Disgraced after admitting to having accepted a bribe to push through Willi Meyer's marriage, he's incinerated by a phosphorous bomb during the RAF raid.

nightclubs are rarely frequented by Deighton's characters, though James Hallam does encounter Samantha Steel in London's fashionable 'Saddle Room' in *Funeral in Berlin*, and the narrator is forced to make a hurried exit from 'Les Chiens' in *An Expensive Place to Die.*

'the night of the buses'. Wartime Londoners' name for the mass arrests and round-ups that follow the resistance bombing of Highgate Cemetery in *SS–GB*. Thousands are detained by the Nazis, and Wembley Stadium, Earls Court Exhibition Hall and the Albert Hall are hurriedly requisitioned as holding centres, while the tenants of the vast riverside apartment block, Dolphin Square, are turned out into the streets, with only two hours' notice, so that their flats can be used for hundreds of simultaneous interrogations.

1924 Society. International society of leading scientists, originally founded to pool information about interstellar communications, but identified by the CIA in *Twinkle, Twinkle, Little Spy* as a major KGB source of secret American scientific data.

Nogin, Guards Major. Soviet GRU officer heading the Baltic Military District team that intercepts Midwinter's agents infiltrated into Latvia in *Billion-Dollar Brain*, and whose arrest of the hapless Ralph Pike is carefully staged to suggest the narrator bought his freedom from Colonel Stok at Pike's expense.

'Normannenstrasse'. The international intelligence community's name for East Germany's State Security Service headquarters, the Ministerium für Staatssicherheit. Twenty-two Normannenstrasse is an anodyne fourteen-storey building, two blocks north of Frankfurter Allee in Berlin-Lichtenberg. Some 1500 senior staff and administrators work in the building, directing foreign and counter-intelligence and controlling the country-wide net of State Security Police, the Stasis. It also houses one of East Berlin's two remand centres for political prisoners—the other is in Berlin-Hohenschönhausen. (Those convicted of political crimes are sent to one of the prisons staffed and maintained by the Stasis outside East Berlin, at Bautzen, Brandenburg, Karl-Marx-Stadt and Erfurt. Inmates of Bautzen earn remission preparing concealment devices and fabricating documents for use by agents of the HVA.)

'Normannenstrasse' looms large in the finale of *Berlin Game*. Detained there by the Stasis following Brahms Four's successful escape to the West, Bernard Samson is interrogated by future defector Erich Stinnes, before being confronted by his treacherous wife Fiona—on the run from London after having been exposed as a Soviet agent.

Nowak, Tony. Senior United Nations security official with 'a six-figure salary and a three-window office', at whose Park Avenue party unidentified gunmen attempt and fail to murder Soviet defector Andrei Bekuv in *Twinkle, Twinkle, Little Spy*.

nuclear devices. Ever since scientists realised the destructive potential of nuclear energy, the acquisition and protection of nuclear weapons secrets has headed the list of intelligence priorities. In *The IPCRESS File*, the extent of Dalby's treachery is revealed when he transmits high-speed TV pictures of the American shot tower on Tokwe Atoll to a waiting Soviet submarine. A CIA plan to deliberately leak American fall-out data to the Chinese Government to restore the credibility of nuclear deterrence, is central to *An Expensive Place to Die*. An elaborate scheme to convince the world that Egypt is in possession of atomic artillery shells is uncovered by Charles Bonnard in *Yesterday's Spy*, and Britain's wartime atomic research secrets are denied to both the Abwehr and the Nazi SD by British resistance leader George Mayhew in *SS–GB*.

NYR. 'Not yet returned' doesn't necessarily mean killed in action, but ground crews wait in vain for 'Volkswagen' and 'S for Sugar' in *Bomber*, and for 'Daniel', 'Happy Daze' and 'Pilgrim' in *Goodbye Mickey Mouse*.

Obersalzburg. The steep hill by the German mountain village of Berchtesgaden on the border with Austria, where Paul Winter inherits land pledged by Petzval as collateral for a loan from Harald Winter's bank at the beginning of *Winter*. The unexpected legacy is fraught with destiny, for several years later Adolf Hitler settles in Haus Wachenfeld on its lower slopes and is soon joined by Bormann, Göring and other camp followers, irrevocably linking Paul Winter to the Nazi Party elite. (Hitler's mountain retreat was hit by Allied bombers on 25 April 1945. His fortified bunker deep in the hillside is now a tourist attraction.)

Office of Naval Intelligence (ONI). Perhaps the fastest growing agency within the American intelligence community, operating a wide array of electronic espionage devices from surface ships and submarines.

However, its endeavours are in no way limited to the high seas, and the Office's unease with the activities of Jay's network in *The IPCRESS File* is revealed when the narrator kills two strangers, later identified as ONI agents, during the rescue of Raven in the Lebanon. An error subsequently exploited by Dalby to deflect suspicion of his own treachery.

Oh! What a Lovely War (GB 1969). *p.c.*: Accord Productions/ Paramount Pictures. *p.*: Len Deighton (not credited), Brian Duffy, Richard Attenborough. *d.*: Richard Attenborough. *sc.*: Len Deighton (not credited). Based on the Joan Littlewood/ Theatre Workshop musical play, adapted from the radio feature *The Long, Long Trail* by Charles Chilton. *ph.*: Gerry Turpin. *ed.*:

Kevin Connor. *p.d.*: Don Ashton. *a.d.*: Harry White. *sfx.*: Ron
Ballanger. *cost.*: Anthony Mendleson. *ch.*: Eleanor Fazan. *tls.*:
Raymond Hawkey. *adv.*: Major-General Sir Douglas Campbell.
m./m.d.: Alfred Ralston. *songs*: 'Oh! What a Lovely War', 'Oh I
Do Like to be beside the Seaside', 'Belgium Put the Kibosh on the
Kaiser', 'Are We Downhearted?', 'Your King and Country Need
You', 'I'll Make a Man of You,' 'We're 'ere because we're 'ere',
'Pack Up Your Troubles', 'Heilige Nacht', 'Christmas Day in the
Cookhouse', 'Goodbyee', 'Gassed', 'Comrades', 'Hush Here
Comes a Whizzbang', 'There's a Long, Long Trail', 'Rule
Britannia', 'I Don't Want to be a Soldier', 'Mademoiselle from
Armentières', 'The Moon Shines Bright on Charlie Chaplin',
'Adieu la Vie', 'They Were Only Playing Leapfrog', 'Forward Joe
Soap's Army', 'We are Fred Karno's Army', 'When This Lousy
War is Over', 'Whiter than the Whitewash on the Wall', 'I Want to
Go Home', 'The Bells of Hell', 'Never Mind', 'Far Far from
Wipers', 'If You Want the Old Battalion', 'Keep the Home Fires
Burning', 'Over There', 'They'll Never Believe Me'. *l.p.*: Ralph
Richardson (*Sir Edward Grey*), Meriel Forbes (*Lady Grey*),
Wensley Pithey (*Archduke Franz Ferdinand*), Ruth Kettlewell
(*Duchess Sophie*), Ian Holm (*President Poincaré*), John Gielgud
(*Count Berchtold*), Kenneth More (*Kaiser Wilhelm II*), John
Clements (*General von Moltke*), Paul Daneman (*Tsar Nicholas
II*), Joe Melia (*The Photographer*) Jack Hawkins (*Emperor Franz
Josef*), John Hussey (*Soldier on Balcony*), Kim Smith (*Dickie
Smith*), Mary Wimbush (*Mary Smith*), Paul Shelley (*Jack Smith*),
Wendy Allnutt (*Flo Smith*), John Rae (*Grandpa Smith*), Kathleen
Wileman (*Emma Smith*), Corin Redgrave (*Bertie Smith*), Malcolm
McFee (*Freddie Smith*), Colin Farrell (*Harry Smith*), Maurice
Roëves (*George Smith*), Angela Thorne (*Betty Smith*), John Mills
(*Field-Marshal Sir Douglas Haig*), Julie Wright (*His Secretary*),
Jean-Pierre Cassel (*French Colonel*), Penny Allen (*Solo Chorus
Girl*), Maggie Smith (*Music Hall Star*), David Lodge (*Recruiting
Sergeant*), Michael Redgrave (*General Sir Henry Wilson*),
Laurence Olivier (*Field-Marshal Sir John French*), Peter Gilmore
(*Private Burgess*), Derek Newark (*Shooting Gallery Proprietor*),
Richard Howard (*Young Soldier at Mons*), John Trigger (*Officer at

Station), Ron Pember (*Corporal at Station*), Juliet Mills, Nanette Newman (*Nurses at Station*), Susannah York (*Eleanor*), Dirk Bogarde (*Stephen*), Norman Jones, Andrew Robertson, Ben Howard, Angus Lennie, Brian Tipping (*Scottish Soldiers*), Christian Doermer (*Fritz*), Tony Vogel (*German Soldier*), Paul Hansard (*German Officer*), John Woodnutt (*British Officer*), Tony Thawnton (*Officer on Telephone*), Cecil Parker (*Sir John*), Zeph Gladstone (*His Chauffeuse*), Stanley McGeagh, Stanley Lebor (*Soldiers in Gassed Trench*), Robert Flemyng (*Staff Officer in Gassed Trench*), Thorley Walters, Norman Shelley, Raymond Edwards (*Staff Officers in Ballroom*), Isabel Dean (*Sir John French's Lady*), Guy Middleton (*General Sir William Robertson*), Natasha Parry (*Sir William Robertson's Lady*), Cecilia Darby (*Sir Henry Wilson's Lady*), Phyllis Calvert (*Lady Haig*), Freddie Ascott (*'Whizzbang' Soldier*), Edward Fox, Geoffrey Davies, Anthony Ainley (*Aides*), Christian Thorogood, Paddy Joyce, John Dunhill, John Owens, P. G. Stephens (*Irish Soldiers*), Vanessa Redgrave (*Sylvia Pankhurst*), Clifford Mollison, Dorothy Reynolds, Harry Locke, George Ghent (*Hecklers*), Michael Bates (*Drunken Lance Corporal*), Charles Farrell (*Policeman*), Pia Colombo (*Estaminet Singer*), Vincent Ball (*Australian Singer*), Gerald Sim (*Chaplain*), Maurice Arthur (*Soldier Singer at Church Parade*), Arthur White (*Sergeant in Dugout*), Christopher Cabot (*Soldier in Shell Hole*), Fanny Carby, Marianne Stone, Christine Noonan (*Mill Girls*), Charlotte Attenborough (*Emma Smith aged 8*). 12,947 feet; 144 minutes.

Len Deighton's wildly cinematic adaptation of Joan Littlewood's anti-war musical fantasy about World War I marked actor Richard Attenborough's directorial début, but drew uneven notices on its release. Encouraged by historian A. J. P. Taylor, Deighton purchased the film rights, wrote the screenplay, and co-produced with Brian Duffy but, dissatisfied with the finished film, he removed his name from the credits prior to its distribution.

one-time pad. Simple encoding method consisting of a random key used only once. Widely used by espionage agents, it's the only code system that is unbreakable both in theory and in practice.

ONLY WHEN I LARF (Michael Joseph/Sphere Books, London, 22 April 1968/**Only When I Laugh**, The Mysterious Press, New York, 25 March 1987; fiction). Deighton's sixth novel marked his first departure from spy fiction, and is a comedy thriller about three English confidence tricksters, Silas Lowther, his girl-friend Liz Mason and junior partner Bob Appleyard. After successfully conning a quarter of a million dollars from a couple of New York businessmen, they return to London and set up a scheme to sell scrap metal in crates labelled 'Arms' to the War Minister of an emergent African nation. The scheme fails, and Bob seizes the opportunity to oust Silas as leader of the group and win Liz's affections as he masterminds the team's final venture—an attempt to gull a vain young titled tycoon with a phoney bank swindle in Beirut.

Only When I Larf (GB 1968). *p.c.*: Beecord Productions. *p.*: Len Deighton, Brian Duffy. *d.*: Basil Dearden. *sc.*: John Salmon. Based on the novel by Len Deighton. *ph.*: Anthony Richmond. *ed.*: Fergus McDonnell. *a.d.*: John Blezard. *m.*: Ron Grainer. *l.p.*: Richard Attenborough (*Silas Lowther*), David Hemmings (*Bob Appleyard*), Alexandra Stewart (*Liz Mason*), Nicholas Pennell (*Honourable Gerald Spencer*), Melissa Stribling (*Diana*), Terence Alexander (*Guthrie Grey*), Edric Connor (*Awana*), Clifton Jones (*General Sakut*), Calvin Lockhart (*Ali Lin*), Brian Grellis (*Spider Cohen*), David Healy (*Johnny Jones*), Alan Gifford (*Karl Poster*). 9,270 feet; 103 minutes.

ONLY WHEN I LAUGH (The Mysterious Press, New York, 25 March 1987; fiction). For nineteen years, *Only When I Larf* remained unavailable in America. Having failed to find anyone to publish the novel in time for the film's première in 1968, Deighton let the book stay on the shelf until the enterprising New York publisher, Otto Penzler, took up the reins. Inside three weeks of its publication in 1987, it sold an astonishing 53,000 copies and reached number 15 on the *Publishers Weekly* best-seller list. A signed limited edition, containing a new introduction by Deighton, was published simultaneously with the trade edition.

opening lines. A personal selection, each one of which immediately puts the reader under the spell of a character or situation. Sources are given at the end of the entry. How many can you identify before checking the list?

I don't care what you say, 18,000 pounds (sterling) is a lot of money. The British Government had instructed me to pay it to the man at the corner table who was now using knife and fork to commit ritual murder on a cream pastry. **(a)**

It was the morning of my hundredth birthday. I shaved the final mirror-disc of old tired face under the merciless glare of the bathroom lighting. It was all very well telling oneself that Humphrey Bogart had that sort of face; but he also had a hairpiece, half a million dollars a year and a stand-in for the rough bits. **(b)**

The birds flew around for nothing but the hell of it. It was that sort of day: a trailer for the coming summer. Some birds flew in neat disciplined formations, some in ragged mobs, and higher, much higher, flew the loner who didn't like corporate decisions. **(c)**

It was a bomber's sky: dry air, wind enough to clear the smoke, cloud broken enough to recognize a few stars. **(d)**

The heavy blue notepaper crackled as the man signed his name. The signature was an actor's: a dashing autograph, bigger by far than any of the text. It began well, rushing forward boldly before halting suddenly enough to split the supply of ink. Then it retreated to strangle itself in loops. The surname began gently but then that too became a complex of arcades so that the whole name was all but deleted by well-considered decorative scrolls. The signature was a diagram of the man. **(e)**

'Himmler's got the King locked up in the Tower of London,' said Harry Woods. 'But now the German Generals say the army should guard him.' **(f)**

(a) *The IPCRESS File*, **(b)** *Billion-Dollar Brain*, **(c)** *An Expensive Place to Die*, **(d)** *Bomber*, **(e)** *Close-Up*, and **(f)** *SS–GB*.

THE ORIENT FLIGHT L.Z.127-GRAF ZEPPELIN (Germany Philatelic Society, Maryland, October 1980; non-fiction). *Co-authored by Fred F. Blau and Cyril Deighton.* A collaboration between Len (Cyril) Deighton and a well-known American airmail collector, this philatelic handbook documents the history of the airship, and in particular the development of the postal service on board. The Orient flight of the *Graf Zeppelin* marked the reintroduction of the air-borne post office, and is distinguished also for being the most controversial (in philatelic terms) of the *Graf Zeppelin*'s history.
  See also: *The Egypt Flight L.Z.127-Graf Zeppelin*.

Orth, Gefreiter. Cunning telephone operator at the Luftwaffe coastal radar station 'Ermine' in *Bomber*. A notorious black marketeer, it's a well known fact that when he hangs the enemy-listening sign on the door it means that the police are tapping the phones for security purposes.

Ostend. Scene of the waterfront confrontation between the narrator, Monsieur Datt, Chief Inspector Claude Loiseau and Maria Chauvet, at the close of *An Expensive Place to Die*.

OÙ EST LE GARLIC (Penguin Books, London, 28 October 1965/Harper & Row, New York, 18 March 1977; non-fiction). Following the early success of the *Observer* cookstrips and the publication of *Action Cook Book*, Deighton's great interest in French cooking prompted him to work on a long-term project in which the fundamental facts of French cooking could be explained in no more than fifty strips. As a guiding principle, he concentrated on the sort of dishes one would hope to find in a small French country restaurant. The result was *Où est.le garlic*, praised by Alex Szogyi in New York's *Village Voice* as 'one of the best arranged and explicated works on French cuisine'.

See also: title changes.

over-the-air-codes used by WOOC(P) are explained for us in a footnote in *Horse Under Water*, after the narrator witnesses the death of Joe MacIntosh in a car-bomb explosion at London-Heathrow—STUDENT: agent or employee; FLAT: dead or presumed dead; SCISSORS: violence.

P

Pace, Billy. RAF navigator aboard the Lancaster 'S for Sugar' in *Bomber*. Forced to evacuate the plane following Himmel's withering attack, he's swept along the fuselage like a shove ha'penny by the 230 m.p.h. air-stream, before drifting whole and unharmed into the zephyr-like warm winds of Altgarten—the only crew member to survive.

Page, Melodie. Cover name assumed by British Intelligence field agent Helen Bishop when put in to investigate Steve Champion's affairs in *Yesterday's Spy*.

Painter, Lieutenant-Colonel Simon. Thin-faced British Army psychiatrist in *The IPCRESS File*. A member of the snatch team that rescues Raven in the Lebanon, he successfully de-programmes the brain-washed Porton biochemist and brings him back to something approaching normality.

Palmer, Harry. Name coined by producer Harry Saltzman for the hero (played by Michael Caine, after Christopher Plummer was originally chosen for the role) in the films of *The IPCRESS File*, *Funeral in Berlin* and *Billion-Dollar Brain*. Palmer's image is now so deeply embedded in the experience of millions of filmgoers and television viewers that many forget the character was unnamed in Deighton's original novels.

Palmer, Private. Shell-shocked veteran of the Somme, a member of the Royal Fusiliers firing squad despatched to Pooglui Camp in *Twelve Good Men And True*.

PAPER CASUALTY. Short story in the collection *Declarations of War*. The surprise outcome of a British Army war-game has far-reaching consequences for the career of a distinguished World War I hero.

Paris, in the mid-1960s, is the setting for much of *An Expensive Place to Die*, whose narrator offers a sardonic portrait of the hard-eyed city. 'The café was on the Boul. Mich., the very heart of the left bank. Outside in the bright sun sat the students; hirsute and earnest, they have come from Munich and Los Angeles sure that Hemingway and Lautrec are still alive and that some day in some left bank café they will find them. But all they ever find are other young men who look exactly like themselves, and it's with this sad discovery that they finally return to Bavaria and California and become salesmen or executives. Meanwhile here they sat in the hot seat of culture, where businessmen became poets, poets became alcoholics, alcoholics became philosophers and philosophers realised how much better it was to be businessmen.'

The French capital provides actor Marshall Stone with a needed respite from his fears in *Close-Up*, is briefly visited by Major Mann and the narrator in *Twinkle, Twinkle, Little Spy*, and also by Bernard Samson in *Mexico Set*, where he is framed for the murder of Paul Biedermann at Charles de Gaulle airport. And in his travel article *Exploring a New City*, Deighton recalls how as a schoolboy he first visited Paris in 1946. 'During one hour in the Gare du Nord, I met more tarts, black marketeers, military cops, deserters and assorted criminals than I did for the next six months . . .'

Parker, Edward. Thickset bear-like Chicago businessman, revealed to be the KGB's Russian-born illegal resident in North America in *XPD*. Assigned to conduct 'Task Pogoni', his safety becomes Moscow Centre's primary concern once Kleiber's bloody pursuit of the Hitler Minutes galvanizes the CIA into action.

Parker, Fusako. Edward Parker's doll-like Japanese wife, whose hurried flight from America leads lovelorn Yuriy Grechko

to commit suicide in the Rousillon Beach Motel at the close of
XPD.

Parkstone, Major-General. Grey-haired World War I hero,
who loses his Divisional Command after being outmanoeuvred by
the new generation of British Army officers during the World War
II war-game in *Paper Casualty*.

parties are the occasion for many first encounters, notably
General Midwinter's lavish costume affair in *Billion-Dollar Brain*,
the reception at a Faubourg St Honoré art gallery in *An Expensive
Place to Die*, Leo Koolman's birthday gala (guests include
Humphrey Bogart, Hoagy Carmichael, Ava Gardner, Gregory
Peck and Dick Powell) in *Close-Up*, Tony Nowak's Park Avenue
cocktail party in *Twinkle, Twinkle, Little Spy*, the glittering
celebration hosted by Sydney Garin and Peter Shetland in Nazi-
occupied London in *SS–GB*, and the rowdy American shindig in
Goodbye Mickey Mouse. In *Berlin Game* Bernard Samson recalls
the party hosted by a Foreign Office clerk at which he first met his
future wife Fiona, and unforeseen consequences arise from Lottie
Danziger's first encounter with Peter Winter at his brother's
twenty-fourth birthday party in *Winter*.
   Other parties with a significant role include General Guerite's
beanfeast on Tokwe Atoll in *The IPCRESS File*, thrown to draw
attention from the crash-reprogramming of the American nuclear
test, the high-society Christmas gathering in Berlin-Wannsee in
London Match where Carol Miller and the private secretary of a
senior Bonn politician are detained following a tip-off from Erich
Stinnes, and Hermann Göring's sumptuous affair for a thousand
guests in *Winter*, at which Erich Hennig is given a welcoming
applause that outmatches that given to any other performer.

Pascal, Jean-Paul. Shallow young Frenchman encountered
by the narrator in *An Expensive Place to Die*. A drugstore cowboy
who 'feels it his duty to make himself available to every girl from
fifteen to fifty', his capricious attempts to ingratiate himself with

both Chief Inspector Loiseau and Monsieur Datt, lead to his messy death at the hands of Datt's henchman Robert.

Pastor, Laurence. One of Hollywood's walking wounded, sought by biographer Peter Anson as he assembles the jigsaw pieces of actor Marshall Stone's life in *Close-Up*. The director of Stone's first smash film 'The Last Vaquero', he made only one more picture before being railroaded for his homosexuality after 'embracing a second assistant who talked'.

Pawlak, Obergefreiter Franz. Trigger-happy forcastle gunner aboard the German coastal flak-ship *Held* in *Bomber*. Washed out of Luftwaffe pilot school, he loathes all aeroplanes with a terrible and sustained hatred, making him only a little less dangerous to his own fliers than to those of the enemy.
See also: Victor von Löwenherz.

Paz, 'Rocky' Ramon. Overgrown ex-wrestler hired by Edward Parker to kidnap Charles Stein at Los Angeles International airport, in a last desperate attempt to secure the Hitler Minutes in *XPD*.

Pearson VC, Pilot Officer. Newly-appointed RAF Educational Officer at Warley Fen in *Bomber*. Recalling the difficulties he'd had to face when discharged in 1918, notwithstanding his Victoria Cross, he worries for the young RAF men who fail to realise how narrow and uncommercial their new-found skills will prove once the war is over.

Peel, Private. Member of the Royal Fusiliers firing squad, 'shorter, younger and more determined to be a man than any there', sent to Pooglui Camp in *Twelve Good Men And True*.

Pelling, James Sidney. Wealthy retired colonel of the Royal Welsh Greys, who some twenty years after World War II misremembers shared wartime adventures during a chance encounter in *It Must Have Been Two Other Fellows*.

Pembroke, Roland. RAF navigator aboard the Lancaster 'Joe for King' in *Bomber*. A public-school-educated young Scot, he returns from the trip over Germany to spring a surprise twenty-first birthday party for skipper Tommy Carter—unaware that the raid went terribly wrong.

Pepper, Kit. Mid-upper gunner aboard the RAF Lancaster 'S for Sugar' in *Bomber*. Struggling to open the fuselage door after the plane is holed by Christian Himmel, his body is atomised into a spray of red foam as the Luftwaffe pilot presses home his attack.

Peterson, Bernard Thomas. Thin neurotic Englishman living in Albufeira under the Portuguese name of Fernie Tomas in *Horse Under Water*. A former Royal Navy officer, who was captured and turned by the Nazis during World War II, he's revealed to be an active partner in Harry Kondit's narcotics operation and willing 'gofer' for Manuel da Cunha—until shot by Kondit after making a full confession to the narrator.

Peterson, Flying Officer Roddy. Canadian pilot of the RAF Lancaster 'Q for Queen' in *Bomber*, who spends a good part of the raid squatting over the Elsan in the rear of the plane, his bowel movements seeming to drain the life out of him.

Petzval, Herr. Bearded young Jewish physicist in *Winter*, who commits suicide in Vienna at the turn of the century after Count Kupka employs secret influence to prevent his joining the German arms manufacturer Krupp.

Phelan, Major Kevin. Amiable Irish-American USAF Operations Officer at Steeple Thaxted in *Goodbye Mickey Mouse*. The fact that he's also a flyer is appreciated by the pilots he despatches on mission after mission to the flak-filled skies over Germany.

'Phelanski's Irish Rose'. USAF P-51 Mustang piloted by the 220th's Ops. Officer, Kevin Phelan, in *Goodbye Mickey Mouse*.

'**Pig Iron**'. Moscow Centre's assignment code for their deep penetration agent, Fiona Samson, in the *Game, Set & Match* trilogy.

Pike, Dr Felix. Impeccably groomed Latvian émigré of about fifty-two in *Billion-Dollar Brain*, whose London medical practice provides masterly cover for his participation in Midwinter's subversive operations against his Soviet-occupied homeland.

Pike, Philippa. Wife of Dr Felix Pike, and a courier for the Facts for Freedom network in *Billion-Dollar Brain*. Sought by the Special Branch following her husband's detention by British Military Intelligence, she's expeditiously removed by WOOC(P) to Milan—guaranteeing her silence and future co-operation.

Pike, Ralph. Younger brother of Dr Felix Pike, a brilliant biochemist and fellow-member of the Facts for Freedom network in *Billion-Dollar Brain*. Infiltrated into Soviet Latvia, he's betrayed by Harvey Newbegin, then later arrested by Major Nogin in a carefully staged scene implicating the narrator in his betrayal.

'**Pilgrim**'. USAF P-51 Mustang piloted by Steeple Thaxted's station commander, Colonel Dan Badger, in *Goodbye Mickey Mouse*.

Piper, Alan. Diffident Oxford-educated Englishman who rises from colonial government service to a senior position within the wartime MI6 in *Winter*. A handsome man with curiously youthful features that earn him the nickname 'Boy', his chance introduction to the Winter family tempts Veronica Winter to betray her husband and abandon their passionless marriage.

Piper, Peter. Talented British film director reduced to running a shabby portrait studio in Nazi-occupied London in *SS–GB*, enlisted by Douglas Archer to secretly process the vital roll of film discovered at the scene of the Shepherd Market murder.

Pippert, Gerda. Fifty-six-year-old spinster and Altgarten schoolteacher in *Bomber*, whose mistaken invitation to join the Mayor's birthday celebrations planned for the night of the RAF raid is 'the most exciting prospect she can remember since her holiday in Heidelberg in 1938'.

Pitman, John Elroy. Retired US Army colonel implicated in the 1945 Kaiseroda robbery, whom Charles Stein entrusts to oversee the Swiss bank founded with the plundered Nazi gold in *XPD*. Distressed by the bank's one hundred million dollar loss at the hands of Peter Friedman, he suffers a fatal heart attack on a Swiss autoroute, ending MI6's search for the elusive Hitler Minutes.

PLAYBOY'S GUIDE TO A CONTINENTAL HOLIDAY. Essay in *Playboy* magazine, May 1968. Debuting as Travel Editor, Len Deighton offers intriguing itineraries for those bent on visiting the Iberian Peninsula, Italy and Scandinavia.

pocket litter. False documents carried by an agent to support an assumed identity—e.g. the Army service card, former residence card, passport and working papers, issued to Ralph Pike when infiltrated by the Facts for Freedom network into Soviet Latvia in *Billion-Dollar Brain*.

Poetsch, ———. American newspaper writer on assignment in West Berlin, whom Johnnie Vulkan finds holding court in the Hilton Hotel bar in *Funeral in Berlin*. After loudly declaring Truth to be 'the most potent weapon in the arsenal of freedom', he spins fantastic tales of being on the communists' black-list before his audience of wide-eyed tourists.

Poland. The country's erratic political fortunes, rooted in centuries of partitioning and the hostile reaction of powerful neighbours to Polish nationalism, is offered as the key to understanding Christian Stakowski—better known as Jay—in *The IPCRESS File*. '. . . Jay has seen governments come and go too often to place too much reliance on them. He remembers the Tsars; government by ignorance; Paderewski, government by gentle pianist; Pilsudski, the general who won the brilliant battle of Warsaw in 1920, and smashed the new Soviet Armies under Voroshilov. He remembers the dictator who seized power by shouting, "This is a whorehouse, all get out," to Parliament. He remembers the government who followed Hitler's example in 1938 by grabbing a piece of Czechoslovakia by force. He remembers the Nazis, and then, after the war, the protégés of London and Moscow fighting each other for power . . .'

Its postwar fate under communist rule is said in *Berlin Game* to have persuaded Jan Kar to open a chess club for fellow expatriates in London when he realised he'd never return to his homeland, while Latvian Roman Catholics in *Billion-Dollar Brain* habitually refer to themselves as 'Poles' after the persecution of the Polish church, and the activities of the KGB's Religious Affairs Bureau—Section 44—are briefly touched on during Erich Stinnes's debriefing in *London Match*.

Porton MRE. Britain's top-secret Microbiological Research Establishment figures in several of the early novels. One of its top biochemists (Raven) is abducted in *The IPCRESS File*; it is said to be keen to acquire the Soviet enzyme scientist Semitsa in *Funeral in Berlin*; and batches of virus-injected hens' eggs are stolen from its laboratories by members of the Facts for Freedom network in *Billion-Dollar Brain*.

Portugal. Principal setting for *Horse Under Water*, at a time when dictators ruled both Portugal (Salazar) and Spain (Franco). 'Portugal is a semi-tropical land; cared-for, cultivated and geometrical. This is not Spain, with leather-hatted civil guards brandishing their nicely oiled automatic rifles every few scorched yards. It's a subtle land, without sign of Salazar on poster or postage stamp.'

'Posh Harry'. Pristine American active on the fringes of the intelligence community in *London Match*. A former CIA employee, he spends half his life on planes and has no address except hotels, shared offices and box numbers. The chosen conduit for the KGB 'float' incriminating Bret Rensselaer as a Soviet mole, he is later used by Bernard Samson to set up the dramatic Stinnes/Volkmann exchange in West Berlin.

Poster, Karl. Tall distinguished-looking New York businessman, 'the type they cast as unfaithful husbands in Italian films that get banned by the League of Decency', in *Only When I Larf*. A partner in the Funfunn Novelty Company, he takes his life by jumping from the top of a building near Wall Street after losing a quarter of a million dollars to the trio of British confidence tricksters.

Prague. Briefly visited by the narrator in *Funeral in Berlin* to interview survivors of the Treblinka concentration camp, in his quest to learn more about the fate of the enigmatic Paul Louis Broum. 'If anyone ever decided to illustrate Hans Andersen with photographs he would start in Prague. The heights of the city are a fairy tale of spikey spires . . .'

Preston, Richard. Twenty-one-year-old 'new wave' director in *Close-Up*, whose film theories learnt from books prove no match for the wiles of Hollywood star Marshall Stone, during the shooting of *Stool Pigeon*.

'The Princess'. Ageing and powdery French *madame* in *Yesterday's Spy*, who continues to run the decrepit flophouse in Nice which once served as a safe house for the Guernica Network during World War II.

prisons. The narrator escapes from a Hungarian one in *The IPCRESS File*—to discover suburban London is just over the wall (a moment vividly realised in the film). Prison life is recalled by Fernie Tomas in *Horse Under Water* and Bob Appleyard in *Only When I Larf*, is endured by Charles Bonnard in *Yesterday's Spy* to win the confidence of Steve Champion, and survived by Lottie

Winter in Nazi Berlin in *Winter*. The most dramatic prison setting is certainly the Tower of London, used by the Germans to hold King George VI following the Nazi occupation of Britain in *SS–GB*.

THE PRIVATE ARMIES. Illustrated essay by Len Deighton, first published in *The Sunday Times Magazine*, 17 September 1967, in which he recalls the work of the Long Range Desert Group and the Special Air Service in the North African campaigns during World War II. One of two essays by Deighton published in *El Alamein and the Desert War*.

private detectives twice make the breakthrough that eludes British Intelligence. Waterman certainly earns his eight guinea fee after spotting the narrator's 'Hungarian' warder, Swainson, entering Dalby's house in *The IPCRESS File*, and Hugo Koch merits every penny of his MI6 retainer when he salvages the Hitler Minutes from Colonel Pitman's wrecked Jaguar on a Swiss autoroute in *XPD*.

quiz. Fifty questions, all of which derive from entries in this book. Many of them will fox you; some of the answers may surprise you.

1. Which novel was to have been called 'A Subtle Smell of Agony'?
2. How many characters appear in all four novels, *Berlin Game*, *Mexico Set*, *London Match* and *Winter*—two? three? or four?
3. In which novel does Margaret Thatcher make a brief appearance?
4. Who was originally chosen to play Harry Palmer in the film *The Ipcress File*, but instead accepted a leading role in *The Sound of Music*?
5. Name the German industrial town chosen as the primary target in *Bomber*, whose fate is spared when the TI markers fall on Altgarten.
6. Identify the odd one out: Earls Court Exhibition Hall, the Royal Albert Hall, the Royal Festival Hall, and Wembley Stadium. The answer lies in Deighton's work.
7. Who is said to have aided the defection of the Foreign Office spies, Burgess and Maclean, in 1951?
8. Who exposes a prized Soviet defector as a KGB provocateur, but is then told he's lucky 'not to be facing grave charges'— Boyd Stuart, Bernard Samson, or the narrator of *The IPCRESS File*?
9. In which city do Edmond Dorf and Captain Maylev meet to arrange a funeral?
10. Name the unknown English actor launched to stardom in the Hollywood western 'The Last Vaquero'.

11. Unscramble the anagram EMBRANDINE to form the name of a character in *Mexico Set*.
12. In which novel are the bones of Karl Marx disinterred from London's Highgate Cemetery?
13. Which novel has the name of a chess opening as its title?
14. What innocent pastime does Madame Tastevin describe as 'a voyage of destruction'?
15. Who accepts an invitation to a business meeting over dinner in Venice, only to wake up in a wooden hut in South Carolina?
16. What is said to be 'the key to WOOC(P)'s reputation'?
17. Identify the odd one out: Frederick Antony, Patrick Armstrong, Charles Bonnard, Harry Palmer, Bernard Samson.
18. Who is parachuted into Nazi-occupied Britain in 1941 to inform the British Resistance that King George VI will *not* be welcome in North America?
19. Identify the member of the Nazi Sicherheitsdienst in *Winter*, who whiles away his days playing bridge with Lisl Hennig in *Mexico Set* and *London Match*.
20. In how many of Deighton's novels does New York appear as a setting—three, four, or five?
21. Who is said to have been run by British *and* Egyptian Intelligence, until he exceeded London's brief and sold classified NATO wavelengths to Cairo?
22. Where is Stalin's son rumoured to be held, following his capture by the Germans on the Eastern Front during World War II?
23. Which is Deighton's shortest novel?
24. Which is his longest novel?
25. Who had a face-to-face encounter with whom at Brûly de Pesche in June 1940?
26. What was taken over by the War Office in 1940 and, like so many other good things seized temporarily by the government, never returned to its former owners?
27. Who murders his wife and her alleged American lover on 'Bad Monday'—Sergeant Major Reg Hardcastle, Sergeant Brand, or Major Albert Dodgson?

28. Where can one find the yellow submarine moored?

29. Who does Frank Harrington describe as 'the Martin Bormann of London South West One'?

30. In which year was *The IPCRESS File* first published—1961, 1962, or 1963?

31. Deighton put aside a novel about a mining company which attempts to restore a tribal chief to his African throne by financing a military coup. In which of his *published* novels does an ambitious African politician plan a similar putsch?

32. Which of these characters appears in only one novel—Alice Bloom, Major Mickey Mann, Colonel Alexeyevitch Stok, Harvey Newbegin?

33. In which country does the narrator of *The IPCRESS File* rescue a Raven, but the Honourable Gerald Spencer lose his bird?

34. Name one of the two James Bond films for which Deighton wrote a draft screenplay.

35. Which female character in the *Game, Set & Match* trilogy does Bernard Samson describe as 'having the coil-spring energy and short fuse of the self-made opportunist'?

36. Which World War II battle does Deighton suggest was 'a pivotal point of the history of this century'?

37. At whose birthday party do the guests include Humphrey Bogart, Ava Gardner, Gregory Peck and Dick Powell?

38. In which short story does Herman Göring appear as the leading character?

39. What fate links Karl Poster in *Only When I Larf*, Douglas Reid-Kennedy in *Twinkle, Twinkle, Little Spy*, Captain Charles Stigg in *Goodbye Mickey Mouse* and Simon Danziger in *Winter*?

40. Identify the document said to reveal Britain's most closely guarded wartime secret—'The Berlin System', 'The Hitler Minutes', or 'The Weiss List'?

41. How many of Deighton's novels have been filmed?

42. What does Silas Gaunt describe as 'the art of the possible' in *Berlin Game*, an art at which Deighton is himself considerably skilled?

43. Which of these cities manifestly doesn't belong: Chicago, Los Angeles, New York, Paris, San Antonio, Washington?

44. Match these ten characters and ten stories: (1) Oberleutnant August Bach; (2) Dicky Cruyer; (3) Colonel Ross; (4) Monsieur Datt; (5) General Midwinter; (6) Harvey Newbegin; (7) Albert Sampson; (8) Colonel Charles Schlegel; (9) Colonel Alexeyevitch Stok; (10) Jacob Weinberger. *Berlin Game* ( ); *Billion-Dollar Brain* ( ); *Bomber* ( ); *Bonus for a Salesman* ( ); *Close-Up* ( ); *An Expensive Place to Die* ( ); *Funeral in Berlin* ( ); *The IPCRESS File* ( ); *Spy Story* ( ); *Yesterday's Spy* ( ).

45. Unscramble the anagram SANDCHIVE to form the name of the narrator's constant friend in *The IPCRESS File*.

46. Who finds it necessary to find a way of proving his real name, after having assumed the identity of a Waffen-SS concentration camp guard—Paul Louis Broum, Max Breslow, or Johnnie Vulkan?

47. In which film of one of Deighton's spy novels does Michael Caine's brother make a brief appearance?

48. Name the two estranged brothers reunited at the IMT war crimes trial in Nuremberg in 1945.

49. Who was in the sixth form at school in Burnley in 1940?

50. In which novel does the CIA deliberately set out to leak classified nuclear fall-out data to the Chinese government?

See answers on p. 327.

R

Radlett, Cynthia. Barmaid at the Bell public house, the RAF crews' local watering-hole in Little Warley in *Bomber*. In common with the other villagers, she finds life dramatically changed by the arrival of the noisy young airmen and their awesome machines that rattle the village window-panes like a thousand furies.

railway stations. An eerily deserted Pooglui Station awaits Sergeant Brand and his detachment of Royal Fusiliers, after the evacuation of the villagers in *Twelve Good Men And True*. In *Yesterday's Spy*, Charles Bonnard sleeps rough among the dossers on Waterloo Station until recruited by 'the Bishop', and later recalls Steve Champion's arrest by the Gestapo at Nice's railway terminus during World War II. London's Nine Elms marshalling yard is the setting for Douglas Archer's unexpected encounter with Reichsführer-SS Heinrich Himmler in *SS–GB*; producer Max Breslow reveals plans to drape Los Angeles' Union Station with fifty-foot tall swastika banners for his proposed film in *XPD*; the ruins of Berlin's famous Anhalter Bahnhof ('Even now old-time Berliners walk out there to look at that slab of broken masonry and fancy they can hear the trains') are chosen by Werner Volkmann for a clandestine rendezvous in *Berlin Game*; a former West Berlin Hochbahn station is the setting for the gun-fight at the climax of *London Match*; and London's Charing Cross and Waterloo stations are the targets of Peter Winter's Zeppelin raid during World War I in *Winter*.

See also: trains.

Rainbow, Ingrid. Aspiring twenty-five-year-old Hollywood ingénue, mother of Marshall Stone's illegitimate daughter Suzy Delft, in *Close-Up*. Paid off by the Koolman Studio in a move to protect their investment in new star Stone, she dies shortly afterwards in a mystifying accident on the San Jorge turnpike.

Rau, Fritz. Frail respected German scientist and businessman, the only member of the Trust to question the violence associated with Operation Siegfried in *XPD*.

'Raven'. WOOC(P)'s cryptonym for the Porton warfare biochemist kidnapped in *The IPCRESS File*, whose disappearance leads the narrator into a labyrinthine investigation of brain-washing and treachery.

The Red Admiral. The player commanding Soviet forces during war-games designed to test NATO defence strategies at the Studies Centre (STUCEN) in *Spy Story*. It's a role usually taken by Ferdy Foxwell, but efforts to secure the defection of a real, live 'Red Admiral', draw Patrick Armstrong into a cunning British Intelligence operation masterminded by his former boss, George Dawlish. (*The Red Admiral* was the novel's pre-publication title.)

The Red Suite. Basement quarters for the Red Admiral and his Red Ops staff at the Studies Centre, in *Spy Story*. Like the opposing Blue Suite upstairs, it receives only the results of reports and analysis, for neither side is permitted access to the big War Table displaying the true state of the game in progress. And since the teams may be locked in battle for several days, the Suite has bedrooms, bathrooms, a well-stocked bar and a sentry to make sure nobody tries to sneak a look at that Table.

Redenbacher, Major Peter. Tough, thirty-three-year-old commander of the Luftwaffe night-fighter airfield at Kroonsdijk in *Bomber*. A barnstorming veteran credited with forty-six victories, he breaks every rule in the book for his men, but is powerless to prevent Himmel's arrest for treason by the Abwehr.

Reichssicherheitshauptamt (RSHA). Formed in 1939 as one of twelve SS administrations, the Reich Central Security Office combined the government's Sicherheitspolizei (the Gestapo and the Kripo) with the Nazi Party's own intelligence service, the Sicherheitsdienst. Although employees of the former continued to be paid by the state, and the latter by the Party, it marked a further step in the realisation of Reinhard Heydrich's ambition to unify all Germany's intelligence services under SS (and thus Party) control.

Sipo Untersturmführer Feldwebel Blessing, detective Theodor Steiner, senior Gestapo administrator Paul Winter and SD officials Lothar Koch and SS-Standartenführer Oskar Huth, all represent the interests of the RSHA, as did Willi Kleiber during the war.

Reid-Kennedy, Douglas. Wealthy American electronics manufacturer, with a major off-stage role in *Twinkle, Twinkle, Little Spy*. A member of the Communist Party since his schooldays and talent-spotted by Moscow Centre while serving with the US Army in Berlin in the mid-1950s, his suicide on the eve of his arrest leads Major Mann and the narrator to identify Gerry Hart as a Soviet agent.

Reid-Kennedy, Marjorie. Common-law name taken by Marjorie Dean, estranged wife of Hank Dean and longtime companion of Douglas Reid-Kennedy, in *Twinkle, Twinkle, Little Spy*.

Reinecke, Stabsfeldwebel Willi. Elderly thickset second-in-command at the Luftwaffe coastal radar station 'Ermine' in *Bomber*. In that curious way that happens sometimes to people with contrasting beliefs and backgrounds, he enjoys a close relationship with his commander, August Bach.

Relay, Dutch. Twenty-four-year-old black American GI in *First Base*, who dies in the urban jungle recreated by Des Jones in an abandoned SAC airbase in war-torn Vietnam.

Remoziva, Katerina. Thin elderly spinster leading the Soviet delegation at the German reunification talks in *Spy Story*. Her arrest by the KGB—in an act of collective family responsibility for the apparent attempt by her brother to defect to the West—brings about the collapse of the talks and the realisation of Dawlish's masterly spoiling operation.

Remoziva, Rear-Admiral Vanya. Ailing Soviet Chief of Staff, Northern Fleet, framed by British Intelligence as a defector in *Spy Story*. The expendable pawn in Dawlish's cunning plot to sabotage German reunifications talks—talks opposed by the British Foreign Office—at which Remoziva's sister heads the key Soviet delegation.

Renseignements Généraux. The French police service responsible for monitoring the activities of foreigners and political militants, whose resources are often called upon by the DST, France's counter-intelligence and domestic security agency.

The narrator of *An Expensive Place to Die* shrewdly elicits an undertaking from Claude Loiseau—a Chief Inspector in the rival Sûreté Nationale—to shield him from the Renseignements Généraux after reluctantly agreeing to break into Datt's Avenue Foch Clinic. But in *Yesterday's Spy*, Charles Bonnard enjoys no such protection as he narrowly escapes death at the hands of RG Inspector Fabre—a handsome youth in his mid-twenties, belatedly identified as an expensive Swiss hit-man hired by Steve Champion.

Rensselaer, Bret. Rich Anglophile grandson of Dottie Turner, a senior British Intelligence officer with a leading role in the *Game, Set & Match* trilogy. A wily bureaucratic infighter, he survives the collapse of his power base within London Central following Brahms Four's escape to the West in *Berlin Game*, only to be framed as a Soviet mole by Erich Stinnes and then seriously injured during the fire-fight in the Berlin finale of *London Match*.

Rensselaer, Cyrus. Distinguished American millionaire, father of Veronica and Glenn Rensselaer in *Winter*. A self-made man, whose standing in New York business and social circles is due as much to his disarming directness and awkward charm as to his luck and financial skills. Unwilling to come to terms with the loss of his daughter to Harald Winter and Imperial Berlin's oppressive salons, he dies aged ninety-three consoled by the knowledge that he's outlived his son-in-law.

Rensselaer, Dottie. *See* Dottie Turner.

Rensselaer, Glenn. Genial cosmopolitan son of New York businessman Cyrus Rensselaer in *Winter*. Devoted to his two nephews, he conforms in every way to the homespun German image of the 'rich *Onkel* from America', frequently visiting his sister in Berlin bearing gifts and news from across the Atlantic. Early to see the threat in Hitler's rise to power and the spread of Nazism, he plays an active role in American and British intelligence operations following the outbreak of war.

Rensselaer, Veronica. *See* Veronica Winter.

reporters endowed with a major role, both against a background of World War II, are the American correspondent Barbara Barga in *SS–GB*, and the Australian-born freelance Henry Scrimshaw in *Goodbye Mickey Mouse*. A pretentious American newspaper writer named Poetsch is encountered in *Funeral in Berlin*, John Koby's days as a streetwise journalist in Berlin are recalled by Bernard Samson in *London Match*, unnamed reporters figure briefly in *Close-Up* and *Goodbye Mickey Mouse*, while the narrators of *Billion-Dollar Brain* and *An Expensive Place to Die* and Charles Bonnard in *Yesterday's Spy* all at times use the profession as cover.

Resident. *See* Berlin Station.

restaurants and **cafés** with a dramatic significance of one kind or another include Leds coffee-house in *The IPCRESS File*, where the narrator first approaches Jay with an offer to buy back Raven; Riga's Luna Café in *Billion-Dollar Brain*, where the narrator unwittingly sets in motion the arrest of Ralph Pike; Le

Petit Legionnaire in *An Expensive Place to Die*, where the narrator first encounters Monsieur Datt; Frenzel's Stube in *Bomber*, patronised by Altgarten's most important citizens; the Terrine du Chef in *Spy Story*, whose cold room is used to store the corpse to be substituted for Rear-Admiral Remoziva; Madame Mauring's Geneva tea room in *XPD*, where Charles Stein caches the Hitler Minutes; the Café Leuschner in *Berlin Game* and *London Match*, chosen by Bernard Samson and Werner Volkmann for various clandestine meetings; Vienna's Café Stoessl, where Harald Winter finds Petzval awaiting him on New Year's Eve 1899, and pre-war Berlin's Romanisches Café, where the marriage is sealed between Paul Winter and Inge Wisliceny, in *Winter*.

In *The IPCRESS File* and *Billion-Dollar Brain* we find the narrator an habitué of Mario and Franco's Trattoria Terrazza, one of London's 'in' restaurants during the 1960s and whose menu is said to have been used as the model for most of London's Italian restaurants. Some twenty years later, Mario's new London restaurant is visited by longtime friend Bernard Samson in *London Match*.

Other well-known restaurants visited or referred to include London's Chez Solange, the Mirabelle, the Savoy and Wiltons, Fouquets's in Paris and the Weinrestaurant Ganymed in East Berlin.

Reuter, Oberzugführer Peter. Middle-aged German Teno officer 'looking more like an art critic than a pioneer officer', with a minor role in *Bomber* restoring order to the havoc wreaked on Altgarten by the RAF bombers.

Rezident. The senior KGB officer stationed within each Soviet embassy—e.g. the Assistant Naval Attaché in Washington, Yuriy Grechko, in *XPD*.

Riga. Capital of the Soviet Federal Republic of Latvia, visited by the narrator in *Billion-Dollar Brain* after having been recruited into the Facts for Freedom network by Harvey Newbegin. 'Latvia—or at least Riga—is more sophisticated than Leningrad or

Moscow. If you ask for breakfast in your room they have difficulty in understanding the idea, but they will do it. A suggestion like that in Leningrad is subversive.'

Riley, Ted. Former British Intelligence Corps captain under the command of Brian Samson in postwar Berlin, ordered by Bret Rensselaer in *London Match* to break into the Cambridge Network's safe house—a foolhardy decision that costs Riley his life.

robberies. Cairo's plan to convince Israel it is in possession of stolen French atomic artillery shells lies at the heart of *Yesterday's Spy*, while the hijacking of Nazi gold and secret papers from a wartime convoy provides the starting-point for *XPD*. Minor incidents with a bearing on the plot include Ossie Butterworth's skilful appropriation of Manuel da Cunha's radio transmitter in *Horse Under Water*, the theft of virus-injected hens' eggs from Porton MRE and the plundering of a Soviet military supply truck in *Billion-Dollar Brain*, and the theft of classified American fall-out data from the narrator's Paris apartment in *An Expensive Place to Die*. Robbery with violence appears to lie behind Serge Frankel's death in *Yesterday's Spy*, but doesn't.

Ross, Colonel. Senior officer in British Military Intelligence, and the narrator's former boss in *The IPCRESS File*. Having dismissed him as a colourless and unimaginative time-server ('People like Ross always gave me a bad time. If I was pally with them I hated myself; when I rowed with them I felt guilty for enjoying it'), Ross saves the narrator's life and masterminds the operation that nets Dalby and the IPCRESS Network.

The Royal Air Force. On 1 April 1918, Britain's Royal Flying Corps and the Royal Naval Air Service were merged into a single, independent service, under the command of General Sir Hugh Trenchard. A history of the service from its inception to its 'finest hour' in the summer of 1940, is lucidly presented in *Fighter* and *Battle of Britain*, while the RAF at war is fictionally portrayed in the short stories *Action*, *Adagio* and *Brent's Deus Ex Machina*, and notably in Deighton's classic work of fiction *Bomber*.

von Ruff, Generalmajor Georg. The senior Abwehr officer in Nazi-occupied Britain in *SS–GB*, whose desire to strike at the prestige of SS-Gruppenführer Kellerman and to deny the SS the opportunity of developing its own atomic research programme, results in the Abwehr's surprising complicity in King George VI's escape from the Tower of London.

Ruysdale, Lieutenant. Cover name provided for the mysterious European physicist, who alone amongst the party landed at Bringle Sands in *SS–GB* knows the importance of the raid in which American lives are sacrificed. Remarkably calm amid the fighting, he supervises the demolition of the Research Establishment's installations, before escorting the aged Professor Frick to the safety of the landing craft.

Ryden, Sir Sydney. Elderly Director General of Britain's MI6 in *XPD*. A man who revels in the lies and deceptions of his craft, he has strong personal grounds for wishing to suppress the Hitler Minutes and safeguard Britain's greatest wartime secret. For, using the cover name of Elliot Castlebridge, he was personally entrusted by Winston Churchill to deliver to Hitler his rejection of the peace terms proposed at their clandestine conference of June 1940.

Ryessman, Walter. Altgarten's fifty-three-year-old Mayor in *Bomber*. After breaking off his birthday celebrations, he copes manfully at the outset of the RAF raid on the town, but is later found entombing himself with rubble on the site of his wrecked home.

S

'S for Sugar'. RAF Lancaster bomber skippered by Flight Lieutenant Sweet, shot down over Altgarten in *Bomber*. Other named crew members are Flight Sergeant Mickey Murphy (flight engineer), Billy Pace (navigator, and only survivor), Kit Pepper (upper gunner) and Sergeant 'Pip' Speke (bomb aimer).

Sachs, Feldwebel Georg. Löwenherz's timid nineteen-year-old radar operator aboard his Ju88 night-fighter in *Bomber*. Armed with the sort of luck that life has always provided for this rich young man, he follows Mrosek out of the doomed plane and makes a perfect descent into occupied Holland.

'sacred'. The slug entered in the NATO computer by Bernard Samson to indicate London Central's priority interest in Paul Biedermann in *Mexico Set*. Done as a favour after he expresses fears for his safety, it has unforeseen consequences for Samson when Biedermann is detained at Charles de Gaulle airport on suspicion of being a KGB courier.

Sadoff, Major Nikolai. Hard-eyed Soviet KGB officer with the work name of Erich Stinnes, who emerges as Bernard Samson's main adversary in the *Game, Set & Match* trilogy. Of a similar age, and sharing the experience of a childhood spent in early postwar Berlin, he materialises as the principal player in a cunning KGB provocation intended to discredit Samson and wreak havoc within London Central.

safe houses. Intelligence parlance for secure meeting places, such as the KGB's 10th Street apartment in New York used by Edward Parker and Willi Kleiber in *XPD*, and London Central's accommodation over a betting shop in Kilburn High Road, chosen by Bernard Samson for a meeting with Giles Trent in *Berlin Game*—both, incidentally, revealed to be insecure. Sometimes they're used to accommodate defectors: thus the CIA's Washington Square townhouse is provided for Professor Bekuv in *Twinkle, Twinkle, Little Spy*, and London Central's Notting Hill Gate apartment is chosen in preference to the London Debriefing Centre for Erich Stinnes in *London Match*. And in *XPD* they're shown to be a convenient place to hold a hostile interrogation when Boyd Stuart detains Billy Stein in an MI6 safe house in London's Pentonville Road, and Edward Parker works over Charles Stein in the KGB's Beverly Hills mansion, 'Bronwyn'.

William Spode is murdered in one in *SS–GB*, as is Julian MacKenzie in *Mexico Set*, and Ted Riley dies after entering the Cambridge Network's booby-trapped safe house in *London Match*. A flophouse in Nice is said to have been used as one by the Guernica Network in *Yesterday's Spy*, but Major Mann declines to accommodate Professor Bekuv in a second safe house ('You might as well take a small-ad in Pravda') following the shooting incident at Tony Nowak's party in *Twinkle, Twinkle, Little Spy*.

Sampson, Albert. Author of the letter in *Bonus for a Salesman*. A former English arms salesman, he recalls how while on a regular sales trip to Latin America in the 1920s he found a local revolution a means of surprising self-advancement—to President of the unnamed country.

(Deighton deliberately took the character's name, with altered spelling, for the hero of *Game, Set & Match*, because he felt that *Bonus for a Salesman* had just the sort of first person energy he wanted for the spy trilogy.)

Samson, Bernard. The narrator and protagonist of the *Game, Set & Match* trilogy. A fortyish British Intelligence officer, son of one-time Berlin Resident Brian Samson, who is summoned back into the field after five years behind a desk when Brahms Four demands to be brought to safety in the face of mounting evidence of treachery within London Central. With Fiona exposed as the KGB mole following her hurried flight to East Berlin, the subsequent conflict between the British and Soviet intelligence services becomes an intimate battle between separated man and wife.

Samson, Brian. Intense young MI6 field agent in *Winter*, whose lack of background and education plainly rules out a career in the snobbish higher echelons of SW1. Fluent in German, he's infiltrated into Nazi Germany and later, wartime Berlin, where he's joined by Peter Winter with orders to assist the anti-Hitler conspirators. Despite their common purpose they make an abrasive team, and when in 1945 Paul Winter absconds from Nuremberg, Samson rues the day he became acquainted with the Winter family.

His postwar assignment as Berlin Resident is frequently evoked in the *Game, Set & Match* trilogy, in which Bernard Samson may be judged to have inherited much of his father's intractable personality.

Samson, Fiona. Rich well-bred wife of Bernard Samson, a senior intelligence officer in London Central until identified by her husband as a Moscow Centre mole in *Berlin Game*. Forced to flee to East Berlin, she wreaks further damage on British Intelligence in *Mexico Set* and *London Match*, masterminding the KGB operation to discredit first Bernard, and later Bret Rensselaer.

San Antonio. The Texas border town where the narrator narrowly escapes arrest at the scene of Signor Fragoli's murder in *Billion-Dollar Brain*. 'Lighted shops painted yellow patches on the pavement and huddles of men stood here and there talking, arguing and gambling. The shop lights illuminated them as though they were valuable items on display in a museum. There was a curious all-enveloping blueness that nights in the tropics have, and on the air was the sweet smell of cumin and hot chilli.'

Sanchez, Phil. Leo Koolman's hatchet-man—inherited from his uncle Max—who proves an important factor in the continuity of the Koolman empire in *Close-Up*.

Sanderson, Mrs. Guthrie Grey's housekeeper in *Only When I Larf*, who finds her employer beaten unconscious by Ali Lin's security agents, following the exposure of Awawa's planned bid for the throne.

'Saracen'. Cryptonym for the former STUCEN employee Mason, assigned by Dawlish in *Spy Story* to monitor Ben Toliver's attempt to secure the defection of Soviet Rear-Admiral Remoziva.

SARDINIA: ITALY'S ALABASTER ISLE. Essay in *Playboy* magazine, December 1968. Len Deighton's final report as Travel Editor offers a hard-eyed look at the jet-set haven.

Schlegel, Colonel Charles. Irascible CIA-trained former Marine Corps officer appointed to run STUCEN in *Spy Story*, then seconded to British Intelligence in *Yesterday's Spy*. Short and thickset 'with that puffed-chest stance that small athletes have', he relishes generating an air of uncertainty but succeeds in earning the grudging respect of his assistants Patrick Armstrong and Charles Bonnard.

Schlegel, Helen. Wife of Charles Schlegel, a New Englander 'with all the crisp assurance of that canny breed', who makes a brief appearance in *Spy Story*.

Schneider, Dr Franz. Said in *Winter* to be Vienna's richest and most successful gynaecologist. A small white-faced man, plump in the way babies are plump, who in the early hours of 1 January 1900, is summoned to deliver the 'child of the new century', Paul Winter.

Schutzstaffel (SS). Formed in 1925 as Hitler's personal bodyguard, the black-uniformed troopers were transformed by

Himmler into a militarily trained and ruthless NSDAP elite. A state within the state, with its own intelligence service, the Sicherheitsdienst, and military arm, the Waffen-SS, it was responsible for setting up and running the concentration camps, and became the most feared and powerful organisation in Nazi Germany and occupied Europe.

SS officers are a disturbing presence in the small German country town of Altgarten in *Bomber*, the organisation casts a giant shadow over Nazi-occupied Britain in *SS–GB* and inevitably figures in *Winter*. Serving officers include SS-Obersturmführer Berger, SS-Sturmbannführer Adolf Fischer, SS-Standartenführer Oskar Huth, SS-Gruppenführer Fritz Kellerman and SS-Standartenführer Wörth. Professor Max Springer, Altgarten's mayor Walter Ryessman and Paul Winter are all made honorary members. Heinrich Brand serves in its military arm, as did Max Breslow and Johnnie Vulkan.

Scotland Yard. London's celebrated former metropolitan police headquarters is depicted under Nazi control, against a background of a defeated and occupied Britain, in *SS–GB*. A genial SS-Gruppenführer has replaced the Commissioner, his powers extending over the whole country, and senior police officers are torn between their sympathy for the resistance movement and their instinctive desire to get on with their work, carefully distancing themselves from the Gestapo and the SD, housed in the same building.

scrambler phones alter the frequencies of transmitted speech to make it unintelligible to eavesdroppers. The most widely available system is the NSA's unit STU-II, which looks like a telephone attached to a small xerox machine. However, the increasing use of cordless phones, and satellite and microwave communications, has hastened the Agency's development of a smaller, easier to use, and cheaper system.

Colonel Schlegel impresses Charles Bonnard with a portable acoustic coupler fitted with an encryption device in *Yesterday's Spy*, while a cautious Boyd Stuart speaks to his contact clerk in Los

Angeles using 'crypto-ciph B' to prevent US Intelligence learning of MI6's anxieties about the Hitler Minutes in *XPD*.

screenplays. Deighton wrote and co-produced *Oh! What a Lovely War* (1969), based on Joan Littlewood's stage musical of the same name, and wrote early drafts of the screenplays for the James Bond films *From Russia With Love* (1963) and *Never Say Never Again* (1983). He's also written one original television play, *Long Past Glory*, produced by Britain's ABC Television in November 1963.

Scrimshaw, Henry. Australian-born veteran freelance reporter in *Goodbye Mickey Mouse*. After securing an exclusive story with American fighter ace Mickey Morse, he's frozen out by the Air Force top brass, who fear their public image will be tarnished by revelations of Morse's affair with Vera Hardcastle.

Scroll, Colonel 'Duke'. Thirty-nine-year-old Executive Officer of the 220th Fighter Group in *Goodbye Mickey Mouse*. A West Point man, pedantic, precise and very hard to please, he's faced with one of the toughest decisions of his career when Jamie Farebrother is trapped in the wreckage of his Mustang on Steeple Thaxted's only serviceable runway.

The Secret Intelligence Service. *See* MI6.

Security Grade Ones (S1s). Important chemists, physicists, electronics engineers, political advisers, etc.—people considered essential to the running of Great Britain—whose movements are analysed by Carswell in *The IPCRESS File* in a statistical analysis of factors common to the disappearance of Raven and other top biochemists.

The Security Service. *See* MI5.

Semitsa, ———. Distinguished Soviet scientist, allegedly under threat of a ten-year prison sentence following an investigation at the Minsk Biochemical Laboratories, whom Colonel Stok offers to sell to WOOC(P) in *Funeral in Berlin*. An elaborate mock funeral procession is set up by Johnnie Vulkan and the Gehlen Bureau for his covert transfer at Checkpoint Charlie, but the narrator soon finds that Stok and Vulkan are not above double-crossing him, and each other.

Sepp, Oberst Max. Plump white-haired friend of August Bach, on the staff of the military governor of the Netherlands, in *Bomber*. Troubled by Sepp's fatalistic reflections on love and the war, Bach subsequently learns he's been ordered to the Russian front—almost certain never to return.

Service de Documentation Extérieure et de Contre-Espionage (SDECE). The former name of France's foreign intelligence and espionage organisation, changed soon after President Mitterand's election in 1981 to the Direction Générale de Sécurité Extérieure (DGSE).

In *An Expensive Place to Die*, Monsieur Datt deliberately encourages speculation that his Avenue Foch 'pleasuredrome' is owned by the SDECE or the Ministry of the Interior, but neither rumour proves true.

Seymour, Sam. Small grey-haired CIA file editor, whose research establishes the critical linkage between Yuriy Grechko, Edward Parker and Willi Kleiber in *XPD*.

Shaw, Sara. Shapely blonde in her mid-twenties, caught up in Ben Toliver's fated attempt to secure the defection of Soviet Rear-Admiral Remoziva in *Spy Story*. Owner of the 'Terrine du Chef', her restaurant's cold store serves as a temporary cache for the corpse to be placed in the simulated helicopter crash to cover Remoziva's disappearance.

Sheenan, Mrs. Warm-hearted Londoner who provides lodgings for displaced widower Douglas Archer and his young son in *SS–GB*, and subsequently supplies a key lead to the whereabouts of Dr John Spode, brother of the Shepherd Market murder victim.

'sheep-dipped'. Personnel (especially military) provided with assumed identities for a clandestine operation to conceal the participation of their agency. Widely practised by the CIA (e.g. the 1961 Bay of Pigs adventure), the term could also be applied to the US Marines involved in the attack on the Bringle Sands Research Establishment in *SS–GB*. For since America is not at war with Nazi Germany, they have been individually discharged from the Marine Corps and re-enlisted as Canadians in the British service.

Shelley, Colonel Lester. Dextrous US Eighth Air Force public relations officer in *Goodbye Mickey Mouse*. A pre-war Hollywood agent and publicist ('I mean this very sincerely, creating heroes in wartime is a lot like creating movie stars'), he manipulates the grounding of fighter ace Mickey Morse to ensure that 'Mr and Mrs America' get the clean-living young heroes they deserve.

Sherlock Holmes. The deductive powers of Conan Doyle's celebrated fictional detective are praised by KGB officer Erich Stinnes ('Holmes is my mentor') in *Berlin Game*, and analysed by longtime fan Len Deighton in his introductions to *The Valley of Fear* and *The Adventure of the Priory School*.
See also: Watson roles.

Shetland, Peter. Hard-eyed partner of Sydney Garin, who provides the aristocratic front for their flourishing art and antiques trade with the German occupation forces in *SS–GB*.

Shields, Sir John. Eminent British pathologist in *SS–GB*, summoned by SS-Standartenführer Huth to conduct the post-

mortem on Peter Thomas—a first measure of the importance the
Nazi Sicherheitsdienst attaches to the Shepherd Market murder
case.

short stories. Many writers enjoy the challenge of writing
them, but publishers are notoriously loth to publish them. Most
books of short stories are collections of pieces which have appeared
previously and at different times in magazines and newspapers.
Never one to conform, Deighton wrote twelve of the thirteen short
stories published together as *Declarations of War* in one go, from
start to finish. He was 'appalled' when his American publisher
decided to omit two of the stories from the US edition, published as
Eleven Declarations of War.

Shumuk, General Stanislav. The legendary head of the
KGB's Executive Action Department, who masterminds 'Task
Pogoni' in *XPD*. Reputedly willing to go to any extreme to provide
results, he wilfully sacrifices Willi Kleiber to British Intelligence to
secure Grechko's disgrace and Parker's safe conduct out of
America, following their failure to secure the Hitler Minutes.

Sicherheitsdienst (SD). The intelligence arm of the SS was
originally established to counter threats to the Nazi Party. With
Hitler's assumption of power in 1933 the Party's enemies became
enemies of the state and under the leadership of Reinhard
Heydrich the SD lost no time in building up an army of informers in
every sphere of German life. Often proving more effective and
dangerous than the Gestapo, it subsequently succeeded in
usurping a role in the governmental terrain of foreign intelligence
and in 1939 was combined with the Sicherheitspolizei in a new
hybrid agency, the Reichssicherheitshauptamt, headed by
Heydrich.

In *Winter*, former detective Lothar Koch is among Heydrich's
early recruits to the service at a time when it operates out of
Munich under the cover name of the *Presse und Informationsdienst*
since Nazi organisations are officially banned. And the SD's
ambition to seize for the SS the spoils of Britain's atomic research

programme lies at the heart of *SS–GB*, resulting in the hurried arrival in Nazi-occupied London of SS-Standartenführer Oskar Huth with orders to lead the Peter Thomas murder investigation.

Sicherheitspolizei (Sipo). The German state security police force, created in 1936 with the merger of the Gestapo and the Kripo (the Criminal Police). Three years later it was brought under the control of the SS, when combined with the Sicherheitsdienst to form the Reichssicherheitshauptamt.

Much to the surprise of his Luftwaffe colleagues at Kroonsdijk in *Bomber*, Feldwebel Blessing identifies himself as an employee of the RSHA with a Sipo rank of Untersturmführer and sets in motion the arrest of Christian Himmel for treason. Another employee is Theodor Steiner, the Gestapo detective whose investigation of a Jewish escape-line leads to the incarceration of Lottie Winter in *Winter*.

'Siegfried'. Cryptonym for the Trust's operation to secure and destroy the Hitler Minutes in *XPD*, which first comes to light when young computer hacker Paul Bock cracks the big new FRÜHLING computer installed by Dr Böttger's German bank.

SIGINT. Signals intelligence is more reliable than HUMINT, and somewhat less vulnerable to misinterpretation than PHOTINT. Pioneered by the French and the Austrians in the early 1900s, it played a major role in World War II, and is today the principal source of Western intelligence data. (The National Security Agency provides over two hundred tons of classified SIGINT material to its American masters every week!)

In *Berlin Game*, the abrupt change of Soviet military codes and wavelengths shortly after a successful British signals intercept, provides further damning evidence that London Central harbours a KGB mole.

Simms, Lieutenant Clive. Union Army officer in *Discipline*, who knowingly sacrifices four of Winkelstein's inexperienced infantrymen for knowledge of the enemy's forward positions.

Simpson, Inspector. Special Branch identity assumed by Lt.-Col. Harriman—since WOOC(P), like MI5, has no powers of arrest—as he and Chico snatch Dr Felix Pike in *Billion-Dollar Brain*.

Singleton, Lieutenant Clive. Twenty-six-year-old Assistant Naval Attaché at the British Embassy in Lisbon, seconded to Operation Alforreca in *Horse Under Water*. Initially unimpressed with his appearance, the narrator quickly finds his underwater clearance experience a considerable asset as they unlock the secrets of the wartime German U-boat lying off Albufeira.

SKIING: FROM A TO V. Essay in *Playboy* magazine, November 1968. Travel Editor Len Deighton reports on America's jet-set snow capitals, Aspen and Vail.

sleeper. A deep cover agent placed or recruited in hostile territory with orders to lie low until activated at a suitable moment—e.g. Dr Walter von Munte in *Berlin Game*. Recruited by Silas Gaunt in 1946, he was kept under wraps during the time the service was rotten with traitors, and then activated to become London Central's prime source of economic intelligence in East Germany.

Smith, Henry. Wealthy British Cabinet Minister, whose efforts to curtail Operation Alforreca in *Horse Under Water* are subsequently explained by his presence on the Weiss List and his active support of the neo-Nazi Young Europe Movement.

Soho, writes Deighton in *Len Deighton's London Dossier*, 'is London's most foreign quarter. Here is the greatest concentration of foreign food shops, restaurants and theatres. Here too are the striptease shows, as well as the confidence tricksters and petty criminals . . .' It is the cosmopolitan backcloth for scenes in *The IPCRESS File*, *Horse Under Water*, *Funeral in Berlin*, *Only When I Larf* and *Berlin Game*, and is the subject of Deighton's first published writing, *Abroad in London*.

'solitaries'. Soviet agents whose real loyalties are known to one or two people at the very top of the command structure, the only record of their assignment a signed contract locked into a safe in Moscow Centre—e.g. Erich Stinnes in the *Game, Set & Match* trilogy.

Sollerod. The village on the Danish island of Sjaelland, chosen by General Shumuk as the neutral location for his clandestine rendezvous with MI6 officer Boyd Stuart in *XPD*.

SOME NOTES ON INDIAN & PAKISTAN COOKING. Article by Len Deighton published in *Elephanta: 2* (1974), the journal of London's White Elephant Club. 'In fact, there is no such thing as Indian cookery,' writes Deighton. 'This vast land, larger than western Europe, with more than four thousand years of recorded history, landscape ranging from desert to jungle (to say nothing of the Himalayas), such widely differing religions that it is never truly at peace, climatic variations and some two thousand dialects—so different as to be almost separate languages—inevitably produced cooking styles as vividly different as its varieties of art, literature and music.'

Somerset, Val. Youthful English actor frequently linked with Suzy Delft in *Close-Up*, whose burgeoning career is stalled by resentful Hollywood star Marshall Stone.

Somló, Boris. Martha Somló's slow and lugubrious son, fathered by Harald Winter in *Winter*. Arrested during a Nazi round-up in Vienna, he escapes from the transport train to Auschwitz-Birkenau and makes his way to Berlin, where he finds sanctuary working alongside Dr Isaac Volkmann in the Jewish cemetery at Weissensee.

Somló, Martha. Harald Winter's petite mistress in *Winter*, whom he installs in a superb apartment on Vienna's Kärtnerstrasse. One of twelve children of a Jewish tailor, she's offered protection by Paul Winter during the Nazi *Anschluss* in

1938, but is later sacrificed by Paul to save his sister-in-law from the camps—a decision which leads to the final estrangement between father and son.

Sontag, Sonny. East End forger used by the narrator to run up a passport in the name of Dempsey, prior to his infiltration of the Facts for Freedom network in *Billion-Dollar Brain*. ('The first time I ever met Sonny he forged a Ministry of Works pass for me in the name of Peter Jolly. Since that day, with a faith in his own handiwork that typified him, he always called me Mr Jolly.')

Soviet Union. The bone-freezing core of winter in Leningrad and Riga is endured by the narrator in *Billion-Dollar Brain*, and Moscow provides a cheerless backdrop in *XPD*.

Stalin's accommodation with Hitler in the early years of World War II is marked in *SS–GB* with the ritualistic disinterment of the bones of Karl Marx from London's Highgate Cemetery following the Nazi occupation of Britain, while the authentic horrors of the war of attrition on the Eastern Front following Germany's invasion in June 1941 are endured by Alex Horner, von Kleindorf, Colonel Weizsäcker and Obergefreiter Winkel in *Winter* and remain uppermost in the minds of several characters in *Bomber*.

The postwar Sovietisation of Eastern Europe ('Between 1945 and 1950 the Reds expanded at the rate of sixty square miles per hour,' claims General Midwinter in *Billion-Dollar Brain*) and the response of the Western Powers to the threat posed by Soviet communism, is the contemporary context of *The IPCRESS File*, *Funeral in Berlin*, *Billion-Dollar Brain*, *Spy Story*, *Twinkle, Twinkle, Little Spy*, *XPD* and the *Game, Set & Match* trilogy.

Spanish Civil War (1936–39). An ideological battleground for a generation of Europeans, the conflict resulted in about a million casualties and widespread devastation. The insurgents, led by General Franco, enjoyed substantial aid from Nazi Germany and Italy, while the Republicans were assisted by Soviet advisers and technicians, and the International Brigades made up of volunteers drawn from many countries.

Several characters have grounds for recalling the War. Fernie Tomas and Major Peter Redenbacher both fought with Franco's forces; Serge Frankel and Gus first met while serving in the International Brigade and Liz Mason sadly recalls how her father also joined up with the Republicans ('Naturally he fought on the losing side'). Barbara Barga and Henry Scrimshaw both witnessed the conflict as war correspondents.

Spartakists. The radical German socialist group, led by Rosa Luxemburg and Karl Liebknecht, took its name from the leader of the slave revolt against Rome in 73 BC. Ostensibly founded as an anti-war movement, the group attempted to seize power in early 1919 and establish a 'free Socialist Republic of Germany'. The subsequent street battles in Berlin as the Freikorps took on the Spartakists are vividly portrayed in *Winter*, with Paul Winter and Fritz Esser entering the thick of the fighting alongside Captain Graf. On 13 January, the Spartakist leaders were finally captured and taken to the Eden Hotel for questioning. After being bundled into separate cars, Liebknecht was murdered in Berlin's Tiergarten and 'Red Rose' was shot through the head and her body then thrown into the Landeswehr Canal (an incident recalled by Bernard Samson in *London Match*). Now, in East Berlin, they name streets after them.

Special Branch. The arresting arm of MI5 was subject to unaccustomed publicity early in 1987 after its officers seized videotapes and documents relating to a proposed BBC television report about the British Government's Zircon spy satellite project. It comprises some 400 detectives attached to local police forces across the country, but is accountable to the Home Secretary through London's Metropolitan Police Commissioner.

A languid Special Branch detective named Blantyre is on hand when Charles Bonnard turns over Steve Champion's London hideaway in *Yesterday's Spy*. Another is encountered by Bernard Samson nosing around the Downing Street Whips Office in *London Match*. And both Lieutenant-Colonel Harriman and Chico impersonate SB officers when they snatch Dr Felix Pike in

Billion-Dollar Brain; a necessary if unlawful ruse since WOOC(P), like MI5, has no powers of arrest.

Speke, Sergeant 'Pip'. Eighteen-year-old RAF bomb-aimer aboard the Lancaster 'S for Sugar' in *Bomber*, who abandons the holed plane without his skipper's permission, only to land in a patch of blazing forest—where Billy Pace later finds his charred body looking like a 'stiff brown doll'.

Spencer, The Honourable Gerald. Vain young English property tycoon, who loses a quarter of a million dollars *and* his girl-friend Rita Marsh in the surprise triple-cross at the end of *Only When I Larf*.

'Spielmaterial'. Espionage slang for chickenfeed information or material, such as the photocopied Cabinet memo passed to Bernard Samson by Posh Harry in *London Match*.

spies, and the cult of espionage. A vivid picture is painted by Colonel Stok for the narrator of *Billion-Dollar Brain*. 'You must imagine, English, that there are two mighty armies advancing towards each other across a vast desolate place. They have no orders, nor does either suspect that the other is there. You understand how armies move: one man a long way out in front has a pair of binoculars, a sub-machine gun and a radiation counter. Behind him comes the armour and then the motors and the medicine-men and finally dentists and the generals and the caviare. So the very first fingertips of those armies will be two, not very clever, men who when they meet will have to decide, very quickly, whether to extend a hand or pull a trigger. According to what they do, either the armies will that night share an encampment, exchange stories and vodka, dance and tell lies; or those armies will be tearing each other to shreds in the most efficient way that man can devise. We are the fingertips.'

However, when the narrator reminds Jean Tonnesen in *Funeral in Berlin* that it's not the role of WOOC(P) to make political decisions, she half-jokingly suggests that 'when Parliamentarians wake up in the small hours of the morning bathed in sweat and screaming, you are what they were dreaming of . . .'

Spode, Dr John. Baby-faced British physicist sought by the Nazis in *SS–GB*, following the murder of his older brother, Dr William Spode. After attempting to pass British atomic research documents to the Americans, he's traced by Douglas Archer to the Little Wittenham POW camp, where he takes a poison capsule believing he faces a ruthless grilling by the Sicherheitsdienst.

Spode, Dr William. Eminent British physicist murdered by George Mayhew to prevent his underselling atomic research secrets to the Americans, whose body is found in the Shepherd Market apartment at the outset of *SS–GB*.

Springer, Professor Max. Solemn German scientist in *SS–GB*. Given a free hand by Reichsführer-SS Himmler to find a way in which the SS can take over the German Army's nuclear research programme, he dies of injuries sustained in the explosion at Highgate Cemetery.

spy satellites. The militarisation of space began in 1960 when the US Navy successfully orbited its Transit satellite and the US Air Force recovered film from the first photo-reconnaissance satellite, Discovery 13. The majority of the intelligence satellites deployed in orbit since then have been Soviet craft, many of which have a life of only 30 to 45 days. American birds tend to have a longer life span, but the January 1986 Shuttle disaster, and the recent failure of several Titan and Atlas-Centaur launch vehicles, have seriously impaired America's short-term ability to restock its space assets— which include jam-proof DSP infrared early warning satellites, Magnum electronic intercept satellites, a KH-11 photo-reconnaissance satellite providing real-time TV pictures from a height of 120 miles, SDS information-relay satellites, and the jam-proof DSCS-3 high-frequency communications satellites. Dramatic evidence of the resulting fall-off in the intelligence 'take' came in late April 1986, with the failure of American analysts to detect the Soviet nuclear reactor accident at Chernobyl, first news of which came from Swedish scientists conducting routine air sampling.

The extension of the Cold War into space becomes a major issue in *Twinkle, Twinkle, Little Spy*, when Professor Bekuv's Sahara ground station is identified as a covert Soviet listening post, tapping American comsats over the Atlantic.

SPY STORY (Jonathan Cape, London, 2 May 1974/Harcourt Brace Jovanovich, New York, 25 September 1974; fiction). Deighton returns to the subject of espionage in his ninth and most cryptic novel, the story of efforts by British Intelligence to sabotage German reunification talks being held in Copenhagen. It marks the reappearance of George Dawlish and Colonel Stok, and while the narrator is never confirmed as our anonymous friend from WOOC(P), he's certainly a close relative. Formerly with British Intelligence, he is now employed under the workname Patrick Armstrong at the war-gaming centre STUCEN, where he suffers a sometimes abrasive relationship with the newly-appointed American boss, Colonel Schlegel. Following a series of puzzling incidents, he finds himself propelled back into field intelligence work in an operation to exfiltrate an alleged defector whose sister heads the key Soviet delegation at Copenhagen.

Spy Story (GB 1976). *p.c.*: Lindsay Shonteff Productions. *p.*: Lindsay Shonteff. *d.*: Lindsay Shonteff. *sc.*: (not available). Based on the novel by Len Deighton. *ph.*: Les Young. *ed.*: John Gibson. *m.*: Roger Wootton, Andrew Hellaby. No further credits issued. *l.p.*: Michael Petrovitch (*Patrick Armstrong*), Philip Latham (*Ferdy Foxwell*), Don Fellows (*Colonel Schlegel*), Michael Gwynne (*George Dawlish*), Nicholas Parsons (*Ben Toliver*), Tessa Wyatt (*Sara Shaw*), Tony Robins (*Mrs Schlegel*), Ciaran Maddan (*Marjorie*), Nigel Plaskitt (*Mason*), Bernard Kay (*Commander Wheeler*), Derren Nesbitt (*Colonel Stok*). 9,182 feet; 102 minutes.

SS nomenclature. Schutzstaffel ranks most commonly found in Deighton's novels, with their equivalent British and American Army ranks: Reichsführer-SS (Field Marshal/US: General of the Army); SS-Gruppenführer (Major-General); SS-Standarten-führer (Colonel); SS-Obersturmbannführer (Lieutenant-Colonel); SS-Sturmbannführer (Major); SS-Obersturmführer (Lieutenant/ US: First Lieutenant); SS-Untersturmführer (Second Lieutenant).

SS—GB (Jonathan Cape, London, 24 August 1978/Alfred A. Knopf, New York, 26 February 1979; fiction). Deighton's twelfth novel is set in a Nazi-occupied Britain in 1941: the King is hostage in the Tower, Churchill has been executed in Berlin by firing squad, men are being deported to work in German factories, and the SS is in charge of Scotland Yard. Linchpin of the story is Douglas Archer, a talented young Detective Superintendent in the Murder Squad. Called upon to investigate an apparently routine murder in London's Shepherd Market, he soon finds himself drawn into an espionage battle for which he is ill-prepared, as the SS and the Abwehr compete to secure Britain's atomic research secrets—which the resistance is determined to deny to both.

Stahl, Hanna. Red-headed American-born Israeli intelligence agent in *Funeral in Berlin*. First encountered by the narrator in London, she unexpectedly turns up in Berlin to secretly take delivery of Semitsa from Johnnie Vulkan, in exchange for her government's agreement to endorse his claim to the Broum fortune.

Staines, Bernard. Birdlike upper-class Englishman, revealed to be the courier between George Mayhew and Washington concerning the King's planned escape to America in *SS—GB*.

Stakowski, Christian. A freelance dealer in people and information, better known by the cryptonym 'Jay', who allegedly had a hand in the defection of Otto John, Bruno Corvo, Guy Burgess and Donald Maclean, and whose efforts to subvert the entire framework of Britain are exposed by the narrator of *The IPCRESS File*. Yet his perfidy brings its rewards, for the British Government subsequently offers him £160,000 to set up a new intelligence department alongside WOOC(P).

See also: Poland.

stamps. A keen philatelist, Deighton is the co-author (under the name Cyril Deighton) of two authoritative studies of Zeppelin post, *The Orient Flight L.Z.127-Graf Zeppelin* and *The Egypt Flight L.Z.127-Graf Zeppelin*.

Simon Danziger shrewdly anticipates the future value of Zeppelin post in *Winter* and despatches mail to friends and business associates during his transatlantic flight to Germany. One of the top ten airmail collections in Europe is said to belong to Steve Champion in *Yesterday's Spy*—Zeppelins, French airships, balloon mail and pioneer flights. 'He likes the drama of it,' suggests the wily old dealer Serge Frankel. 'He likes to have the sort of collection he can run with, and unload quickly.' Though as Dicky Cruyer recalls in *Berlin Game*, retrieving such a collection proved a costly mistake for Karl Busch when the Erfurt Network was rolled-up by East German counter-intelligence. And Deighton offers modern investors some cautionary advice in *Why not invest your money in valuable postage stamps?* (His verdict: you might do better to put it on a horse.)

See also: collaborators.

Starkhof, Dr Hans. Temperate German Abwehr officer assigned to investigate Luftwaffe pilot Christian Himmel's alleged treason, following his theft of a report on human freezing experiments conducted at Dachau, in *Bomber*. The epilogue records that he was himself arrested after the attempt on Hitler's life in 1944, and died in a concentration camp.

Stasis (Staatssicherheitspolizei). East Germany's State Security Police, the domestic guardians of the communist regime responsible for counter-intelligence, internal security and political repression, come under the centralised command of Minister Erich Mielke's assistant, Generalleutnant Rudolf Mittig.

The service is organised into fifteen departments responsible for each of the country's fourteen *Bezirke* (regional districts) plus East Berlin. It maintains a country-wide net of local offices, controls an army of 'unofficial workers' and secret informers placed in every sphere of the nation's life, and is responsible for running the political prisons.

A copy of every visa application by Western visitors and tourists is sent to its Normannenstrasse headquarters (if you've ever stayed in West Berlin and taken one of those daily sightseeing coach tours into East Berlin—you're on its files), and each hotel has a State Security officer permanently on its staff.

It is government policy, remarks Bernard Samson in *Berlin Game*, that Stasis never wear beards or moustaches, and dress in plain clothes that make them immediately recognisable to every East German who sees them. But—he goes on to caution—everyone except the most naive realise that there are other plainclothes policemen who aren't so easy to spot.

See also: Wachregiment Felix Dzerzhinsky.

Steel, Samantha. Otherwise known as Hanna Stahl, an Israeli intelligence agent encountered by the narrator in *Funeral in Berlin*, and in whose apartment Ossie Butterworth discovers passports in both names.

Steeple Thaxted. 'Mud, shit, and tents' is Vince Madigan's acerbic description of the 220th Fighter Group's wartime airbase in Cambridgeshire, England, in *Goodbye Mickey Mouse*. Built as an RAF satellite field, it wasn't designed to hold over sixteen hundred Americans who want to bathe every day in hot water.

Stein, Billy. Artless, twenty-four-year-old son of Charles Stein in *XPD*. Though eager to prove his manhood, he proves a walkover for Boyd Stuart in his efforts to acquire the Hitler Minutes from his father.

Stein, Charles. Brusque, guileful American in his late fifties, with a leading role in *XPD*. A wartime corporal in Patton's Third Army, he's revealed as the mastermind behind the hijacking of Nazi gold and documents recovered from the Kaiseroda Mine in 1945. Secure in the knowledge that the theft was always denied by the Allied Reparations Agency, he enjoys an affluent lifestyle in California until becoming the focus of competing efforts to obtain the Hitler Minutes—a fatal battle for which he is ill-prepared.

Steiner, Theodor. Beer-bellied Gestapo detective in *Winter*, who in 1937 cracks a Berlin forgery ring producing American passports for fugitive Jews, leading to the arrest and incarceration of Lottie Winter.

Stewart, Josephine. Influential London film critic in *Close-Up*, with the dubious distinction of having seen *The Sound of Music* three times, after panning it in her review: 'I can't afford to tell my readers to go and see schmaltz.'

Stigg, Captain Charles. Easy-going young American B-24 pilot, with a minor role in *Goodbye Mickey Mouse*. A close friend of Jamie Farebrother since their days at flying school in California, his tragic suicide is a measure of the harrowing pressures facing the bomber crews flying mission after mission over Nazi Germany in 1943–4.

Stinnes, Erich. Work name of Soviet KGB officer, Major Nikolai Sadoff, in the *Game, Set & Match* trilogy. Belatedly, Bernard Samson and Werner Volkmann conclude that his provocative choice of name—Hugo Stinnes was a well-known German capitalist obsessed by the threat of world Bolshevism—could only have been made by a very, very confident communist, a man 'so trusted by his KGB masters that he could select such a name without fear of being contaminated by it'.

Stok, Colonel Alexeyevitch. Deeply human, occasionally cynical KGB officer of about sixty, with leading roles in *Funeral in*

Berlin and *Billion-Dollar Brain*, and a minor part in *Spy Story*. A supreme pragmatist whose weary manner conceals a Machiavellian cunning, he probes, tests and sometimes teases British Intelligence, rarely seeking a direct confrontation, but nevertheless always departing the battle with an equal share of the spoils.

Stone, Marshall. Gifted forty-nine-year-old English actor and charismatic member of Hollywood's elite, with the leading role in *Close-Up*. An overnight discovery back in 1948, his films have since earned him millions and worldwide acclaim for his talents. But for all that, he's racked with anxieties and fears, lusting for reassurance and yearning for the one gift he most desires—everlasting youth.

Stuart, Boyd. Rootless thirty-eight-year-old MI6 field officer, ordered to retrieve the Hitler Minutes and suppress evidence of Britain's greatest wartime secret in *XPD*. 'A handsome, dark-complexioned man whose appearance—like his excellent German and Polish and fluent Hungarian—enables him to pass himself off as an inhabitant of anywhere in that region vaguely referred to as central Europe.'

Stuart, Jennifer. Tedious estranged wife of Boyd Stuart in *XPD*, whose intercession with her father—MI6 Director General, Sir Sydney Ryden—ensures that Boyd receives an overseas assignment during their divorce.

STUCEN. The fictional London war-games centre ('a particularly appalling example of Gothic revival, that in anywhere but Hampstead would have been too conspicuous to house secrets') in *Spy Story*, where NATO defence strategies are matched against theoretical Soviet strike threats. Selected by Ben Toliver as the ideal safe house in which to debrief Soviet defector Rear-Admiral Remoziva, its staff includes Colonel Schlegel, Patrick Armstrong and Ferdy Foxwell.

Sturmabteilung (SA). The SA was formed in August 1921 under the anodyne name of the Gymnastics and Sports Division of the Nazi Party, drawing its nucleus from the Freikorps. Its original purpose was to keep order at political meetings, but by 1934 its numbers had swelled to four million, brownshirt stormtroopers were a familiar sight on every German street, and SA commander Ernst Röhm seemed ready to threaten Hitler's leadership of the Nazi revolution. Encouraged by Himmler (who had his own private army, the SS), Hitler led a bloody purge of its leaders on the night of 29–30 June 1934, and brought to a violent end the factionalism that had consumed the Party.

Several leading characters in *Winter* are implicated in the rise and fall of the SA. Fritz Esser follows Captain Graf into its ranks before shrewdly recognising that the future lies with Hitler rather than Röhm, and Paul Winter is summoned to play a necessary role on the 'Night of the Long Knives', then dispassionately witnesses the summary execution of his former Freikorps commander Graf.

submarines. A sunken German XXI U-boat lying off the coast of Portugal is the focus of attention in *Horse Under Water*. Submarines also feature in *The IPCRESS File*, when Dalby transmits high-speed TV pictures of the American shot tower to a Soviet one lying off Tokwe Atoll, and in *Spy Story*, when an American nuclear submarine is used for the provocative rendezvous with Soviet Rear-Admiral Remoziva. Charles Bonnard recalls being landed in Occupied France by one in *Yesterday's Spy*, and classified plans for new hunter-killer submarines are planted on Paul Biedermann in a KGB ploy to discredit Bernard Samson in *Mexico Set*.

suicides. Captain Charlie Stigg's tragic suicide in *Goodbye Mickey Mouse* is a measure of the harrowing pressures endured by the bomber crews flying mission after dangerous mission over Nazi Germany in 1943–4. Karl Poster leaps from a building near Wall Street after losing a quarter of a million dollars to the trio of confidence tricksters in *Only When I Larf*, and Simon Danziger steps into the traffic on Berlin's Potsdamer Platz on learning he's been wiped out by the Wall Street crash in *Winter*. Sergeant Major Reg Hardcastle turns a gun on himself after murdering his wife and her presumed Yank lover in *Goodbye Mickey Mouse*, and a melancholy Yuriy Grechko takes his life at the Rousillon Beach Motel after losing Fusako Parker in *XPD*. Dr John Spode takes a cyanide pill fearing a ruthless grilling by the Nazi Sicherheitsdienst in *SS–GB*, Petzval dies by his own hand as a result of Count Kupka's Machiavellian scheming in *Winter*, and Douglas Reid-Kennedy puts a shotgun to his head minutes before his arrest for spying in *Twinkle, Twinkle, Little Spy*.

Sûreté Nationale. France's national police force operates directly for the Ministry of the Interior on the rue de Saussaies. Chief Inspector Claude Loiseau, a leading character in *An Expensive Place to Die*, works for the Sûreté, as does Chief Inspector Gérard Nicol (known as 'the Cardinal' among colleagues in the Ministry) in *Mexico Set*.

surveillance. 'Hot' surveillance is when a person is openly tailed or bugged for harassment or intimidation purposes, such as Chief Inspector Loiseau's handling of the narrator in *An Expensive Place to Die*. 'Cold' surveillance is covert, and intended to go unnoticed by the target.
See also: consort watch.

Swainson, ———. Flat-featured Lithuanian employed by Jay to mind the narrator in the 'Hungarian' prison in *The IPCRESS File*. Subsequently identified entering Dalby's home, establishing the latter's treachery and complicity in Jay's IPCRESS Network.

Sweet, Flight Lieutenant. Ambitious twenty-two-year-old RAF pilot, whose unquestioning readiness to flatter and defer to the voice of authority earns him few friends among the aircrews at Warley Fen in *Bomber*. Killed in the raid on Altgarten, when his Lancaster is shot down by Luftwaffe night-fighter pilot Christian Himmel.

Switzerland. Briefly visited by Charles Bonnard in *Yesterday's Spy*, for a clandestine meeting with double-agent Aziz, and a major setting in *XPD*, where the bloody quest for the Hitler Minutes reaches its unexpected conclusion.

T

TACTICAL GENIUS IN BATTLE by Simon Goodenough. *Introduced by Len Deighton* (Phaidon Press, Oxford and New York, October 1979). An illustrated analysis of the principal tactics employed in major battles throughout history, edited and introduced by Deighton.

Tarrant, Major Harry. Poker-faced commander of the Military Police Company at Steeple Thaxted in *Goodbye Mickey Mouse*. Although priding himself on his flexibility and perception, he's not the most popular officer around the base—a 'narrow-eyed, barrel-chested know-it-all' in the words of station commander Colonel Dan Badger.

Tarrant, Private. Member of the Royal Fusiliers firing squad despatched to Pooglui Camp in *Twelve Good Men And True*, who lives solely for his cheap beer and weekly visit to the brothel.

Tarrant, ———. Frank Harrington's inscrutable old valet, employed to guard the portals of the Grunewald mansion in the *Game, Set & Match* trilogy.

'Task Pogoni'. Moscow Centre's cryptonym for the KGB operation to secure the Hitler Minutes in *XPD*. The first recorded use of the name comes in an unexpected two-part radio transmission beamed from Moscow to the Soviet Embassy in Washington, intercepted by the National Security Agency.

Tastevin, Monsieur. The narrator's Paris landlord in *An Expensive Place to Die*. It's said he once had his own restaurant on Boul. Mich., which during the war was a meeting place for members of the communist-dominated resistance organisation, Front National. After the liberation he almost got a certificate signed by General Eisenhower, but when his political past became clearer to the Americans, he got his restaurant declared out of bounds and searched by the Military Police every week for a year instead.

telephone tapping. *See* wire-tapping.

television adaptations. The short stories *Discipline* and *It Must Have Been Two Other Fellows* were dramatised for Melvyn Bragg's profile of Len Deighton in the BBC television programme 'The Lively Arts' (BBC2), transmitted 18 December 1977. At the time of writing, the *Game, Set & Match* trilogy is being filmed by Granada Television for transmission in the UK and US, autumn 1988. Produced by Brian Armstrong, the thirteen-part series is being shot on location from November 1986 to October 1987, with a storyline stretching from Gdansk on the Baltic to Guerrero on the Pacific. See individual entries for cast lists and principal production credits.

Teno (Technische-Nothilfe). The German wartime emergency rescue and repair service. Their specialists (among whom are Fuchs Ueberall and Bodo Reuter) spend hours digging into the burning wreckage after the RAF raid on Altgarten in *Bomber*, and work ceaselessly to release people trapped beneath the rubble in Berlin in *Winter* as 22,000 Soviet guns lay waste to what is left of the city in April 1945.

Thatcher, Margaret (1925–   ). Britain's first woman Prime Minister makes a brief appearance in *XPD*, when only days after the general election of May 1979 Sir Sydney Ryden alerts her to the possible disclosure of the country's most closely guarded wartime secret—the clandestine meeting between Winston Churchill and

Adolf Hitler in June 1940 to discuss the terms of Britain's surrender.

third-person narratives. A necessary device for stories that cannot be told from a single or narrow point of view. Five of Deighton's eighteen novels, *Bomber*, *SS–GB*, *XPD*, *Goodbye Mickey Mouse* and *Winter*, and eleven of the short stories in *Declarations of War*, are written in the third person. However, the decison is not always easily arrived at. He rewrote *SS–GB* from page one after having written three-quarters of it in the first person, and abandoned his plan to write each chapter of *Goodbye Mickey Mouse* as the first-person narrative of a different character only after completing several chapters of the first draft in this way.

Thomas, Peter. The presumed identity of the body discovered in an apartment over a Shepherd Market antiques shop owned by 'Peter Thomas', at the beginning of *SS–GB*. However, Detective Superintendent Douglas Archer subsequently learns that the shop is a front for the resistance movement, who use it to launder money raised to fight the Nazi occupation forces, and that the murder victim is the eminent British physicist, Dr William Spode.

378 File. Periodic review of the loyalty of Security Grade Ones (i.e. persons considered essential to Britain's national interest) undertaken by WOOC(P). 'I knew that Dawlish had another nasty little bomb called the 378 file sub-section 14, which was a file about trade union officials . . . I dreaded that file landing on my desk,' confesses the narrator of *Billion-Dollar Brain*. 'None of those public-school boys would be able to do that job with the instinct that I would be able to bring to it. Yet some of the people concerned would be people I was at school with; and in any case it would call upon questions and allegiances that I had continuously pushed into the rear recesses of my mind.'

'Tinkle Bell'. Nickname of a WOOC(P) heavy who makes a couple of asthmatic appearances in *Horse Under Water*. ('Tinkerbell' is also the alleged sobriquet of Britain's national wire-tapping facility in a concealed building off Ebury Bridge Road, London SW1, operated by telephone engineers on behalf of MI5 and the Special Branch.)

Tiptree, Henry. Gauche upper-class MI6 Internal Security officer, whose yearning for cloak-and-dagger experience leads to a chaotic showdown at the conclusion of *Mexico Set*.

title changes. When a novel has been with us for some years, the title becomes so identified with the story that it is difficult to imagine any other could have been seriously considered. Three of Deighton's novels underwent late title changes: *Funeral in Berlin* was to have been called 'Night Flight to Berlin' (he later decided 'My Funeral in Berlin' was much more the title he wanted, and some foreign language editions of the novel have this title), *An Expensive Place to Die* 'A Subtle Smell of Agony', and *Spy Story* 'The Red Admiral'. For a long time his English publisher dickered with 'A Child of the Century' as the title for *Winter*. And Deighton's preferred title for his first French cookbook was 'Où est le boeuf de ma tante'. While the book was in production it was suggested the pages might be impregnated with garlic. The publisher's warehouse staff protested, the idea was dropped and the book acquired the ironic title *Où est le garlic*. He counts *Bomber* among the titles he wishes he could have improved, so as to tell potential readers more clearly what sort of book it was, 'a story about wartime Germany that devoted more pages to the Germans than to the RAF'.[20]

Tokwe Atoll. The isolated Pacific site for the American bomb test in *The IPCRESS File*, where Dalby reveals the extent of his treachery and the narrator is abducted by members of Jay's IPCRESS Network. You'll not find it in any atlas for it's entirely written from Deighton's imagination, who wanted the island 'to be a mysterious place that was not exactly like any other'.[21]

Toliver, Ben. Self-seeking Member of Parliament, businessman and bon viveur in *Spy Story*. Set up by Dawlish to believe Soviet Rear-Admiral Remoziva wishes to defect to the West, his fated exfiltration plans lead to the arrest of Remoziva, his family and relatives, and to the collapse of German reunification talks as the Foreign Office had intended.

Tomas, Fernie. Portuguese identity assumed by the traitorous British wartime naval officer, Bernard Thomas Peterson, in *Horse Under Water*.

Tonnesen, Jean. Dark, calm and dangerous-looking twenty-six-year-old employee of WOOC(P), transferred from the Macao desk to work as the narrator's assistant in *The IPCRESS File*. 'She could have been top kick in the Bolshoi, Sweden's first woman ship's captain, private secretary to Chou-en-lai, or Sammy Davis's press agent . . . she was fine, my very first beautiful spy.' Born in Cairo of a Norwegian father and Scottish mother, fluent in five languages, she goes on to prove an invaluable and sometimes tantalising presence—on and off duty—in *Horse Under Water*, *Funeral in Berlin* and *Billion-Dollar Brain*.

————, **Topaz.** Provocative British honours graduate in thermo-chemistry, with an ambiguous role in Steve Champion's household in *Yesterday's Spy*. Nominally employed as a nanny for Champion's young son Billy, she's in bed with Bonnard when shot by Mebarki prior to the evacuation of the Tix mansion.

The Tower of London. The ancient fortress-palace on the banks of the Thames has been used for centuries as a prison for kings and queens, captive foreign sovereigns, eminent prisoners awaiting trial, and others destined for the axe or the scaffold, and is the dramatic setting for King George VI's imprisonment following the Nazi occupation of Britain in *SS–GB*.

trains are the setting for dramatic sequences in several novels. Defector Harvey Newbegin survives an attempted XPD by American (or are they British?) agents while en route to Leningrad by train in *Billion-Dollar Brain*; Charles Bonnard is finally recruited by Steve Champion during a rail journey in *Yesterday's Spy*; a train ticket to Bringle Sands proves a vital clue in the Shepherd Market murder enquiry and Douglas Archer comes face-to-face with Reichsführer-SS Heinrich Himmler aboard a closely guarded train, in *SS–GB*; and Franz Wever provides a vivid account of the transfer of Reichsbank gold and Nazi documents to the Kaiseroda Mine aboard Adolf Hitler's *Führersonderzug* in *XPD*.

The romance of steam arouses Grenade's Gallic enthusiasm in *Funeral in Berlin* ('He was in the Resistance during the war. He destroyed any number of locomotives. Now that they are being exterminated by progress he feels he has a task to protect and preserve them'), but 'only two young people very much in love could have endured so cheerfully' the wartime train journey to Wales undertaken by Jamie Farebrother and Victoria Cooper in *Goodbye Mickey Mouse*.

Trent, Giles. Vain British Intelligence officer in *Berlin Game*, recruited by the KGB in a skilful gambit to protect their mole within London Central. Broken and turned by Bernard Samson, he's later murdered by Rolf Mauser in the mistaken belief he's about to blow the Brahms Network.

Trent, Miss. Frustrated middle-class spinster in *Berlin Game*, whose burgeoning affair with Chlestakov leads her brother Giles into the KGB ploy to deflect suspicion from their highly-placed agent within London Central.

The Trust. The secret fund established by some of the most powerful interests in West Germany to maintain a strong and prosperous Federal Republic, whose trustees approve Willi Kleiber's efforts to secure the Hitler Minutes in *XPD*—unaware they're being used as a front for an operation masterminded by Moscow Centre.

Tucker, Major Spurrier. Tense thirty-year-old American pilot, commanding the USAF's 199th Squadron at Steeple

Thaxted in *Goodbye Mickey Mouse*. A West Pointer, his cold pedantic manner and air of condescension add to his unpopularity among his fellow fighter jocks—until he unexpectedly opposes the grounding of Lieutenant Mickey Morse, whom he restores to flying duties after he inherits command of the 220th Group.

Turner, Dottie. Scheming American widow in *Winter*, who marries Cyrus Rensselaer in the twilight of his life and finds fortune for herself and her three sons—one of whom fathers Bret Rensselaer, a leading character in the *Game, Set & Match* trilogy.

'Turnstone'. Cryptonym for WOOC(P)'s operation to net the recalcitrant Harvey Newbegin at the close of *Billion-Dollar Brain*.

TWELVE GOOD MEN AND TRUE. Short story in the collection *Declarations of War*. Twelve privates in the Royal Fusiliers stationed in the Punjab are drafted 500 miles for a brief special mission during the British rule of India in the early 1920s.

'Twin Beeches'. Marshall Stone's elegant country mansion in *Close-Up*, providing an analgesic retreat from a capricious and aggressive world. A shrine to his success, it records nothing of his family, his background or his days as a struggling young actor.

TWINKLE, TWINKLE, LITTLE SPY (Jonathan Cape, London, 17 June 1976/**Catch a Falling Spy**, Harcourt Brace Jovanovich, New York, 27 September 1976; fiction). Deighton's eleventh novel, and the third to team a British Intelligence officer with an American boss, finds the narrator joining CIA electronics expert Major Mickey Mann to take custody of a defecting Soviet scientist in the Sahara desert, from where a trail of blood leads to Manhattan, Paris, Dublin and halfway back across Africa—where they uncover a covert Soviet listening post tapping American comsats stationed over the Atlantic.

220th Group. The fictional USAF Fighter Group flying P-51 Mustangs from Steeple Thaxted, portrayed in *Goodbye Mickey*

Mouse. Originally activated by a typewritten order that made 'Duke' Scroll and Sergeant Kinzelberg its first personnel and provided them with a dilapidated office near the flight line at Hamilton Field, California, the Group is posted to the European theatre to protect the fleets of Allied bombers penetrating deep into Nazi Germany in 1943–4.

U

Ueberall, Zugwachtmeister 'Fuchs'. Elderly red-haired Saxon Teno engineer in *Bomber*, who despite his strong dislike of military life, is at the forefront of efforts to restore order to Altgarten following the holocaust unleashed by the RAF bombers.

Uhl, Leutnant. Spindly young Wehrmacht officer in *Winter*, who shares Colonel von Kleindorf's horror and shame on finding trainloads of Jews being transported eastward for 'resettlement' in Poland.

underwater sequences figure in *Horse Under Water*, with the narrator leading the search for a sunken wartime U-boat off the coast of Portugal, and in *Spy Story*, when the American nuclear submarine USS *Paul Revere* undertakes a hazardous Arctic rendezvous with Soviet Rear-Admiral Remoziva.

United States Air Force. Wartime USAF fighter jocks flying escort missions from their Steeple Thaxted base in England are the heroes of *Goodbye Mickey Mouse*, and the USAF's role in the modern nuclear age is briefly scrutinised in *The IPCRESS File*, *An Expensive Place to Die* and *Spy Story*. A deserted SAC airbase in Vietnam is the eerie setting for the short story *First Base* and USAF fighter pilots flying Phantom F-4s during the Vietnam War were the subject of a novel Deighton put aside when almost finished.

United States Federal Narcotics Bureau. Before coming into the British service in 1953, Adem is said to have freelanced for the Bureau in the Middle East (an equitable arrangement after he'd been caught running Indian hemp across the Syrian border as a section of a chain to New York). And to the narrator's astonishment, sexy Charlotte Lucas-Mountford boldly identifies herself as a Bureau undercover agent when she corners Harry Kondit at the conclusion of *Horse Under Water*.

United States Medical Department. The USMD is found to have been infiltrated by Jay's agents in *The IPCRESS File*, who abduct the narrator from Tokwe Atoll by telling the British authorities that the Americans are holding him, and the Americans that the British have asked for his return.

USS Paul Revere. The American nuclear submarine deployed to carry Patrick Armstrong, Colonel Schlegel and Ferdy Foxwell to the provocative Arctic rendezvous with Rear-Admiral Remoziva in *Spy Story*. Identified as an intelligence submarine, the midships section is crammed with electronic counter measures (ECM) and radio monitoring and recording equipment, instead of the usual banks of sixteen missiles.

Vaclav, ———. Officer of the Czech OBZ (the Military Security Police), dismissed by Colonel Stok in *Funeral in Berlin* as 'a mass round-up man' who'd use an armoured division to shadow a suspect and wonder why he vanished.

Valentin, Lucie Simone. Henry Hope Dean's lover in *Twinkle, Twinkle, Little Spy*. A lot older than the boy, she supplies the narrator and Major Mann with the important lead that sends them hurrying to Ireland in pursuit of traitorous Douglas Reid-Kennedy.

THE VALLEY OF FEAR by Arthur Conan Doyle. *Introduced by Len Deighton.* (John Murray/Jonathan Cape, London, January 1974/Doubleday, New York, May 1977.) A longtime Sherlock Holmes fan, Deighton relates in his introduction how Conan Doyle became the chronicler and occasional prophet of the remarkable new world of forensic science.
See also: Watson roles.

Valmy Complex. The French atomic weapons research establishment at the heart of the military testing range known as 'the Atelier', from which it is alleged Steve Champion intends to steal atomic artillery shells in *Yesterday's Spy*. The complex 'was built in 1890, and the name of the great victory for French artillery is carved in stone above the main entrance. It's a curious-looking place: probably designed by some architect who had waited all his life for a chance to use poured concrete, for almost every wall is curved.'

Vienna. Although no longer the capital of an empire, Vienna is unchanging. Sachers is still serving the Sacher Torte cake that it served at the turn of the century—an era notably depicted at the beginning of *Winter*, in which we find Veronica Winter in the first stages of labour as her husband is summoned to a meeting with the secret police chief, Count Kupka. Thirty-eight years later, Paul Winter returns to the city of his birth, to find the restaurants and shops filled with German tourists who've arrived within hours of the German Army crossing the frontier to enforce the Nazi *Anschluss*.

Vietnam War (1965–73). The war aroused more discontent in America than any previous military engagement in its history, and is the setting for the short story *First Base*. Deighton also wrote half a million words and notes for a novel about Phantom F-4 fighter pilots in the war, but the Pentagon delayed so long in granting him access to USAF bases in Vietnam that the war ended and the book was abandoned.

'Vitamin'. Cryptonym for the controversial British Intelligence operation referred to in *London Match*, which was conducted at the behest of the Prime Minister to test security at certain very sensitive British establishments in West Germany. In a determined bid to frame Bret Rensselaer as a second traitor within London Central, the KGB deliberately leaks the fact that a copy of the Cabinet Memo on the operation subsequently reached Moscow Centre. (The 200-lb car bomb detonated inside the huge Rheindahlen headquarters of the British Army of the Rhine in late March 1987, is evidence of the very real threat facing these installations in Germany.)
See also: Hauptverwaltung Aufklärung

VNV (Vós não vedes). Portuguese revolutionary movement committed to the overthrow of the Salazar regime in the early 1960s, whose request for covert financing in *Horse Under Water* sets in motion WOOC(P)'s operation to recover counterfeit Nazi money from the sunken wartime U-boat lying off Albufeira.

Volkmann, Dr Isaac. Fashionable Berlin dentist in *Winter*, whose patients include the Winter brothers and many of the city's famous film and theatre stars. However, Paul Winter is powerless to help as Goebbels decimates Berlin's Jewish community, forcing Dr Volkmann and his wife to seek refuge in the Hennigs' house off Kantstrasse, where in 1943 Lily gave birth to a son. (The ageing Lisl Hennig should be forgiven for misremembering the actual date as 1 March 1943, in *Berlin Game*. Werner Volkmann must have been born several months later, on 23 November 1943, for it was on that night that an Allied bomb hit the Kaiser Wilhelm Memorial Church on Berlin's Ku'damm.)

Volkmann, Werner. The son of Dr Isaac and Lily Volkmann, with a central role in the *Game, Set & Match* trilogy as Bernard Samson's close friend and alter ego. He possesses a natural talent for spy errantry, and although no longer enjoying the confidence of MI6's Berlin Station, proves a brother-in-arms amid lengthening shadows of treachery when Samson returns to fieldwork after five years behind a London desk.

Volkmann, Zena. Small dark twenty-two-year-old wife of Werner Volkmann in the *Game, Set & Match* trilogy. A restless *provocatrice*, social-climber and talent spotter, with the 'coil-spring energy and short fuse of the self-made opportunist'.

'The Volkswagen'. RAF Lancaster skippered by Cornelius Fleming, shot down as it crosses the Dutch coast in *Bomber*. Fleming, Bertie (flight engineer) and Robin (bomb aimer), all perish in the encounter with Luftwaffe night-fighter ace, von Löwenherz.

Vopos (Volkspolizei). East Germany's 'People's Police Force' is controlled by the Ministry of the Interior, under the command of Generaloberst Friedrich Dickel. Its headquarters is near Alexanderplatz in what is now Hans-Beimler-Strasse. In addition to normal policing activities, it has ABV (Abschnittsbevollmächtiger) officers with the rank of lieutenant or second lieutenant stationed in residential areas to keep watch on political developments, and maintains 'on call' armoured battalions quartered in barracks in each industrial district. Three battalions are permanently stationed in East Berlin.

In *Twinkle, Twinkle, Little Spy*, Hank Dean's intelligence job in Berlin during the early 1950s is said to have been to build a complete picture of the service, and Vopo officers are inevitably encountered by British Intelligence agents active in East Berlin in *Funeral in Berlin* and the *Game, Set & Match* trilogy.

Voss, Herr. Wealthy German tailor in *Bomber*, who while deploring his loss of skilled Jewish staff, prospers supplying uniforms to the Nazis until killed in the RAF raid that consumes Altgarten.

Vulkan, Johnnie. Waffen-SS guard murdered during the evacuation of the Treblinka concentration camp in 1945, whose identity is assumed by Paul Louis Broum until unmasked by the narrator in *Funeral in Berlin*.

Wachregiment Felix Dzerzhinsky. An elite arm of East Germany's Ministerium für Staatssicherheit, charged with guarding government buildings and enforcing internal repression. Comprising some 3,500 armed soldiers equipped with tanks and armoured carriers, the regiment's most notorious engagement occurred in East Berlin in June 1953, when it was deployed alongside the Volkspolizei to put down the strikes and demonstrations which threatened to topple the communist regime—a crisis recalled some thirty years later by Pavel Moskvin in *Mexico Set*.

Waffen-SS. The military arm of the Nazi SS provided front-line troops as well as guards for the concentration camps, and by the war's end numbered about 900,000 men, including divisions of 'non-Germanic' volunteers and conscripts from almost every occupied country.

Communist assassin Paul Louis Broum finds it expedient to assume the identity of Treblinka camp guard Johnnie Vulkan in *Funeral in Berlin*, but the postwar legacy of the Waffen-SS is feared by Max Breslow in *XPD*, who risks deportation should American newspapers ever learn of his service record. In *London Match* an embittered Gerda Koby is quick to blame her husband's downfall on her brother's brief attachment to the 'Liebstandarte Adolf Hitler', the same division to which SS-Sturmbannführer Adolf Fischer is attached in *Bomber*, and in *Winter* General Alex Horner's worst fears are realised when Heinrich Brand's Waffen-SS division executes captured Allied soldiers during the battle for France in 1944.

Wald Hotel. The once elegant hotel in Altgarten set in two and a half acres of parkland, which before the war attracted guests from all corners of Europe—and from America too. Because of the high walls and barbed wire, as well as the constant howls of fierce dogs, it's widely believed by the townsfolk to be a secret SS centre of considerable importance—one rumour suggests it's a stud farm for SS men on leave; another that Stalin's son, captured on the Eastern Front, is being held there. In reality, it's a Waffen-SS dog-training centre.

Waley, Captain. US Marine Corps officer killed leading the raid on the Bringle Sands Research Establishment in *SS–GB*. (Since America is neutral at the time, lawyers insist on the Marines being discharged from the USMC and re-enlisted as Canadians in the British service.)

Walker, Corporal. Balding middle-aged United States Air Force medic, who works tirelessly alongside 'Doc' Goldman in the fight to save the life of Jamie Farebrother in *Goodbye Mickey Mouse*.

warfare. 'When old men decided to barter young men for pride and profit the transaction was called war,' writes Deighton in *Winter's Morning*. His almost paradoxical hatred of war and compassion for those engaged in combat is evident in the superbly mobilised tragedy *Bomber*, in *Goodbye Mickey Mouse* and *Winter*, and is the resonating theme of his underrated collection of short stories *Declarations of War*. The human costs of the historical conflicts depicted in these books were enormous. It is a sobering thought that at this moment some twenty wars are raging around the world.

war-gaming. Already in 1824, Prussian Lieutenant von Reisswitz was simulating military combat on a determined field, with rules taking into account such factors as the increased power of cavalry when charging and troops being slowed by forestation. Millions are now spent on modern exercises in sanitised warfare and they have interested Deighton ever since he watched a naval battle organised by a war-games club in the 1950s. Following a reader's letter which suggested *Bomber* made an admirable basis for a war-game, he decided to explore the subject in *Spy Story*, creating a highly convincing war studies centre—STUCEN— where computers are used to match NATO defence strategies against theoretical Soviet strike threats.

It is also the subject of the short story *Paper Casualty*, in which a World War I hero is outmanoeuvred by the new generation of army officers during a World War II war-game.

Warley Fen. The fictional Royal Air Force Bomber Command airfield from which the raid on the Ruhr is launched in *Bomber*. Adjacent to the Fen village of Little Warley, it was constructed shortly after the outbreak of World War II and 'in no time at all it seemed as though the village had always known the bustle of one thousand and eighty-three noisy airmen . . . There were girl airmen too, to the villagers' dismay. They flaunted painted lips and waved hair and worked as hard as the men. Sometimes they were heard to swear as hard as the men, too. They set an awesome example to the village girls.'

Washington, DC. Briefly visited by Major Mann and the narrator of *Twinkle, Twinkle, Little Spy* to confront Senator Greenwood with evidence of Gerry Hart's treachery. 'They are made of marble, steel, chromium and tinted glass, these gleaming governmental buildings that dominate Washington, D.C., and from the top of any one of them, a man can see half-way across the world—if he's a politician.' Fifty years earlier, in 1925, it's a State Department officer rather than a politician to whom Glenn Rensselaer reports in *Winter*, visiting his gloomy little intelligence bureau on K Street where he finds him more concerned about the size of Britain's navy than the spread of Nazism in Germany.

Waterman, ———. Down-at-heel private detective hired by the narrator of *The IPCRESS File* after arranging a meeting with Dalby. Not the brightest PI to walk the streets, his crucial sighting of Swainson entering Dalby's house certainly merits his eight guinea fee.

Dr Watson roles. One of Conan Doyle's outstanding contributions to crime fiction was to provide Sherlock Holmes with Dr Watson as a simple and effective means of explaining the plot through dialogue. Characters in Deighton's novels cast in a 'Dr Watson' role include Harvey Newbegin in *Billion-Dollar Brain*, Colonel Charles Schlegel in *Spy Story* and *Yesterday's Spy*, Major Mickey Mann in *Twinkle, Twinkle, Little Spy* and Werner Volkmann in the *Game, Set & Match* trilogy.

the weather. An Englishman's favourite topic of conversation, it prompts a stream of splendid, sometimes wry comments from the narrators of the novels—'Someone from the Meteorological Office should discover why it is that every time I fly into London Airport it is raining' (*Funeral in Berlin*)—'Outside was February and the first snow of the year . . . the sort of snow that a sharp P.R. man would make available to journalists' (*Billion-Dollar Brain*).

And, of course, it plays a decisive role in the two novels about the air war of 1943–4: *Bomber* ('It was a bomber's sky: dry air, wind enough to clear the smoke, cloud broken enough to recognize a few stars'), and *Goodbye Mickey Mouse* ('Spring was creeping over northern Europe. The continental landmass had warmed up enough to form dome-shaped cumulus, the sort of cloud artists use to depict a perfect summer's day. Above the formation of Mustangs, the sky was a vivid cerulean blue that in a painting might have seemed a vulgar overstatement').

Wein, Lieutenant Rube. Taciturn, scholarly USAF pilot flying as Morse's wingman in *Goodbye Mickey Mouse*. A 'sad-eyed kid with jug ears', his fear of ending up as a Jewish POW in Nazi-occupied Europe is cruelly realised when he's forced to bail out over Holland as his Mustang runs out of fuel.

Weinberger, Jacob. Former Koolman Studios publicity

vizier turned successful agent in *Close-Up*, with the appearance of 'a gigantic teddy-bear that had survived several generations of unruly childen'. Friend and father-confessor to actor Marshall Stone for a quarter of a century, he proves a master of the big-daddy world in which stars are bought and sold like slaves at an auction.

Weiss List. The sensational Nazi document at the centre of *Horse Under Water*. About the size of a paperback novel, it's said to list British nationals who'd been willing to support a Nazi-sponsored government following Hitler's planned invasion in the early years of World War II. Prominent among the names on the list is that of postwar British Cabinet Minister, Henry Smith.

Weizsäcker, Colonel. Chauvinistic Wehrmacht officer serving under General Alex Horner on the Eastern Front in *Winter*. Trapped in the snow-covered approaches to Moscow by heavier than expected Soviet resistance, Weizsäcker's blind faith in Hitler astonishes and saddens his commander.

Wentworth, Major-General. Elderly British Army officer in *SS–GB*, whose celebrated final stand against the invading German army in 1940 is recalled by Douglas Archer when he encounters the brave old soldier in the Little Wittenham prisoner-of-war camp.

West German Intelligence. Foreign intelligence and espionage is the responsibility of the Bundesnachrichtendienst (BND), the agency established by the Americans shortly after World War II, and known as the Gehlen Bureau until handed over to the West German Government in 1956. Counter-intelligence and domestic security are handled by the Bundesamt für Verfassungsschutz (BfV), which has its national headquarters in Cologne and locally administered regional offices in each of the ten Federal States and Berlin. Military counter-intelligence is conducted by the Armed Forces' own service, the Militärischer Abschirm Dienst (MAD), which became the subject of domestic scorn in 1984 after mistakenly accusing four-star general, Günther

Kiessling, of being a member of a notorious homosexual club in Cologne.

West Germany. *See* Germany, West.

Wever, Franz. Former Wehrmacht signals officer, who accompanied Hitler's personal papers to their hiding place in the Kaiseroda Mine in early 1945, with a minor but key role in *XPD*. Murdered by Willi Kleiber after having been interviewed by Boyd Stuart, Wever is later revealed as the author of the Hitler Minutes—the secret record of Winston Churchill's discussions with Adolf Hitler at their clandestine meeting of June 1940.

Wheeler, Commander. A member of Ben Toliver's cabal in *Spy Story*, 'with the kind of ruddy face that comes with those dual benefits of sea-faring: open air and duty-free drink'.

WHODUNIT? A Guide to Crime, Suspense & Spy Fiction. Edited by H. R. F. Keating (Windward, London, August 1982/Van Nostrand Reinhold, New York, August 1982). Contains Deighton's illuminating essay *Even on Christmas Day*, in which he discusses his writing and research methods, and reproduces some notes and drawings made while preparing *Goodbye Mickey Mouse*.

WHY DOES MY ART GO BOOM? Essay in *Playboy* magazine, May 1966. Author Len Deighton files a personal report on the spy craze phenomenon.
See also: *Beat the Devil*.

WHY NOT INVEST YOUR MONEY IN VALUABLE POSTAGE STAMPS? Article by Len Deighton published in *Elephanta* (Christmas 1975), the journal of London's White Elephant Club. 'Technology and valuables are recurring ingredients of modern fiction,' writes Deighton, and for his novel *Yesterday's Spy* rare stamps had the sort of magic and nostalgia that interested him. After talking with experts and dealers and learning of the deceptions that can trap the unwary, his advice for anyone who has ever thought about stamps as an investment is that they might do better to put their money on a horse.

Winkel, ———. German sergeant-major on the Western front in *Winter*. Gassed by the British, he takes his disability pension, a pretty young wife and the two horses that come as her dowry, and opens a riding stables at Bernau near Berlin.

Winkel, Obergefreiter. Winkel's son in *Winter*, who joins the Wehrmacht expecting to use the expertise with horses that he's learned in his father's stables, but spends all his time driving General Horner's half-track command car.

Winkelstein, Sergeant Karl-Heinz. Short thickset thirty-two-year-old German émigré in the Union Army, with the central role in *Discipline*. Despised for his foreign name and heavy accent, he finds an enemy ambush a convenient way to revenge himself on the soldiers who ridicule him.

Winkler, Claude. Enigmatic BND officer, who thirty years after World War II is reunited with members of the Guernica Network in *Yesterday's Spy*. Part French, he passed for a national during the war, and admits to Charles Bonnard that he was an Abwehr agent while active with the Network. 'I was never a Nazi—*never*! I hated those people. But I am a German, and I did my duty then as I do it now.'

WINTER (Hutchinson, London, 22 October 1987/Alfred A. Knopf, New York, 5 January 1988; fiction). In his eighteenth and longest novel, Deighton takes leave of the postwar intelligence community and presents a richly detailed portrait of a Berlin family, set against the backcloth of the turbulent history and bellicose ambitions of the German nation through the first half of this century. At the heart of the story are two brothers: Paul Winter, born on the first day of January 1900, who rises to a senior administrative role in the Gestapo, earning for himself a minor celebrity status as he smoothes the path for the Nazi tyranny; and his elder brother Peter Winter, an authoritarian figure nostalgic for the old *Kaiserzeit*, who opposes the spread of Nazism and chooses exile in America. With a cast of superbly drawn characters—including several, and their parents, from the *Game, Set & Match* trilogy—the novel delivers the summation to twenty-five years of Deighton's fiction.

Winter, Harald. Imperious German businessman, head of the Winter family in *Winter*. Quick to grasp the opportunities afforded by the new century, he parlays an investment by his father-in-law into a fortune supplying Zeppelin airframes, survives the collapse of Germany in 1918, and makes a second killing in the great inflation of 1923. Smarter about money than his women, he's mostly undeserving of his American wife's loyalty and suffers a distant, sometimes abrasive relationship with their sons Peter and Paul. Like so many men of the *Kaiserzeit*, he's offended by the coarseness of the Nazis, and dies in 1944 with his country once again facing defeat.

Winter, Inge. Eldest of the Wisliceny daughters in *Winter*. A tall, self-sufficient girl with a full mouth that smiles easily, she marries Paul Winter after having set her heart on capturing his elder brother. Corrupted by her status as the wife of one of the Nazi regime's top layer, she embarks on an affair with Deputy Reichsminister Fritz Esser then flees Berlin in the final days of the war, and finds employment singing in a nightclub in the American occupation zone.

Winter, Lottie. Outspoken jazz-loving daughter of American entrepreneur Simon Danziger, who wins the heart of Peter Winter during a trip to Europe in the 1920s in *Winter*. Married and settled in Berlin, she finds life increasingly precarious as the tide of anti-Semitism sweeps Germany and is drawn into an underground cell forging travel documents for a Jewish escape-line. Arrested by the Nazis, she's saved from the camps by the intervention of her brother-in-law and hidden with the Volkmanns in the Hennig household—only to perish in an American air-raid on Berlin.

Winter, Paul. Compelling linchpin of *Winter*, the 'child of the new century' born to Veronica Winter on 1 January 1900. Charming, efficient, at times indecisive, he survives World War I to take up criminal law, and finds the emerging Nazi Party's demands on his practice providing him with needed self-respect as he strives to win his autocratic father's affection. Though apolitical and somewhat liberal in outlook, he quickly rises to a senior administrative role in the Gestapo and earns a minor celebrity status as one of the Nazi regime's elite. Arrested by the Allies in 1945, he absconds from Nuremberg in a bid to reach the Austrian border and sanctuary in Switzerland.

Winter, Peter. Eldest son of Harald and Veronica Winter, who elects for exile in America for himself and young daughter Helena, following the pre-war imprisonment in Berlin of his Jewish wife in *Winter*. Recruited into US Intelligence by his uncle Glenn Rensselaer, at the war's end he's sent by the US Army's attorney general's department to the IMT war crimes trial in Nuremberg, where he's forced to choose between loyalty to his brother Paul—who has saved his life not once, but many times—and loyalty to his adopted country.

Winter, Major Richard. Veteran World War I German fighter pilot, with the central role in *Winter's Morning*. A nerveless and relentless killer in the skies over France, he takes pride in seeing his victims die, believing only such men can become aces.

Winter, Veronica, Tall, elegant daughter of American businessman Cyrus Rensselaer, sister of Glenn Rensselaer and stoical wife of Harald Winter in *Winter*. Notwithstanding her husband's mistresses in Berlin and Vienna, she selflessly holds together the family through the vicissitudes of two wars and a revolution, twice finding her adopted country called to arms against America. Widowed in 1944, she's reunited after the Allied victory with the Englishman for whom she once might have abandoned it all.

WINTER'S MORNING. Short story in the collection *Declarations of War*. A World War I German fighter pilot survives a zipper patrol over the Western Front; his new young wingman does not.

wire-tapping. 'When you talk into a telephone, you shout from the roof,' warns Ivor Butcher in *Horse Under Water*. The clandestine interception of phone conversations is an industry in America, while Britain's burgeoning state operations are now centralised in a concealed building in London's Ebury Bridge Road, linked to a network of local facilities covering the country.

Instances in the novels range from the crude attempt by Egyptian Intelligence to tap Samantha Steel's phone in *Funeral in Berlin*, to the massive CIA-BND operation to monitor some eighteen thousand lines between West Germany and Switzerland to trap Willi Kleiber in *XPD*.

See also: bugging *and* 'Tinkle Bell'.

Wisliceny, Frau. Mother of Inge and Lisl Wisliceny in *Winter*, a big, handsome, matronly woman whose Berlin salon off Kantstrasse attracts the finest musicians, poets, novelists and painters. An early champion of Peter Winter's ambition to become a concert pianist, she uncovers a brilliant talent in Erich Hennig, whose interpretations of Bach win him acclaim throughout Germany.

Wisliceny, Inge. *See* Inge Winter.

Wisliceny, Lisl. *See* Lisl Hennig.

wives. 'How many husbands have not felt a pang of uncertainty at some unexplained absence, some careless remark or late arrival of his spouse?' admits a confused Bernard Samson in *Berlin Game*. Certainly Elena Bekuv, Vera Hardcastle, Tessa Kosinski, Zena Volkmann and Inge Winter stand condemned of marital betrayal, while Marjorie Dean and Fiona Samson betray both their husbands and their countries. However, wives cast in a supportive role, not always deserved, include Mary Anson, Teresa Foxwell, Ruth Lambert, Bessie Mann, Frau von Munte, Helen Schlegel, Lottie Winter and Veronica Winter.

WOOC(P). The small but important department at the heart of British Intelligence depicted in *The IPCRESS File*, *Horse Under Water*, *Funeral in Berlin* and *Billion-Dollar Brain*. Envied, criticised, and sometimes opposed by the other intelligence services, the department's conspiratorial energies are revealed through the eyes of the anonymous narrator, who first serves under Dalby in *The IPCRESS File*, then under Charles Dawlish in the subsequent novels. The acronym WOOC(P) is fictive. There's no account of the department's full name.

Woodhall, Flying Officer. Cranwell-trained RAF Hurricane fighter pilot whose 60-second dog-fight during the Battle of Britain is reconstructed in action-filled slow motion in *Adagio*.

Woods, Detective Sergeant Harry. Elderly police officer in Scotland Yard's Murder Squad, with a leading role alongside surrogate son Douglas Archer in *SS–GB*. Of the generation that fought and won in the filth of Flanders, his inability to come to terms with defeat leads to his involvement with the resistance—until forced to become SS-Gruppenführer Kellerman's informant to save Archer's young son from being sent to a youth camp in Nazi Germany.

Woods, Joan. Harry Woods's shrewish, embittered wife, sought out by Douglas Archer following her husband's detention in *SS–GB*.

Wool, ———. Garrulous confectionery salesman, and wartime corporal in the Royal Welsh Greys, who recalls shared exploits in a chance encounter with his former commanding officer in *It Must Have Been Two Other Fellows*.

word-counts. A total word-count for the period 1962–87 reveals that Deighton has written over two million words of published fiction—over 250 words every day for twenty-five years.

These individual counts are arrived at using a constant calculation base: *The IPCRESS File* c.90,200; *Horse Under Water* c.81,900; *Funeral in Berlin* c.97,400; *Billion-Dollar Brain* c.97,300; *An Expensive Place to Die* c.85,400; *Only When I Larf* c.86,700; *Bomber* c.172,800; *Declarations of War* c.69,700; *Close-Up* c.134,600; *Spy Story* c.78,100; *Yesterday's Spy* c.79,900; *Twinkle, Twinkle, Little Spy* c.87,300; *SS–GB* c.138,700; *XPD* c.158,200; *Goodbye Mickey Mouse* c.159,700; *Berlin Game* c.110,600; *Mexico Set* c.142,100; *London Match* c.176,700; *Winter* c.242,700.

WORD PROCESSORS. Article by Len Deighton, who has always believed electronic hardware to be a good investment, published in *Author* magazine, Autumn 1983.

word processors. *Bomber*, written in 1968–9, was probably the first book written on a word processor (though the name 'word processor' was not then in current usage). It was entirely recorded on magnetic tape for the IBM 72 IV, enabling Deighton to redraft many chapters over twenty times, and by means of memory-coding to select certain technical passages at only a moment's notice. He replaced this with an Olivetti TES 501, bought second-hand from Richard Condon who had already written a couple of books on it, and then an Olivetti 1010. Deighton presently works with a Hewlett Packard Portable Plus, using Microsoft's 'Word' software programme.

World War I (1914–18). Technically, Britain and Germany went to war in August 1914 over the neutrality of Belgium, supposedly guaranteed under a Treaty of 1839 to which both countries were among five signatories. The United States entered the war against Germany as an 'associated power' in April 1917.

It was the first war to see aerial combat, and the exploits of those early fighter pilots are the subject of *Lord Nick Flies Again* and

Winter's Morning, and are recalled by August Bach in *Bomber*. Harald Winter builds a fortune supplying the German fliers with airframes in *Winter*, while his sons Peter and Paul respectively serve their country in the Imperial Navy's Airship Division and in an infantry regiment on the Western Front. The novel paints a grim picture of life in the German trenches, and reconstructs in detail a Zeppelin air raid on London, viewed from the ground and the air.

World War II (1939–45). It is often forgotten that, as in 1914, Britain declared war on Germany in 1939 and not the other way round. It is the convincingly realised setting for the novels *Bomber*, *SS–GB* and *Goodbye Mickey Mouse*, the short stories *Adagio*, *Brent's Deus Ex Machina* and *Paper Casualty*, and inevitably comes to dominate the lives of many characters, ending the lives of several, in *Winter*. Vivid recollections of the war figure notably in *Horse Under Water*, *Funeral in Berlin*, *Only When I Larf*, *Yesterday's Spy*, *XPD*, *Berlin Game* and *London Match*, and in the short stories *Action* and *It Must Have Been Two Other Fellows*.

Wormwood Scrubs is one of London's dismal Gothic prisons. Bob Appleyard and Spider Cohen are reunited in *Only When I Larf* after having met serving time there, and Charles Bonnard endures an uncomfortable stay in its remand cells in a ploy to win the confidence of Steve Champion in *Yesterday's Spy*. Bonnard, and Colonel Ross in *The IPCRESS File*, both recall working there at the outbreak of World War II, after the prisoners had been evacuated and the buildings were taken over by British Military Intelligence—a disastrous move, since a German bomb subsequently destroyed the section housing MI5's huge system of files (and one may speculate how *that* served the careers of Soviet agents Anthony Blunt, Guy Burgess, Donald Maclean and Kim Philby).

Wörth, SS-Standartenführer. Sickly commanding officer of the SS unit billeted in Altgarten's Wald Hotel in *Bomber*.

Worthington, Flight Sergeant. Senior groundcrew chief at RAF Warley Fen in *Bomber*, who after twenty-eight years service is inclined to regard airmen who joined up after World War II began as nothing better than 'amateurs'.

Wright, Lieutenant Peter. Novice Royal Flying Corps airman, who enacts the heady exploits of comic book hero Lord Nicolas Beau-de-Ville as he pilots his flimsy biplane across the Channel in *Lord Nick Flies Again*.

Wynn, Todd. Thin wiry twenty-five-year-old member of the CIA team which bugs the KGB's New York safe house and later abducts Willi Kleiber from Europe, in *XPD*.

X

XPD (Hutchinson, London, 9 March 1981/Alfred A. Knopf, New York, 30 April 1981; fiction). Deighton's thirteenth novel is constructed around the sensational supposition that Winston Churchill secretly met with Adolf Hitler in June 1940 to discuss the terms of Britain's surrender. Reportedly prepared to hand over most of the Empire to bring an end to the war, the Prime Minister finally rejected the German proposals and a cloak of secrecy was drawn over the meeting—with anyone learning of it having their file stamped 'XPD'. But when Hitler's personal minutes of the discussions threaten to surface two generations later, Britain's MI6, the CIA, the KGB and a group of influential West German businessmen are drawn into a relentless search stretching from Hamburg to Hollywood.

XPD: expedient demise. A term coined by Deighton in the novel *XPD*, describing sanctioned acts of murder, or 'wet ops'—e.g. the deaths of Dalby in *The IPCRESS File*, Willi Kleiber in *XPD* and Pavel Moskvin in *London Match*.

Y

'the yellow submarine'. The jocular nickname for the London Data Centre, the secret computer facility three levels below Whitehall in *Berlin Game*.

YESTERDAY'S SPY (Jonathan Cape, London, 29 May 1975/ Harcourt Brace Jovanovich, New York, 6 October 1975; fiction). Deighton's tenth novel once again teams a British Intelligence officer with the irascible CIA-trained Colonel Schlegel, and draws together surviving members of the Guernica Network—a resistance group who operated in occupied France during World War II—when the activities of their former leader, Steve Champion, arouse the concern of intelligence mandarins in London and Bonn.

Young Europe Movement. The network of European neo-Fascists uncovered in *Horse Under Water*, whose supporters include Manuel da Cunha, Fernie Tomas, and British Cabinet Minister, Henry Smith.

Z

Zeppelins. In 1900—long before a manned flight by an aeroplane—Graf Ferdinand von Zeppelin's rigid airship was making short flights across Lake Constance. By 1910 he had formed the world's first airline company and was running the world's first airline service between German cities (although most flights were no more than joy-rides). The airships were subsequently pressed into service by both the German Army and Navy during World War I. They bombed Antwerp, Liège, Paris and Warsaw, and made fifty-three raids on England (twelve on London), killing 556 civilians. With the return of peace they resumed their commercial role, flying regularly across the Atlantic until in 1937 the *Hindenburg* dramatically burst into flames as it was about to moor at Lakehurst, New Jersey, with the loss of thirty-five of the ninety-six passengers and crew on board.

The Zeppelin's short-lived history is recalled in *Airshipwreck* (readers of which were offered a record on which Deighton introduced the voices of Graf von Zeppelin and Hugo Eckener, together with an American eye-witness radio commentary on the *Hindenburg* disaster) and in *Flying the Atlantic*, while the development of the postal service on board is documented in *The Orient Flight L.Z.127-Graf Zeppelin* and *The Egypt Flight L.Z.127-Graf Zeppelin*. In his massive novel *Winter*, Deighton takes us through their early development, vividly recreates a Zeppelin air raid over England during World War I, and captures the exhilaration of a transatlantic crossing aboard the *Graf Zeppelin* on the final leg of the world cruise sponsored by the American newspaper magnate William Randolph Hearst in 1929.

the 'Ziggurat'. The 'curious, truncated, pyramidal building' on the south side of London's River Thames, which serves as MI6's modern headquarters in *XPD*. With rust stains dribbling on the façade and cracks in the basement, the panelling, paintings and antique furniture in Sir Sydney Ryden's office are said to be all part of an attempt to recapture the elegance that MI6 once enjoyed in the beautiful old houses in St James's.

Alphabetical List
of Themes Explored

The following are given individual entries in the book:

abandoned novels
abduction
Abwehr
access controls
acoustic couplers
action codes
actors
adultery
advertising
aerial warfare
agents
agents of influence
airports
airships
Albufeira
Algeria
Algiers
America
American Civil War
American Intelligence
Americans
anonymous narrators
anti-heroes
appendices
Arabs
The Arctic
assumed identities
Austria
autobiographical
  content
avalizing

awards
bacteriological warfare
Baltic States
banks and bankers
The Battle of Britain
Beirut
Belgium
The Bendlerblock
Berlin
Berlin (East)
Berlin Resident
Berlin Wall
Berlin (West)
Berliners
betrayal
blackmail
black marketeering
Bonn
Bordeaux
border crossings
brainwashing
breaking & entering
British Intelligence
British Military
  Intelligence
British Union of Fascists
bugging
Bundesamt für
  Verfassungsschutz
Bundesnachrichten-
  dienst

business proprietaries
cars
case officer
Central Intelligence
  Agency
Central Registry
changing papers
Checkpoint Charlie
chess
children
China
Christmas
ciphers
cities
city drop
class
closing lines
clubs
codes
the Cold War
computers
concentration camps
confidence tricks
consort watch
cookery
The Cookstrip
counter-espionage
counterfeit money
counter-intelligence
country drop
couriers

cover
cover names
Criminal Records Office
crossword puzzles
cryptanalysis
cryptonyms
Czechoslovakia
dead drop
deep cover agents
defectors
denied areas
Denmark
desk officer
detectives
detention centres
dinner parties
Direction de la
  Surveillance du
  Territoire
Direction Générale de
  Sécurité Extérieure
disguises
double-agents
drugs
East German
  Intelligence
Egyptian Intelligence
England
The English
enrolment v.
  recruitment
espionage
Eton
exfiltration
ex-wives
Federal
fictional settings
field agents
film adaptations
Finland
first-person narratives
flashbacks
Flugwachkommando

food
Foreign Office
France
Freikorps
French Intelligence
French Resistance
games
Geneva
German reunification
Germans
Germany (East)
Germany (West)
Gestapo
Gibraltar
Glavnoye
  Razvedyvatelnoye
  Upravleniye (GRU)
goodbye codes
Government
  Communications
  Headquarters
Graf Zeppelin
Grepos
Gruinard
Hamburg
Hauptverwaltung
  Aufklärung
helicopters
Helsinki
Hendaye-plage
Highgate Cemetery
history as hypothesis
hitch-hiking
Holland
Hollywood
homicides
hotels
HUMINT
Hungary
illegals
India
infiltrations
informants

intelligence
interrogation
Ireland
islands
Italy
Jews
jokes
the Kaiseroda Mine
kill file
Komitet
  Gosudarstvennoi
  Bezopastnosti (KGB)
Krefeld
Latvia
laundered money
Lebanon
legals
legend
Leningrad
Lichterfelde Barracks
London
Los Angeles
The Luftwaffe
Madrid
mark
masers
master file
Mexico
Mexico City
MI5
MI6
Miami
Ministerium für
  Staatssicherheit
mole
Morocco
Moscow
moving drop
Munich
music
National Security
  Agency
Nazi Intelligence

necrology
neo-Nazism
New York
Nice
nightclubs
Normannenstrasse
nuclear devices
Obersalzburg
Office of Naval
    Intelligence
one-time pad
opening lines
Ostend
over-the-air-codes
Paris
parties
pocket litter
Poland
Porton MRE
Portugal
Prague
prisons
private detectives
railway stations
Reichssicherheitshaupt-
    amt
Renseignements
    Généraux
reporters
Resident
restaurants and cafés
Rezident
Riga
robberies
The Royal Air Force

safe houses
San Antonio
Schutzstaffel (SS)
Scotland Yard
scrambler phones
screenplays
Security Grade Ones
Service de
    Documentation
    Extérieure et de
    Contre-Espionage
sheep-dipped
short stories
Sicherheitsdienst
Sicherheitspolizei
SIGINT
sleeper
Soho
solitaries
Sollerod
Soviet Union
Spanish Civil War
Spartakists
Special Branch
Spielmaterial
spies
spy satellites
SS nomenclature
stamps
Stasis
Sturmabteilung (SA)
submarines
suicides
Sûreté Nationale
surveillance

Switzerland
Technische-Nothilfe
telephone tapping
television adaptations
third-person narratives
title changes
The Tower of London
trains
underwater sequences
US Air Force
US Federal Narcotics
    Bureau
US Medical Department
Vienna
Vietnam War
Vopos
Wachregiment Felix
    Dzerzhinsky
Waffen-SS
warfare
war-gaming
Washington DC
Dr Watson roles
weather
West German
    Intelligence
wire-tapping
wives
word-counts
word processors
World War I
World War II
Wormwood Scrubs
XPD
Zeppelins

REGISTER OF CHARACTERS BY NATIONALITY

A note of all the characters given individual mention:

African
Ibo Awawa
Ali Lin

American
Pte. Joshua Ashton
Col. Dan Badger
Red Bancroft
Barbara Barga
Danny Barga
Barney Barnes
Battersby
Col. Alexander Bohnen
Kagan Bookbinder
Sgt. Harry Boyer
Mary Breslow
Joe Brody
Lt. Busby
Col. Bill Callaghan
Simon Danziger
Hank Dean
Henry Hope Dean
Marjorie Dean
Jerry Delaney
Capt. Jamie Farebrother
Pfc. Fred Fryer
Sgt. 'Tex' Gill
Milton Goldman
Pte. Green

Harvey Kane
  Greenwood
Corp. Steve Harmon
J. B. D. Harrison
Gerry Hart
Major Skip Henderson
Hudson
Pte. Des Jones
Johnny Jones
Melvin Kalkhoven
Sgt. Kinzelberg
John Koby
Lt. Earl Koenige
Harry Kondit
Leo Koolman
Max Koolman
Erich Loden
Bernie Lustig
Miles MacIver
Capt. Vince Madigan
Lt. Stefan Madjicka
Bessie Mann
Major Mickey Mann
General Midwinter
Jamie Morse
Lt. Mickey Morse
Harvey Newbegin
Mercy Newbegin
Tony Nowak
Edward Parker
Fusako Parker

Laurence Pastor
'Rocky' Ramon Paz
Major Kevin Phelan
Col. John Pitman
Poetsch
'Posh Harry'
Karl Poster
Ingrid Rainbow
Douglas Reid-Kennedy
Pte. Dutch Relay
Bret Rensselaer
Cyrus Rensselaer
Glenn Rensselaer
Phil Sanchez
Col. Charles Schlegel
Helen Schlegel
Col. 'Duke' Scroll
Sam Seymour
Col. Lester Shelley
Lt. Clive Simms
Billy Stein
Charles Stein
Capt. Charles Stigg
Major Harry Tarrant
Major Spurrier Tucker
Dottie Turner
Capt. Waley
Corp. Walker
Lt. Rube Wein
Jacob Weinberger
Wilson

Lottie Winter
Veronica Winter
Todd Wynn

Australian
Flt. Sgt. Digby
Henry Scrimshaw

Austrian
Count Kupka

British
Prof. Allenby
Mary Anson
Peter Anson
Frederick L. Antony
Bob Appleyard
Douggie Archer
Det. Supt. Douglas
  Archer
Patrick Armstrong
Arthur
Nora Ashton
Pete Barrett
Sgt. Ted Battersby
Sir Robert Benson
Bernhard
Albert Bingham
Helen Bishop
'The Bishop'
Blantyre
Alice Bloom
Paul Bock
Charles Bonnard
Flt. Sgt. Booth
Sgt. John Brand
FO Michael Brent
Angela Brooks
Sylvia Brummage
Ivor Butcher
Ossie Butterworth
Martin Langley Byrd
Capt. J. F. Carswell
Sgt. Tommy Carter

Kevin Cassell
Charlie Cavendish
Steve Champion
Philip Chilcott-Oakes
Stanley Childs
Sir Henry Clevemore
Emmy Cohen
Mr Cohen
Sgt. Simon Cohen
'Spider' Cohen
Peter Colfax
Sgt. 'Tapper' Collins
Dr Bernard Cooper
Margaret Cooper
Victoria Cooper
Daphne Cruyer
Dicky Cruyer
Dr Curtiss
Dalby
George Dawlish
Alun Davies
Det. Sgt. Davis
Suzy Delft
Percy Dempsey
Major Albert Dodgson
Air Marshal John Dover
Det. Con. Jimmy Dunn
CPO Edwards
Dr Eichelberger
Lt. Fane
PO Cornelius Fleming
Flynn
Ferdy Foxwell
Teresa Foxwell
Lt. Frazer
Brigadier Bunny
  Frederick
Prof. Frick
Eric Friendly
Fuller
Sgt. Ben Gallacher
Sydney Garin
Flt. Lt. John Garrard
Silas Gaunt

Flt. Lt. 'Jammy' Giles
Glynn
Sgt. 'Flash' Gordon
Dorothy Graham
Guthrie Grey
Sgt. Jimmy Grimm
James Hallam
Bert Hanratty
Sgt. Major Reg
  Hardcastle
Vera Hardcastle
Lt.-Col. Harriman
Frank Harrington
Mrs Harrington
PO Alan Hill
Mabel Hogarth
Maisie Holroyd
Peter Hutchinson
'Ipcress Man'
Gp. Capt. Jarman
Pte. Johnson
Sgt. Binty Jones
Col. Joyce
Alf Keating
Capt. Keightley
Gloria Kent
David Kimber-
  Hutchinson
Kitty King
George Kosinski
Tessa Kosinski
Corp. Ruth Lambert
Flt. Sgt. Sam Lambert
Col. Lee
Dennis Lightfoot
FO Longfellow
Graham Loveless
Silas Lowther
Charlotte Lucas-
  Mountford
Flt. Lt. Ludlow
MacGregor
FO MacIntosh
Joe MacIntosh

Julian MacKenzie
Sylvia Manning
Marjorie
Rita Marsh
Liz Mason
Mason
George Mayhew
Ac McDonald
Carol Miller
Brigadier Mitchell
Michael Moncrieff
Morgan
Gp. Capt. John Munro
Flt. Sgt. Mickey Murphy
'Newmarket Tony'
Edgar Nicholson
Billy Pace
Lt.-Col. Simon Painter
Harry Palmer
Major-General
    Parkstone
PO Pearson
Pte. Peel
Sidney James Pelling
Roland Pembroke
Kit Pepper
Bernard Peterson
Dr Felix Pike
Philippa Pike
Ralph Pike
Alan 'Boy' Piper
Peter Piper
Richard Preston
Cynthia Radlett
Ted Riley
Col. Ross
Sir Sydney Ryden
Albert Sampson
Bernard Samson
Brian Samson
Fiona Samson
Mrs Sanderson
Sara Shaw
Mrs Sheenan

Peter Shetland
Sir John Shields
Lt. Clive Singleton
Henry Smith
Val Somerset
Sonny Sontag
Sgt. 'Pip' Speke
Hon. Gerald Spencer
Dr John Spode
Dr William Spode
Bernard Staines
Josephine Stewart
Marshall Stone
Boyd Stuart
Jennifer Stuart
Flt. Lt. Sweet
Pte. Tarrant
Tarrant
Henry Tiptree
Ben Toliver
Jean Tonnesen
Topaz
Giles Trent
Miss Trent
Waterman
Major-General
    Wentworth
Commander Wheeler
FO Woodhall
Det. Sgt. Harry Woods
Joan Woods
Wool
Flt. Sgt. Worthington
Lt. Peter Wright

Canadian
FO Roddy Peterson

Chinese
Kuang-t'ien

Czechoslovakian
Jan-im-Glück
Josef-the-Gun
Vaclav

Egyptian
Aziz
Mebarki

Finnish
Olaf Kaarna
Signe Laine

French
Chief Insp. Baix
Caterina Baroni
Marius Baroni
Pina Baroni
Maria Chauvet
Annie Couzins
Monsieur Datt
Ercole
Serge Frankel
Grenade
Gus
Chief Insp. Loiseau
Monique
Chief Insp. Nicol
Jean-Paul Pascal
'The Princess'
Monsieur Tastevin
Lucie Simone Valentin

German
Anna-Luisa
OL. August Bach
Lt. Beer
SS-Obersturmführer
    Berger
Paul Biedermann
Poppy Biedermann
Max Binder
'Black Peter'
Fw. Blessing
Gerd Böll
Col.-General Erich Borg
Dr Paul Böttger
Heinrich Brand
Marie-Louise Breslow

Max Breslow
Paul Louis Broum
Fritz Esser
SS-Sturmbannführer
   Adolf Fischer
Erwin Fischer
Richard Fischer
Herr Frenzel
Dr Hans Furth
Captain Graf
Hauser
Erich Hennig
Lisl Hennig
Capt. Hans Hesse
OL. Hildmann
Uffz. Christian Himmel
Frau Hinkelburg
Herr Holländer
Alex Horner
SS-Standartenführer
   Oskar Huth
Johannes Ilfa
SS-Gruppenführer Fritz
   Kellerman
Frau Kersten
Klara
Willi Kleiber
Rudolf von Kleindorf
Lt. Klimke
Fk. Knobel
Gerda Koby
Lothar Koch
Lt. Kokke
Konrad
Helmut Krebs
Ofw. Krugelheim
OL. Victor von
   Löwenherz
Axel Mauser
Rolf Mauser
Hans-Willy Meyer
Dr Ernst Mohr
Lt. Mrosek
Klaus Munte

Dr Walter von Munte
Baron Wilhelm von
   Munte
Frau von Munte
Oberstabsmeister Nagel
Andi Niels
G. Orth
OG. Franz Pawlak
Petzval
Gerda Pippert
Fritz Rau
Major Peter
   Redenbacher
Stsw. Willi Reinecke
Peter Reuter
Generalmajor Georg
   von Ruff
Walter Ryessman
Fw. Georg Sachs
Dr Franz Schneider
Oberst Max Sepp
Prof. Max Springer
Dr Hans Starkhof
Theodor Steiner
'Fuchs' Ueberall
Lt. Uhl
Dr Isaac Volkmann
Werner Volkmann
Zena Volkmann
Herr Voss
Johnnie Vulkan
Col. Weizsäcker
Franz Wever
OG. Winkel
Winkel
Sgt. Karl-Heinz
   Winkelstein
Claude Winkler
Harald Winter
Inge Winter
Paul Winter
Peter Winter
Major Richard Winter
Frau Wisliceny

SS-Standartenführer
   Wörth

Hungarian
Boris Somló
Martha Somló

Israeli
Hanna Stahl

Italian
Signor Fragoli

Lebanese
Adem
Papa Kimon

Polish
Jan Kar
Christian Stakowski

Russian
Prof. Andrei Bekuv
Elena Bekuv
Chlestakov
Erikson
Yuriy Grechko
Col. Pavel Moskvin
Major Nogin
Katerina Remoziva
Rear-Admiral Vanya
   Remoziva
Major Nikolai Sadoff
Semitsa
General Stanislav
   Shumuk
Col. Alexeyevitch Stok
Swainson

South American
Humberto Costa

Swiss
Hugo Koch
Madame Mauring

BIBLIOGRAPHY

FICTION 1962–1987

THE IPCRESS FILE

First British edition:
Publisher: Hodder & Stoughton, London | 12 November 1962 | 15s. | large Crown 8vo | 224pp. | word-count c.90,200

D/Wrapper: Black and white photographic d/w. Designed by Raymond Hawkey, photography by Ken Denyer. Deighton has a very high regard for the design, which so successfully caught the gritty, yet witty, flavour of the book. The jacket went against the prejudice of the book trade at the time in that it was monochromatic, used discreet typography and a photographic rather than a drawn illustration.*

Binding: Orange boards, gold blocked on spine. Plain endpapers.

Print-run: 4,000

Proof: Bound in green Hodder & Stoughton proof wrappers.

Proof d/w: As published.

First serialisation: *Evening Standard*, London | 19–30 November 1962.

First American edition: *The Ipcress File*
Simon & Schuster, New York | 29 October 1963 | $3.95 | 287pp.

First (UK) paperback: Panther, 1964, 3s. 6d. Reproduces the jacket design

of the hardcover edition, which was most unusual, if not a precedent at the time.

25th Silver Jubilee paperback (UK):
Grafton, January 1987, £2.95. Limited edition published only in 1987, with a new preface by Len Deighton.

Motion Picture: *The IPCRESS FILE*
Screenplay by Bill Canaway & James Doran | Directed by Sidney Furie
Rank/Steven/Lowndes, 1965.

* Encouraged by Len Deighton, Hawkey himself has written three highly acclaimed thrillers, the first of which, *Wild Card*, was published in 1974. It was followed by *Side-Effect* (1979), and *It* (1983). The three were reissued by Sphere Books in 1988 as *The Presidential Trilogy*.

HORSE UNDER WATER

First British edition:
Publisher: Jonathan Cape, London | 21 October 1963 | 16s. | Crown 8vo | 255pp. | word-count c.81,900

D/wrapper: Black and white photographic d/w. Designed by Raymond Hawkey, photography by Ken Denyer.

Binding: Red boards, gold blocked on spine. Black 'office stamp' motif and blind-stamped DOWNGRADED TO UNCLASSIFIED on front board. Endpapers illustrated with crossword clues.

Print-run: 15,000

Note: Published with *Horse Under Water* crossword competition entry form laid in.

Proof: Bound in green and white Cape proof wrappers.

Proof d/w: Differs from the published d/w in many details. The proof design was judged to be too cluttered, rightly so in the opinion of Hawkey, with too many items of ephemera beneath the skull on the front cover. The publisher's blurb on the rear cover is different, and the inside front flap carries a photograph of Len Deighton watching two Royal Navy frogmen demonstrating high-speed dressing at H.M.S. Vernon, Portsmouth.

First American edition: *Horse Under Water*
G. P. Putnam's Sons, New York | 5 January 1968 | $4.95 | 256pp.

First (UK) paperback: Penguin, 1965, 4s. 6d. Original cover design by Raymond Hawkey. Publisher's biography of Len Deighton states: '*Description*—Dark complexion, 14 stone, 6 feet tall. Cruel, sardonic sense of humour. *Experience*— Railway lengthman, Piccadilly waiter, Madison Avenue adman, *Vogue* fashion artist, photographer RAF Mosquitoes, manager Aldgate gown factory. Seen Vista-Vision blue films in pre-Castro Cuba, typhoon in Tokyo, hurricane passing New York. Given talk over Soviet radio. Once fell into Hong Kong harbour, fatty tissue saved him.'

Compare with the author's contrasting biography in the Penguin edition of *Funeral in Berlin*! The whole of the first paperback printing of *Horse Under Water*—over 60,000 books—sold out completely within 48 hours of publication.

25th Silver Jubilee paperback (UK): Grafton, January 1987, £2.95. Limited edition published only in 1987, with a new preface by Len Deighton.

FUNERAL IN BERLIN

First British edition:
Publisher: Jonathan Cape, London | 17 September 1964 | 18s. | Crown 8vo | 320pp. | word-count *c.*97,400

D/wrapper: Black and white photographic d/w. Designed by Raymond Hawkey, photography by Adrian Flowers.

Binding: Black boards, gold blocked on spine. Blue-grey 'office stamp' motif and blind-stamped DOWNGRADED TO UNCLASSIFIED on front boards. White and black endpapers, reproducing part of the official membership list of the Nazi SS. (The first name is that of Heinrich Himmler.)

Print-run: 14,000

Proof: Bound in green and white Cape proof wrappers.

Proof d/w: Differs from the published d/w, with the title in Gothic lettering on the front cover and spine.

Special promotional material: A facsimile of Len Deighton's British passport in black which, when opened, becomes a chessboard with plastic pieces sealed in a buff envelope stamped 'Top Secret'. Produced as an advance promotional item for the trade, and not issued with the book.

First American edition: *Funeral in Berlin*
G. P. Putnam's Sons, New York | 11 January 1965 | $4.95 | 320pp.

First (UK) paperback: Penguin, 1966, 5s. Original cover design by Raymond Hawkey. Publisher's biography of Len Deighton states: '*Description*—Fair complexion, 9 stone, five feet six tall. Warm generous sense of humour. *Background*—Eldest son of a Governor-General of the Windward Islands. *Experience*—After working as a translator for the BBC Welsh service, clerk in the Ministry of Agriculture and Fisheries and manager of a chain of boutiques in Leeds, he became the Manchester stringer for *The Times*. He was unable to find a publisher for his first book which was lavishly praised by Kingsley Amis. Likes: being under the bonnet of a vintage motor car, public bars, ballroom dancing and cricket.' Compare with the author's biography in the Penguin edition of *Horse Under Water*! (Apocryphal accounts still abound of the publisher's Berlin beano which helped launch the book!)

25th Silver Jubilee paperback (UK): Grafton, February 1987, £2.95. Limited edition published only in 1987, with a new preface by Len Deighton.

Motion Picture: *Funeral in Berlin* Screenplay by Evan Jones Directed by Guy Hamilton Paramount/Saltzman, 1966.

THE BILLION DOLLAR BRAIN

First American edition:
Publisher: G. P. Putnam's Sons, New York | 11 January 1966 | $4.95 | Demy 8vo | 320pp. | word-count c.97,300
D/wrapper: Two colour graphic d/w. Designed by R. Schneider.
Binding: Red fictionette boards, gold blocked on spine. Plain endpapers.
Print-run: 20,000
Special promotional material: A replica of one of Deighton's small tan-coloured notebooks containing—in addition to notes and drawings related to the novel—facsimiles of an Aeroflot baggage ticket, a ticket to Verdi's *Otello* at Leningrad's Maly Opera House, and a Finnish ferry ticket. Produced by Jonathan Cape for Putnam's as an advance promotional item for the trade, and not issued with the book.

First British edition: *Billion-Dollar Brain*
Publisher: Jonathan Cape, London | 31 March 1966 | 21s. | Crown 8vo | 312pp. | word-count c.97,300
D/wrapper: Black and silver photographic d/w. Designed by Raymond Hawkey, photography by Ken Denyer (whose helmeted face appears on the front cover).
Binding: Blue boards, gold blocked on spine. Computer punch-tape stamped in white on front board. Endpapers illustrated with black and white Automath Statement.
Print-run: 25,000
Proof: Bound in green and white Cape proof wrappers.
Proof d/w: The publisher's blurb

beneath the title on the front cover differs from that on the published d/w.

Special promotional material: Identical to the American item, except for the references to page numbers in the novel, which differ in the British edition. Produced as an advance promotional item for the trade, and not issued with the book. (So convincing was the notebook that some bookshop owners returned their copy to the publisher, with a note of thanks to Len Deighton for lending it to them.)

First (UK) paperback: Penguin, 1967, 5s. Original cover design by Raymond Hawkey. Publisher's biography of Len Deighton similar to that in the Penguin edition of *Horse Under Water*. The tongue-in-cheek biography is of course that in the Penguin edition of *Funeral in Berlin*!

25th Silver Jubilee paperback (UK): Grafton, February 1987, £2.95. Limited edition published only in 1987, with a new preface by Len Deighton.

Motion Picture: *Billion-Dollar Brain* Screenplay by Joe McGrath | Directed by Ken Russell United Artists/Saltzman, 1967.

AN EXPENSIVE PLACE TO DIE

First American edition:

Publisher: G. P. Putnam's Sons, New York | 26 April 1967 | $4.95 | Demy 8vo | 256pp. | word-count *c*.85,400

D/wrapper: Red, black, and white graphic d/w. Designed by John Van Zwienen.

Binding: Three-piece case with red fictionette boards and white spine. Gold blocked on spine. Red endpapers.

Print-run: 20,000

First British edition: *An Expensive Place to Die*

Publisher: Jonathan Cape, London | 11 May 1967 | 21s. | Crown 8vo | 254pp. | word-count *c*.85,400

D/wrapper: Colour photographic d/w. Designed by Raymond Hawkey, photography by Adrian Flowers.

Binding: Black boards, gold blocked on spine. Endpapers illustrated with a black and white Art Nouveau design.

Print-run: 30,000

Note: Published with a TOP SECRET buff wallet containing ten letters and documents, laid in. They purport to have originated from the President of the United States, the Secretary of Defense, the Central Intelligence Agency and the Prime Minister of Great Britain, and trace the sequence of events leading up to the start of the novel.

Proof: Bound in green and white Cape proof wrappers.

Proof d/w: As published.

First serialisation: The complete text was serialised prior to publication in *Playboy* magazine (US): December 1966, January, February and March 1967.

First (UK) paperback: Panther, 1969, 5s. Original cover design by Raymond Hawkey, photography by Adrian Flowers.

25th Silver Jubilee paperback (UK): Grafton, March 1987, £2.95.

Limited edition published only in 1987, with a new preface by Len Deighton.

ONLY WHEN I LARF

First British edition:

Publisher: Michael Joseph, London | 22 April 1968 | 25s. | large Crown 8vo | 233pp. | word-count c.86,700

D/wrapper: Colour photographic d/w. Designed by Raymond Hawkey, photography by Brian Duffy.

Binding: Dark brown boards, gold blocked on spine. Plain endpapers.

Print-run: 9,000

Proof: Bound in brown Michael Joseph proof wrappers.

Proof d/w: As published.

Note: An edition of 150 copies was privately printed by Len Deighton in 1967 to establish the copyright whilst negotiating the motion picture deal with Paramount Pictures. It thus precedes the first published edition. Foolscap size, with white plastic comb-binding, it features an English £5 note in blue on the front and rear card covers.

First serialisation: *Playboy* magazine was going to serialise the novel, but as Deighton reveals in his introduction to the limited edition of *Only When I Laugh*, they eventually decided against it on the grounds that 'their policy precluded publishing stories in which women outwitted men'.

First American edition: *Only When I Laugh*

The Mysterious Press, New York | 25 March 1987 | $16.95 | 241pp. A limited edition of 250 numbered copies signed by Len Deighton, containing a new introduction by the author, was published simultaneously with the trade edition.

First (UK) paperback: Sphere, 22 April 1968, 5s. (print-run 250,000). Sphere Books acquired the UK publishing rights, then sub-licensed the hardcover rights to Michael Joseph. The two editions appeared simultaneously and feature the same 'smiling lips' cover photograph by Brian Duffy. The paperback cover design was to have been an English £5 note. Massed displays of what at first sight would have looked like bundles of £5 notes would, in the opinion of Deighton and Ray Hawkey, have been quite irresistible to the public. But the idea was finally killed, fearing an action by the Bank of England.

Motion Picture: *Only When I Larf* Screenplay by John Salmon | Directed by Basil Dearden | Paramount/Beecord (Deighton, Duffy, Attwooll), 1968.

BOMBER

First British edition:

Publisher: Jonathan Cape, London | 10 September 1970 | 35s. | Demy 8vo | 494pp. | word-count c.172,800

D/wrapper: Colour d/w, reproducing a detail from Turner's 'Fishermen at Sea off the Needles'. Designed by Raymond Hawkey.

Binding: Blue boards, silver blocked on spine. Black endpapers.

Print-run: 50,000

Note: The first edition contains a

number of errors, which crept in after the proof had been passed for printing. These were corrected in the second edition published in 1970.

Proof: Bound in green and white Cape proof wrappers.

Proof d/w: As published.

First American edition: *Bomber* Harper & Row, New York | 30 September 1970 | $7.95 | 424pp.

First (UK) paperback: Pan, 1972, 50p.

25th Silver Jubilee paperback (UK): Grafton, March 1987, £3.95. Limited edition published only in 1987, with a new preface by Len Deighton.

DECLARATIONS OF WAR

First British edition:

Publisher: Jonathan Cape, London | 21 October 1971 | £1.50 | Demy 8vo | 205pp. | word-count *c.*69,700

D/wrapper: Colour d/w, reproducing a painting by Christopher Foss. Designed by Raymond Hawkey.

Binding: Black boards, gold blocked on spine. Maroon endpapers.

Print-run: 22,500

Proof: Bound in red and white Cape proof wrappers.

Proof d/w: As published:

Special promotional material: A black, imitation leather folder bearing the Royal insignia in gold, and containing reproductions of six historical documents relating to the theme of the book. Produced as an advance promotional item for the trade, and not issued with the book.

First American edition: *Eleven Declarations War*

Harcourt Brace Jovanovich, New York | 6 March 1975 | $6.95 | 180pp. Omits two of the stories in the British edition.

First (UK) paperback: Panther, 1973, 35p.

25th Silver Jubilee paperback (UK): Grafton, April 1987, £2.95. Limited edition published only in 1987, with a new preface by Len Deighton.

Television adaptation: *Discipline* and *It Must Have Been Two Other Fellows*

Adapted by Peter Prince | Directed by Ben Rea

BBC Television, 18 December 1977.

CLOSE-UP

First British edition:

Publisher: Jonathan Cape, London | 1 June 1972 | £1.95 | Demy 8vo | 381pp. | word-count *c.*134,600

D/wrapper: Colour photographic d/w. Designed by Raymond Hawkey, photography by Peter Williams.

Binding: Black boards, silver blocked on spine. Plain endpapers.

Print-run: 45,000

Proof: Bound in red and white Cape proof wrappers.

Proof d/w: As published.

First American edition: *Close-Up* Atheneum, New York | 19 June 1972 | $7.95 | 381pp.

First (UK) paperback: Pan, 1974, 45p.

25th Silver Jubilee paperback (UK): Grafton, April 1987, £3.50. Limited edition published only in 1987, with a new preface by Len Deighton.

SPY STORY

First British edition:
Publisher: Jonathan Cape, London |
2 May 1974 | £2.25 | Demy 8vo |
224pp. | word-count *c*.78,100
D/wrapper: Colour photographic d/w.
Designed by Raymond Hawkey,
photography by Peter Williams.
Binding: Black boards, gold blocked
on spine. Red endpapers.
Print-run: 27,000
Proof: Bound in red and white Cape
proof wrappers.
Proof d/w: As published.
First American edition: *Spy Story*
Harcourt Brace Jovanovich, New
York | 25 September 1974 | $6.95 |
224pp.
First (UK) paperback: Panther, 1976,
60p.
25th Silver Jubilee paperback (UK):
Grafton, May 1987, £2.95. Limited
edition published only in 1987, with
a new preface by Len Deighton.
Motion Picture: *Spy Story*
Screenplay credit not available |
Directed by Lindsay Shonteff |
Gala/Shonteff, 1976.

YESTERDAY'S SPY

First British edition:
Publisher: Jonathan Cape, London |
29 May 1975 | £2.75 | Demy 8vo |
224pp. | word-count *c*.79,900
D/wrapper: Colour photographic d/w.
Designed by Raymond Hawkey,
photography by Adrian Flowers.
Binding: Brown boards, gold blocked
on spine. Plain endpapers.
Print-run: 83,000

Proof: Bound in red and white Cape
proof wrappers.
Proof d/w: As published.
First American edition: *Yesterday's
Spy*
Harcourt Brace Jovanovich, New
York | 6 October 1975 | $7.95 |
282pp.
First (UK) paperback: Panther, 1977,
60p.
25th Silver Jubilee paperback (UK):
Grafton, May 1987, £2.95. Limited
edition published only in 1987, with
a new preface by Len Deighton.

TWINKLE, TWINKLE, LITTLE SPY

First British edition:
Publisher: Jonathan Cape, London |
17 June 1976 | £3.25 | Demy 8vo |
240pp. | word-count *c*.87,300
D/wrapper: Colour photographic d/w.
Designed by Raymond Hawkey,
photography by Adrian Flowers.
Binding: Black boards, gold blocked
on spine. Endpapers illustrated with
blue and white stellar photographs.
Print-run: 42,500
Proof: Bound in red and white Cape
proof wrappers.
Proof d/w: As published.
First American edition: *Catch a
Falling Spy*
Harcourt Brace Jovanovich, New
York | 27 September 1976 | $7.95 |
268pp.
First (UK) paperback: Triad/Panther,
1977, 60p.
25th Silver Jubilee paperback (UK):
Grafton, June 1987, £2.95. Limited
edition published only in 1987, with
a new preface by Len Deighton.

SS—GB

First British edition:
Publisher: Jonathan Cape, London |
    24 August 1978 | £4.95 | Demy 8vo |
    350pp. | word-count *c*.138,700
D/wrapper: Colour graphic d/w.
    Designed by Raymond Hawkey.
Binding: Black boards, silver blocked
    on spine. Red endpapers.
Print-run: 110,000
Proof: Bound in red and white Cape
    proof wrappers.
Proof d/w: As published.
Special promotional material: A book
    of 1941 United Kingdom postage
    stamps in three denominations (6 at
    2½d, 6 at 2d and 6 at ½d), each
    bearing the head of Adolf Hitler.
    Also, a sepia-tinted postcard with a
    photo(montage) of Hitler taking the
    salute in Whitehall, London, on his
    52nd birthday. Both produced as
    advance promotional items for the
    trade, and not issued with the book.
First American edition: *SS—GB*
    Alfred A. Knopf, New York | 26
    February 1979 | $9.95 | 344pp.
First (UK) paperback: Triad/Panther,
    1980, £1.25.
25th Silver Jubilee paperback (UK):
    Grafton, July 1987, £3.50. Limited
    edition published only in 1987, with
    a new preface by Len Deighton.

XPD

First British edition:
Publisher: Hutchinson, London | 9
    March 1981 | £6.95 | Demy 8vo |
    397pp. | word-count *c*.158,200
D/wrapper: Colour photographic d/w.

Designed by Carroll & Dempsey,
    photography by Andy Seymour.
Binding: Black boards, gold blocked
    on spine. Red endpapers.
Print-run: 50,000
Proof: Bound in orange Hutchinson
    proof wrappers.
Proof d/w: As published.
First American edition: *XPD*
    Alfred A. Knopf, New York | 30
    April 1981 | $12.95 | 339pp.
First (UK) paperback: Granada, 1982,
    £1.95.
25th Silver Jubilee paperback (UK):
    Grafton, August 1987, £3.50.
    Limited edition published only in
    1987, with a new preface by Len
    Deighton.

GOODBYE MICKEY MOUSE

First British edition:
Publisher: Hutchinson, London | 20
    September 1982 | £8.50 | Demy 8vo |
    395pp. | word-count *c*.159,700
D/wrapper: Colour illustrated d/w.
    Designed by David Pelham,
    illustration by Chris Moore.
Binding: Red boards, silver blocked
    on spine. Plain endpapers.
Print-run: 40,000
Proof: Bound in orange Hutchinson
    proof wrappers.
Proof d/w: As published.
First American edition: *Goodbye,*
    Mickey Mouse
    Alfred A. Knopf, New York | 28
    October 1982 | $14.95 | 337pp.
First (UK) paperback: Granada, 1983,
    £1.95.
25th Silver Jubilee paperback (UK):
    Grafton, August 1987, £3.50.

Limited edition published only in 1987, with a new preface by Len Deighton.

BERLIN GAME

First British edition:
Publisher: Hutchinson, London | 3 October 1983 | £8.95 | Demy 8vo | 304pp. | word-count *c*.110,600
D/wrapper: Colour illustrated d/w. Designed by Raymond Hawkey, illustration by Hargrave Hands.
Binding: Black boards, silver blocked on spine. Red endpapers.
Print-run: 40,000
Proof: Bound in yellow Hutchinson proof wrappers.
Proof d/w: As published, except for minor layout and typographical differences to the publisher's blurbs.
First American edition: *Berlin Game* Alfred A. Knopf, New York | 5 January 1984 | $15.95 | 345pp.
First (UK) paperback: Panther, 1984, £1.95. The cover, designed by Raymond Hawkey, features the Hargrave Hands illustration used on the hardcover edition.
25th Silver Jubilee paperback (UK): Grafton, September 1987, £3.50. Limited edition published only in 1987, with a new preface by Len Deighton.
Television adaptation: Granada Television is producing a thirteen-part series of the *Game, Set & Match* trilogy for transmission in the UK and USA in the autumn of 1988. See the *Game, Set & Match* entry in the Companion for cast list and production credits.

MEXICO SET

First British edition:
Publisher: Hutchinson, London | 22 October 1984 | £8.95 | Demy 8vo | 381pp. | word-count *c*.142,100
D/wrapper: Colour illustrated d/w. Designed by Raymond Hawkey, illustration by Hargrave Hands.
Binding: Black boards, silver blocked on spine. Red endpapers.
Print-run: 45,000
Proof: Bound in orange Hutchinson proof wrappers.
Proof d/w: Differs from the published d/w, in respect of the publisher's blurb and minor typographical details.
First American edition: *Mexico Set* Alfred A. Knopf, New York | 28 February 1985 | $16.95 | 374pp.
First (UK) paperback: Granada, 1985, £2.50. The cover, designed by Raymond Hawkey, features the Hargrave Hands illustration used on the hardcover edition.
25th Silver Jubilee paperback (UK): Grafton, September 1987, £3.50. Limited edition published only in 1987, with a new preface by Len Deighton.
Television adaptation: see *Berlin Game.*

LONDON MATCH

First British edition:
Publisher: Hutchinson, London | 10 October 1985 | £9.95 | Demy 8vo | 432pp. | word-count *c*.176,700
D/wrapper: Colour illustrated d/w. Designed by Raymond Hawkey, illustration by Hargrave Hands.

Binding: Black boards, silver blocked on spine. Red endpapers.

Print-run: 45,000

Proof: Bound in a special 2-colour Astralux cover, reproducing Hargrave Hands' d/w illustration.

Proof d/w: Differs from published d/w, in respect of the publisher's blurb.

First American edition: *London Match*
Alfred A. Knopf, New York | 3 January 1986 | $16.95 | 408pp.

First (UK) paperback: Grafton, 1986, £2.50. The cover, designed by Raymond Hawkey, features the same Hargrave Hands illustration used on the hardcover edition.

25th Silver Jubilee paperback (UK): Grafton, October 1987, £3.50. Limited edition published only in 1987, with a new preface by Len Deighton.

Television adaptation: see *Berlin Game*.

GAME, SET & MATCH

Omnibus edition of *Berlin Game*, *Mexico Set* and *London Match*. With a new preface by Len Deighton.

First British edition:
Publisher: Hutchinson, London | 9 October 1986 | £12.95 | Royal | 858pp. |

D/wrapper: Colour photographic d/w. Designed by Raymond Hawkey, photography by Peter Williams.

Binding: Black boards, gold blocked on spine. Endpapers illustrated with a map of Berlin, identifying key locations in the trilogy.

Print-run: 7,000

Proof: None.

Proof d/w: As published.

WINTER

First British edition:
Publisher: Hutchinson, London | 22 October 1987 | £11.95 | Royal | word-count *c.*242,700

D/wrapper: Colour illustrated d/w. Designed by Raymond Hawkey, illustration by Hargrave Hands.

Binding: Blue boards, silver blocked on spine. Red and black Edwardian floral design endpapers.

Print-run: 50,000

Proof: None.

Proof d/w: Differs from the published d/w, in respect of some of the text, and the layout, of the publisher's blurb. Lacks the author's photograph, and lacks the title on the back of the jacket.

First American edition: *Winter*
Alfred A. Knopf, New York | 5 January 1988 | $19.95 | 578pp.

First (UK) paperback: Grafton, 1988, £3.50. The cover, designed by Raymond Hawkey, features the Hargrave Hands illustration used on the hardcover edition.

NON-FICTION 1954–1987

ACTION COOK BOOK
Len Deighton's Guide to Eating

First British edition:
Publisher: Jonathan Cape, London |
   18 March 1965 | 25s. | ob. 4to |
   138pp., text and drawings.
Binding: Colour printed boards, with
   a .38 Smith & Wesson firing off
   parsley, on the front cover.
   Designed by Raymond Hawkey.
   Endpapers illustrated with black and
   white drawings showing various cuts
   of meat.
Print-run: 7,500
Proof: Bound in green and white Cape
   proof wrappers.
   Note: Publication was originally
   announced for November, 1963.
   The Swiss designer Paul Piech was
   commissioned to provide additional
   drawings, but Deighton felt the
   result was not in keeping with his
   intended style. New illustrations
   were commissioned, although some
   of Piech's work survives in the final
   published edition.
First American edition: *Cookstrip
   Cook Book*
   Bernard Geis, New York | 9
   September 1966 | $3.95 | 132pp.
First (UK) paperback: Penguin, 1967,
   10s. 6d. With an additional seven-
   line introduction by Len Deighton.

OU EST LE GARLIC
or, Len Deighton's French Cook Book

First British edition:
Publisher: Penguin Books, London |
   28 October 1965 | 10s. 6d. | ob. large
   Crown 8vo | 224pp., text and
   drawings.
Binding: Soft covers, with colour
   photographic design. Designed and
   photographed by Jacques
   Dehornois.
Print-run: 30,000
Proof: Unbound galleys.
First American edition: *Où est le
   garlic, or, French cooking in 50
   Lessons*, Harper & Row, New York
   | 18 March 1977 | $6.95 | 224pp. With
   minor amendments to the Penguin
   text.

THE ASSASSINATION OF PRESIDENT KENNEDY
*Compiled and edited by Michael Rand,
   Howard Loxton and Len Deighton*

First British edition:
Publisher: Jonathan Cape, London |
   23 March 1967 | 13s. 6d.
Description: Dark blue portfolio
   measuring 23cm × 36cm, containing
   12 reproductions of contemporary

documents, 1 cut-out model, and 5 explanatory broadsheets.
Print-run: not available
Proof: Galleys.

LEN DEIGHTON'S LONDON DOSSIER

Compiled and annotated by Len Deighton

With contributions from Adrian Bailey, Drusilla Beyfus, Eric Clark, Daniel Farson, Adrian Flowers, Spike Hughes, Steve Race, Milton Shulman, Godfrey Smith, Nick Tomalin, Frank Norman, John Marshall, Michael Wale and Jane Wilson.

First British edition:
Publisher: Jonathan Cape, London, in association with Penguin Books | 27 April 1967 | 30s. | Crown 8vo | 352pp.
D/wrapper: Colour photographic d/w. Designed by Raymond Hawkey, photography by Adrian Flowers.
Binding: Red boards, gold blocked on spine. Endpapers illustrated with black and white aerial photograph of London.
Print-run: 5,600
Proof: Bound in green and white Cape proof wrappers.
Proof d/w: As published.
First (UK) paperback: Penguin, 27 April 1967, 7s.6d. (Print-run 75,000.) Published simultaneously with the Cape hardcover edition. Designed by Raymond Hawkey, the front cover features a distinctive cut-out keyhole motif. The eye peering through the keyhole from the first tipped-in colour page is that of

Twiggy, photographed by Adrian Flowers. Hawkey pioneered the use of cut-out covers with his design for the 1963 Pan paperback edition of Ian Fleming's *Thunderball*.

LEN DEIGHTON'S CONTINENTAL DOSSIER

A Collection of Cultural, Culinary, Historical, Spooky, Grim and Preposterous Fact

Compiled by Victor and Margaret Pettitt

Foreword by Len Deighton

First British edition:
Publisher: Michael Joseph, London, in association with Wylton Dickson Publishing | 11 November 1968 | 25s. | Demy 8vo | 60pp., with maps
Binding: Printed boards with six-colour photographic design by Max Robinson. Plain endpapers. On cover and at head of title page: 'The World of Peter Stuyvesant Presents'.
Print-run: 20,000
Proof: Bound in proof wrappers reproducing the photographic cover design.

FIGHTER

The True Story of the Battle of Britain

Introduced by A. J. P. Taylor

First British edition:
Publisher: Jonathan Cape, London | 15 September 1977 | £4.95 | Demy 8vo | 304pp., illus.
D/wrapper: Colour d/w, featuring Paul Nash's painting 'Under the

Cliff'. Designed by Raymond
Hawkey.
Binding: Dark blue boards, gold
blocked on spine. Red endpapers.
Print-run: 40,500
Proof: Bound in plain proof wrappers.
Proof d/w: As published.
First American edition: *Fighter*
Alfred A. Knopf, New York | 25
May 1978 | $12.50 | 261pp., illus.
Contains additions and changes to
the Cape text.
First (UK) paperback: Triad/Panther,
1979, £1.50. Includes those additions
and changes to the Cape text in the
American edition.
25th Silver Jubilee paperback (UK):
Grafton, June 1987, £3.50. Limited
edition published only in 1987, with
a new preface by Len Deighton.

AIRSHIPWRECK

*Len Deighton and Arnold
Schwartzman*

First British edition:
Publisher: Jonathan Cape, London | 5
October 1978 | £4.95 | Crown 4to |
74pp., illus.
D/wrapper: Colour photographic d/w.
Designed by Arnold Schwartzman,
photography by Harry Peccinotti.
Binding: Black boards, silver blocked
on spine and front board. Endpapers
illustrated with side view and plan
drawings of the *Hindenburg*,
reversed white out of black.
Print-run: 40,000
Note: Published with one of a set of
six monochrome postcards
reproducing rare photographs from
the book, laid in.
Proof: Unbound galleys.

Proof d/w: As published.
Special promotional material: The full
set of six postcards, plus a record on
which Len Deighton introduces the
voices of Graf von Zeppelin, Hugo
Eckener and an eye-witness
commentary on the *Hindenburg*
disaster, could be purchased from
the publisher.
First American edition: *Airshipwreck*
Holt Rinehart Winston, New York |
15 March 1979 | $12.95 | 74pp., illus.

BASIC FRENCH COOKING

Revised and enlarged from Où est le
garlic

First British edition:
Publisher: Jonathan Cape, London | 1
March 1979 | £3.95 | ob. Crown 4to |
222pp., text and drawings
D/wrapper: Colour photographic d/w.
Designed by Raymond Hawkey,
photography by Peter Williams.
Binding: Green boards, gold blocked
on spine and front board. Plain
endpapers.
Print-run: 10,000
Proof: Unbound galleys.
Proof d/w: As published.

BLITZKRIEG

From the Rise of Hitler to the Fall of
Dunkirk

*Foreword by General W. K. Nehring,
aD*

First British edition:
Publisher: Jonathan Cape, London | 3
September 1979 | £5.95 | Demy 8vo |
320pp., illus.

D/wrapper: Red, black and white graphic d/w, with a reproduction of the Totenkopf (Death's Head) emblem worn by all members of the German Panzer units in 1940. Designed by Raymond Hawkey.

Binding: Black boards, gold blocked on spine. Endpapers illustrated with a black and yellow chart showing the organisation of a Panzer division in 1940.

Print-run: 70,000

Proof: Bound in red and white Cape proof wrappers.

Proof d/w: Differs from the published d/w, lacking the Totenkopf emblem on the front cover.

Special promotional material: A limited number of wall charts reproducing the endpaper illustration could be purchased from the publisher.

First American edition: *Blitzkrieg* Alfred A. Knopf, New York | 22 May 1980 | $14.95 | 295pp., illus.

First (UK) paperback: Triad/ Granada, 1981, £1.95.

25th Silver Jubilee paperback (UK): Grafton, July 1987, £3.50. Limited edition published only in 1987, with a new preface by Len Deighton.

BATTLE OF BRITAIN

First British edition:

Publisher: Jonathan Cape, London | 11 September 1980 | £8.50 | small Crown 4to | 224pp., illus.

D/wrapper: Colour d/w, reproducing a painting by Frank Wootton. Designed by Adrian Field.

Binding: Light blue boards, silver blocked on spine. Plain endpapers.

Print-run: 130,000

Proof: Unbound galleys.

Proof d/w: As published.

First American edition: *Battle of Britain* Coward McCann & Geoghegan, New York | 12 September 1980 | $19.95 | 224pp., illus.

THE ORIENT FLIGHT L.Z.127-GRAF ZEPPELIN

Fred F. Blau and Cyril Deighton

First American edition:

Publisher: Germany Philatelic Society, Maryland | October 1980 | $17.50 | large Demy 8vo | 144pp., illus.

Binding: Dark blue non-woven material over boards. Gold stamped on spine and front board. Plain endpapers.

Print-run: 1,000

Proof: Unbound galleys.

The publisher is an American philatelic society for collectors specialising in German stamps. The book is G.P.S. Philatelic Handbook No. 7.

THE EGYPT FLIGHT L.Z.127-GRAF ZEPPELIN

Fred F. Blau and Cyril Deighton

First American edition:

Publisher: Germany Philatelic Society, Maryland | September 1981 | $14.00 | large Demy 8vo | 94pp., illus.

Binding: Light blue card cover. Title printed in dark blue on spine and front cover. No endpapers.

Print-run: 500

Proof: Unbound galleys.
Published by the same American
philatelic society, this book is G.P.S.
Philatelic Handbook No. 8.

OTHERS

Edited by Len Deighton. *Drinks-man-
ship: Town's Album of Fine Wines &
High Spirits*. London: Haymarket
Press, November 1964, 50s., 136pp.,
illus.

'Ironmongery of the Desert' and 'The
Private Armies'. In *El Alamein and
the Desert War*, edited by Derek
Jewell. London: Sphere Books,
October 1967, 7s. 6d., 208pp., illus.
New York: Ballantine Books, July
1968, 95¢, 208pp., illus.

'Introduction'. In *The Valley of Fear* by
Arthur Conan Doyle. London:
Murray/Cape, January 1974, £1.95,
192pp. New York: Doubleday, May
1977, $7.95, 192pp.

'Foreword'. In *Guilt-Edged* by Merlin
Minshall. London: Bachman &
Turner, October 1975, £4.50,
320pp., illus.

'Recipes'. In *How to be a Pregnant
Father* by Peter Mayle. Illustrations
by Arthur Robins. Secaucus, NJ:
Lyle Stuart, October 1977, $12.00,
56pp., illus. London: Macmillan,
March 1980, £5.95, 56pp., illus.

'Introduction'. In *Tactical Genius in
Battle* by Simon Goodenough.
Oxford: Phaidon Press, October
1979, £8.95, 144pp., illus. New
York: Phaidon Press, October 1979,
$16.95, 144pp., illus.

'Even on Christmas Day'. In
*Whodunit? A Guide to Crime,
Suspense & Spy Fiction*. Edited by
H. R. F. Keating. London:
Windward, August 1982, £7.95,
320pp., illus. New York: Van
Nostrand Reinhold, August 1982,
$18.95, 320pp., illus.

'Introduction'. In *The French Foreign
Legion* by John Robert Young.
London: Thames & Hudson,
September 1984, £12.95, 212pp.,
illus. New York: Thames & Hudson,
September 1984, $24.95, 212pp.,
illus.

'Introduction'. In *The Adventure of the
Priory School* by Arthur Conan
Doyle. Preface by Marvin P.
Epstein. Santa Barbara: Santa
Teresa Press, August 1985, $45.00,
100pp. A limited edition of 350
copies signed by Len Deighton, with
an additional twenty-six deluxe
copies bound in leather and cloth
and slipcased, and a limited number
of Presentation Copies marked thus
on colophon page. Twenty-five
copies of Len Deighton's
introduction were separately printed
in January 1985 for copyright
purposes.

'Introduction'. In *Literary Agents* by
Anthony Masters. Oxford: Basil
Blackwell, October 1987, £12.95,
272pp., illus.

ARTICLES

'Abroad in London'. *Ark*, London,
Issue 10, 1954.

'Impressions of New York'. *Ark*,
London, Issue 13, 1955.

'My File on Surprising Places'. *Daily
Express*, London, February 1964.

'Why Does My Art Go Boom?'
Playboy, Chicago, May 1966.

'The Private Armies'. *Sunday Times Magazine*, London, 17 September 1967.

'Ironmongery of the Desert'. *Sunday Times Magazine*, London, 24 September 1967.

'Playboy's Guide to a Continental Holiday'. *Playboy*, Chicago, May 1968.

'Hawaiian Aye'. *Playboy*, Chicago, June 1968.

'It Happens in Monterey'. *Playboy*, Chicago, July 1968.

'Exploring a New City'. *Playboy*, Chicago, August 1968.

'Mexico!'. *Playboy*, Chicago, October 1968.

'Skiing: From A to V'. *Playboy*, Chicago, November 1968.

'Sardinia: Italy's Alabaster Isle'. *Playboy*, Chicago, December 1968.

'Some Notes on Indian & Pakistan Cooking'. *Elephanta*, London, Issue 2, 1974.

'Flying the Atlantic'. *Elephanta*, London, Spring 1975.

'Why not invest your money in valuable postage stamps?' *Elephanta*, London, Christmas 1975.

'Word Processors'. *Author*, London, Autumn 1983.

SCREENPLAYS

Oh! What a Lovely War. Based on Joan Littlewood's stage production of the same name. Directed by Richard Attenborough. Paramount/Accord, 1969.

From Russia With Love. Early draft screenplay. Eon Productions, 1963.

Never Say Never Again. Early draft screenplay. Woodcote/A Taliafilm Production, 1983.

TELEVISION PLAY

Long Past Glory. Directed by Charles Jarrott. ABC Television, 17 November 1963.

Answers to the
quiz on page 231

1. *An Expensive Place to Die*, a title derived from Oscar Wilde's observation, 'Dying in Paris is a terribly expensive business for a foreigner'.
2. Only two: Frank Harrington and Lisl Hennig.
3. *XPD*. Only days after the general election of May 1979, MI6 Director General Sir Sydney Ryden alerts her to the possible disclosure of Britain's most closely guarded wartime secret.
4. Christopher Plummer.
5. Krefeld.
6. London's postwar Royal Festival Hall. The other three are hurriedly requisitioned by the Nazis in *SS–GB* to house the thousands rounded up following the Highgate Cemetery bombing.
7. Christian Stakowski, better known as 'Jay', in *The IPCRESS File*.
8. Bernard Samson in *London Match*.
9. Berlin in *Funeral in Berlin*. 'Edmond Dorf' and 'Captain Maylev' are the respective cover names of the narrator and Colonel Stok.
10. Marshall Stone, the subject of Peter Anson's biography in *Close-Up*.
11. Biedermann.
12. *SS–GB*, a novel set in a Nazi-occupied Britain of 1941. The ritualistic disinterment of Karl Marx is one of the final ceremonies of German-Soviet Friendship Week.
13. *Berlin Game*.
14. The game of 'Monopoly', in *An Expensive Place to Die*.
15. Willi Kleiber in *XPD*, whom the CIA abduct in Europe and fly to the United States for interrogation.
16. Its IBM collator.
17. Harry Palmer. Michael Caine's portrayal of Palmer in *The Ipcress File*, *Funeral in Berlin* and *Billion-Dollar Brain* is now so deeply embedded in the experience of millions of filmgoers and television viewers, that many forget the character was unnamed in Deighton's novels. The other four are named narrators.
18. Danny Barga.
19. Lothar Koch.
20. New York appears in five novels: *Billion-Dollar Brain*, *Only When I Larf*, *Twinkle, Twinkle, Little Spy*, *XPD* and *Winter*.
21. Steve Champion in *Yesterday's Spy*.

22. Altgarten's Wald Hotel in *Bomber*. The rumour is unfounded.

23. *Spy Story*.

24. *Winter*.

25. In the novel *XPD*, Winston Churchill is alleged to have met with Adolf Hitler at this Belgian frontier town to discuss a negotiated settlement between Great Britain and Nazi Germany.

26. Berwick House, also known as the London Debriefing Centre, in the *Game, Set & Match* trilogy.

27. Sergeant Major Reg Hardcastle in *Goodbye Mickey Mouse*.

28. Whitehall, London. The 'yellow submarine' is the jocular nickname given the London Data Centre, British Intelligence's secret computer facility in *Berlin Game*.

29. Morgan, Sir Henry Clevemore's brazenly ambitious assistant in *Mexico Set* and *London Match*. Martin Bormann was Hitler's secretary, but by controlling the paperwork of Hitler's office and by deciding who was permitted to have an audience with the Führer, he became the power behind the throne.

30. *The IPCRESS File* was first published in England on 12 November 1962. It first appeared in America, published by Simon & Schuster, in October 1963.

31. *Only when I Larf*. The African politician is Ibo Awawa, whose brazen quest for weapons to mount a coup and seize his country's throne, makes him easy prey for the trio of confidence tricksters.

32. Major Mickey Mann, the narrator's American boss in *Twinkle, Twinkle, Little Spy*.

33. The Lebanon.

34. *From Russia With Love* (1963) and *Never Say Never Again* (1983).

35. Werner Volkmann's twenty-two-year-old wife, Zena.

36. The Battle of Britain, examined at length in *Fighter* and *Battle of Britain*.

37. Leo Koolman, heir to the Koolman Studios in *Close-Up*.

38. *A New Way to Say Goodnight*.

39. All four characters commit suicide.

40. The Hitler Minutes in *XPD*. The only documentary evidence of the secret meeting between Winston Churchill and Adolf Hitler in June 1940.

41. Five. *The IPCRESS File* (1965), *Funeral in Berlin* (1966), *Billion-Dollar Brain* (1967), *Only When I Larf* (1968) and *Spy Story* (1976).

42. Cooking.

43. Chicago, the only one of these cities *not* used as a setting in Deighton's novels.

44. *Berlin Game* (2) Dicky Cruyer; *Billion-Dollar Brain* (5) General Midwinter; *Bomber* (1) Oberleutnant August Bach; *Bonus for a Salesman* (7) Albert Sampson; *Close-Up* (10) Jacob Weinberger; *An Expensive Place to Die* (4) Monsieur Datt; *Funeral in Berlin* (6) Harvey Newbegin; *The IPCRESS File* (3) Colonel Ross; *Spy Story* (9) Colonel Alexeyevitch Stok; *Yesterday's Spy* (8) Colonel Charles Schlegel.

45. Cavendish.

46. Paul Louis Broum, who assumes the identity of murdered camp

guard Johnnie Vulkan in *Funeral in Berlin*.

47. *Billion-Dollar Brain*. Stanley Caine makes a brief appearance as a Post Office delivery boy.
48. Peter and Paul Winter in *Winter*.
49. The narrator of *The IPCRESS File*. 'Looking back now it was capricious to say that he was from the northern town of Burnley,' says Deighton. 'I had picked the place at random having remembered it on parcels I'd sorted for the post office while on vacation jobs from college.'[22]
50. *An Expensive Place to Die*.

SOURCES

1 Len Deighton, 'Even on Christmas Day' in *Whodunit? A Guide to Crime, Suspense & Spy Fiction*, ed. H. R. F. Keating, Windward, London, 1982.

2 Len Deighton, preface to the 25th Silver Jubilee edition of *Twinkle, Twinkle, Little Spy*, Grafton Books, London, 1987.

3 Len Deighton, preface to the 25th Silver Jubilee edition of *Horse Under Water*, Grafton Books, London, 1987.

4 Unidentified source, Donald McCormick, *Who's Who in Spy Fiction*, Elm Tree Books, London, 1977.

5 Miles Copeland, *The Real Spy World*, Weidenfeld & Nicolson, London, 1975.

6 Anthony Burgess, *Ninety-Nine Novels*, Allison & Busby, London, 1984.

7 Len Deighton to the author.

8 Miles Copeland. Ibid.

9 Len Deighton to Alan Road, 'The Deighton File', *Observer Magazine*, London, 28 April 1974.

10 Julian Symons, *Sunday Times*, London, 3 April 1966.

11 Len Deighton to Alan Road. Ibid.

12 Len Deighton, *Newsweek*, European edition, 24 December 1962.

13 George Grella, *Crime and Mystery Writers*, St James Press, London, 1985.

14 T. J. Binyon, *Times Literary Supplement*, London, March 1981.

15 Len Deighton, preface to the 25th Silver Jubilee edition of *XPD*, Grafton Books, London, 1987.

16 Julian Symons, *Sunday Times*, London, 11 November 1962.

17 Len Deighton, preface to the 25th Silver Jubilee edition of *Mexico Set*, Grafton Books, London, 1987.

18 Ibid.

19 Len Deighton to the author.

20 Len Deighton, preface to the 25th Silver Jubilee edition of *Bomber*, Grafton Books, London, 1987.

21 Len Deighton, preface to the 25th Silver Jubilee edition of *The IPCRESS File*, Grafton Books, London, 1987.

22 Len Deighton, preface to the 25th Silver Jubilee edition of *Horse Under Water*, Grafton Books, London, 1987.

Other sources I have found most useful:

Christopher Andrew, *Secret Service*, Heinemann, London, 1985.
Susanne Everett, *Lost Berlin*, Hamlyn, London, 1979.

David Kahn, *The Codebreakers*, Sphere Books, London, 1973.

Victor Marchetti and John D. Marks, *The CIA and the Cult of Intelligence*, Jonathan Cape, London, 1974.

Alexander Walker, *Hollywood, England*, Michael Joseph, London, 1974.

David Wise, *The Politics of Lying*, Random House, New York, 1973.

David Wise, *The American Police State*, Random House, New York, 1976.

Personal Notes

Personal Notes

Personal Notes

Personal Notes